Rebel Russia

For Masha

Rebel Russia

Dissent and Protest from the Tsars to Navalny

ANNA ARUTUNYAN

polity

First published in 2025 by Polity Press

Polity Press
65 Bridge Street
Cambridge CB2 1UR, UK

Polity Press
111 River Street
Hoboken, NJ 07030, USA

ISBN-13: 978-1-5095-5229-0

A catalogue record for this book is available from the British Library.

Library of Congress Control Number: 2024948524

Typeset in 11 on 14pt Warnock Pro
by Cheshire Typesetting Ltd, Cuddington, Cheshire
Printed and bound in Great Britain by CPI Group (UK) Ltd, Croydon

For further information on Polity, visit our website:
politybooks.com

Contents

Note on Spelling

Historically, Ukraine's capital was commonly spelled Kiev, not Kyiv, as it is today. When referencing events that took place before 1991, the original spelling of Kiev will be retained. For events that took place after 1991, the modern Ukrainian spelling of Kyiv will be used.

Preface

This project began in a different time, and in a different Russia. In 2021, when I was still based in Moscow, I undertook to write a history of Russian dissenters. My initial, unquestionably ambitious, project hoped to meld field research with a history tracing Russian dissent from the earliest days to the modern dissident Alexei Navalny, at that time still alive, albeit in a prison camp. But the war and the changing political climate made it practically impossible to continue working in Russia and I left in March 2022. More to the point, however, the transformations that occurred in the country blindsided not just me, but a whole generation of Russian writers and observers.

Russia, it has been said, is a country with an unpredictable past. As I tried to make sense of why things happened the way they did – why, from a period of unprecedented pluralism, the country returned to some of its most autocratic traditions – my concept of this book project changed as well. Rather than a history, it turned into a way of reckoning with the present, with the events of the last decade as a prism through which to examine the past – the things that have brought us to the present.

Rebel Russia became, in many ways, a personal voyage to find answers to painful questions Russians and Russia watchers have been asking themselves since February 24, 2022, when Vladimir Putin launched the invasion of Ukraine. Why have dissenters fighting to resist state tyranny so rarely succeeded? In the process of researching and writing this book, I discovered answers that surprised me and questioned my own assumptions, and that I hope will challenge some of the prevailing stereotypes of the day – namely, that Russia's story is one of descending darkness set on repeat, or that Russia is somehow abnormal, even cursed, or that "good" dissenters struggle and usually lose against a "bad" government. In fact, history shows that Russian dissenters have repeatedly defeated tyrannical governments, as they did in February 1917 and, again, in August 1991. The rebel has often put a crown upon his own head, but remains only as strong as the civil society that he governs. His repeating oppression is a function of his weakness, and the cycle repeats.

This book interrogates that cycle and traces how it has evolved and shows promises of transforming. It rejects the popular bigotry masquerading as analysis: the notion that Russians are somehow civically backwards, predestined either to lawlessness and submission to tyranny, or to brutality and imperialism – a notion that is, perversely, shared by some members of an older generation of Russian dissidents, by Ukrainian nationalists and some of their most ardent Western supporters, and, in a telling irony, by Vladimir Putin himself.

Ultimately, this is a book about the choices and agency of the human beings at the heart of history, describing the capacity of people to make hard decisions about resisting (or not resisting) in a constrained environment. It shows how those constraints have changed, sometimes thanks to the efforts of both the Russian people and their government combined. It challenges the lazy analysis of Russia as a mystery and its people as being predisposed to their "learned helplessness" before state power.

(There is, after all, little mystery to learned helplessness, if only those who apply the concept to Russians bothered to read the psychiatric literature on it.) It traces, instead, not just how the constraints of this environment shaped and continue to shape the choices of those who oppose, rebel against, or try to change the Russian government (and these are entirely different objectives, with entirely different outcomes, as this book explores), but also how those constraints – including the very decisions of those who resist – shape the choices of Russian rulers who, by turn, decide to oppress, reform, or tolerate, so long as they retain their power. It shows how the choices of a variety of dissenters – from pro-Western liberals to Communists to xenophobic nationalists – end up shaping their environment.

The roles of the dissident, the insurgent, and the opposition activist are all inherently different. The dissident, as it came to be defined during the Soviet period, was one morally opposed to the governing regime, whether or not he or she actively resisted (at which point they could also be considered activists), and usually opposed violent means. The insurgencies throughout history – from the Pugachev rebellion to the Decembrist uprising to the Bolshevik Revolution and even the Russian Spring that sparked the conflict in Eastern Ukraine – ultimately turned to organized violence either to defeat the state or to compel it to change course. Others would turn instead to non-violent activism, writing, publishing, protesting, or even campaigning for political office. In Putin's Russia, until the start of the war, there was a whole assortment of such groups and individuals, working at a time when political activity was, indeed, made possible by the government. By focusing on the *rebel*, this book explores the things they all have in common: the different ways in which they try to resist or change state power, and the different ways in which they fail and succeed.

This book is by no means a comprehensive history or analysis of Russia's various types of dissenters, rebels, insurgents, or dissidents, nor will it pretend to name-check every brave man or woman who stood up to state power. There are omissions. The resistance of seventeenth-century Archpriest Avvakum against the church reforms of Patriarch Nikon and the birth of the Old Believers are only briefly addressed, though even a chapter would not do justice to the profound implications of the great schism – the *Raskol* – for Russia's religious and political trajectory. There is, also, certainly a limit to what can be said about one of the biggest rebellions in world history – the Bolshevik Revolution – in one chapter. Rather, this book explores, through examples of each, some of the fundamental questions about the nature of the Russian government and those who have opposed it.

Underpinning this relationship between the rebel and the tsar was a strong alienation between society and the government and also between estates or classes within society – an alienation that ensured each perennially feared or mistrusted the other. It was this distance that made rule over Russia so precarious for any leader, and, thus, made repression and abuse all the more common. But it was also this distance that, strangely enough, made the rebel and the tsar so close: rarely has a Russian ruler felt secure enough to be able to afford *not* to respond to criticism, to ignore challenges, or to ally with one kind of rebel against another.

Finally, at a time when it is popular to view Russia's future as bleak, I believe it imperative to try to envisage a constructive, progressive trajectory, and to think beyond the patterns of revolt and repression that have comprised its history. History, as I hope this book will demonstrate, is not destiny. Although these days, paradoxically enough, it can seem heretical to think and say certain things, even in the freedom of Western democracies, I will say this: I love Russia, and, most of all, I believe in it, even in its current darkness.

I am indebted to Louise Knight and the team at Polity for undertaking this project and for their continual encouragement.

There are too many people without whom this book would not have been possible to name them (and some for whom it might be dangerous to do so), but I hope they know who they are. The Kennan Institute, its library, and the Russian scholars there who informed and supported this project with their invaluable insight, Russian opposition journalists who have worked tirelessly to document the struggle against the state, and a great deal more people all have my gratitude. Finally, I want to thank my husband, Mark Galeotti, for sharing in the blood, sweat, and tears that were shed over this book, and my daughter, Masha, for her insights.

Anna Arutunyan, Kent, 2024

1

The Optimists

To confront Putin – and walk away

"My name is Alena Popova. Vladimir Vladimirovich, you are a colossus standing on feet of clay. We all despise you. And we want you to leave."

It is a truism that to understand the present, you need to understand the past. In the case of Russia's malleable history, to understand the past, sometimes you first need to understand the present.

To this day, Alena Popova, an entrepreneurial Russian politician who is now – like many independent activists – in exile, is at a loss to pinpoint what exactly made her do it. But that day in 2013, when the Russian opposition still had hope, before half of them were jailed and the other half had emigrated, before their most prominent leader, Alexei Navalny, died in an Arctic prison cell, something had accumulated in the pit of her stomach – a potent, dark nausea – and she stood there, less than a meter away, and called out Vladimir Putin to his face.

"At first, I had no desire to talk to him," she recalls. Part of a delegation of oppositionist voices invited to Putin's annual Valdai conference, back when the Kremlin was still trying to look vaguely democratic and inclusive, she found herself in a banquet hall following his official speech, where she and her colleagues were discussing Russia's future. Suddenly Putin emerged into their midst. "It was just making me nauseous. I didn't want to be a part of this. I thought, this man is absolute evil."

Popova went instead to the bathroom. But as she tried to get out, the door was jammed. When she heaved at it, she found herself catapulted through, right into the arms of one of the president's bodyguards. In the commotion, she somehow got thrown at the president himself.

"I turned to him, and he turned to me. I told him my name. He asked, 'who?' and I repeated. Then something just clicked, all these things I didn't even know I wanted to say burst forth." Suddenly, she knew she had to say them. "I spoke calmly and firmly. I told him that I was disgusted to stand next to him, that he was weak, that he needed to leave power, that he was so afraid of his own people that he had to find ways to prevent critics from running even for local elections."

Putin's spokesman, Dmitry Peskov, started pointing to his wrist, signaling to the president that it was time to leave. Peskov, a former diplomat, knew the drill and was making sure Putin had an out. To Alena, and to anyone who has observed such interactions, the subtle gesture was a tell-tale sign of the autocrat's fragility – of a ruler afraid of his people, in spite of his efforts to seem close to them, willing to appear among crowds, chat with his subjects unscripted, and take their side against oligarchs and governors alike. It was a precarious dance that Putin had tried to maintain throughout his rule: be apparently open to spontaneity and criticism, but withdraw at the first sign of danger. This time, Putin hesitated and turned back to Popova. "Can you say that again?" he asked.

"And I told him everything again. He has to leave."

Nearly a decade had passed when Popova told me this story. By that point, she, like so many Russians who opposed Putin's invasion of Ukraine in 2022, had left Russia, knowing that she could go to prison simply for voicing the thoughts she held in her head. But back then, in a different Russia, nothing happened after that encounter. No arrests, no raids. Alena continued to do the work she thought necessary. "This story didn't really mean anything. Not to him, not to me. It was a tragicomedy more than anything else."[1]

When she told me about her encounter with Putin, I already had a sense of her spirit – her belief that, with her determination alone, she could effect change. She was part of a new generation of Russians – savvy enough to understand how their world worked, they also believed they were entitled to their rights and to their voice, and they were not afraid to speak out. A lawyer, journalist, and successful entrepreneur by her mid-twenties, Alena Popova became a part of a fledgling institutional democracy when she began volunteering in 2010. That summer, a massive heatwave sparked wildfires all over Russia, exposing a government that, however much it was awash with oil revenue, was catastrophically unprepared for what had been a predictable emergency. Ordinary Russians began organizing volunteer brigades to fight the fires, and Alena joined one of them, traveling to the Moscow region and as far as Siberia. Those experiences inspired her to found the Civil Corps, one of a number of volunteer groups that started cropping up at the time, focused on anything from finding missing children to helping domestic abuse victims. In 2016, she launched a network of support for domestic abuse survivors called "You Are Not Alone," and began to lobby hard to change legislation to protect women. She would go on to set up a group that would engage lawyers to draft domestic violence legislation. Even though this was not passed, her network proceeded to help women win lawsuits against harassment. As late as 2021 – a time far more politically repressive than a decade earlier, but not quite yet the quasi-totalitarianism in which Russians would find themselves just a year later – Alena was stuffing parliamentarians' mailboxes with pictures of abused women. By then, she had already acquired a great deal of access to the halls of Russia's State Duma – first as an assistant to parliamentarian Ilya Ponomaryov, then as a parliamentary candidate in her own right. "When they see me coming, they turn the other way," she told an American journalist.[2]

It was hard for me to imagine that, even in those relatively liberal times, knowing what she knew about the Kremlin then, she could have so brazenly told Putin to his face how much he disgusted her.

It was so hard for me to imagine, almost impossible, because I myself am not a dissident. About a year before the events she described, I too had stood in front of Vladimir Putin, less than a meter away, called out his name . . . and walked away.

It was 2012, and I was a reporter at Russia's oldest English-language weekly, *The Moscow News*. Putin's Russia was still relatively pluralistic and even a government-funded news outlet was free to criticize Kremlin policies. As editor of the news desk and chief political correspondent, I had been covering corruption and human rights abuses for several years. We had minimal interference from the Presidential Administration: I remember only one phone call from its offices on Staraya Ploschad, Old Square, inquiring about my reporting on a whistleblower cop who was exposing police corruption. Even the head of our news agency encouraged us to resist self-censorship. There was only one red line, really. "Criticize the Kremlin and its policies as much as you want. But attacking Putin personally is off limits." That was the unwritten rule in those days, and I stuck to it.

But the story I had been working on when I got accredited to Putin's yearly press conference was testing even my own impartiality. A vindictive piece of legislation had banned the adoption of Russian orphans by American foster parents. It was passed quickly by Putin's party in direct retaliation for the US Magnitsky Law, which sanctioned Russian officials over the death in custody of jailed tax lawyer Sergei Magnitsky. Officially the authors of the so-called Dima Yakovlev Law claimed that they were defending Russian orphans, after four adoptees, including one Dima Yakovlev, had died over several years while in the care of American families. But given that thousands of children died each year from abuse or neglect at the hands of Russia's own neglected foster care system, the only people Putin's government was hurting were Russian orphans themselves. I had meant to confront Putin about this paradox: had he done the math, and did he know that by banning adoptions, he was sentencing thousands of Russian orphans to death?

With the press conference over, a crowd of reporters surrounded the president, and as I tried to get close, I found myself buoyed by the throng, but feeling curiously pressurized. It was as though the air within a two-meter radius of the Russian leader was charged, warping the very thoughts and words of those in the vicinity.

"Vladimir Vladimirovich!" I called out. At that moment, he was in an apparent argument with another journalist about corruption: "Look at me, I am talking to you," he was telling her, and I clearly needed to wait. My question, formulated at the start of the conference, softened: surely I wouldn't accuse Putin of sentencing children to death? Maybe I should actually ask if he knew that the deaths would increase by the thousands? Perhaps he didn't. Perhaps it was my job to be useful and helpful, and point it out to him. Perhaps that way I could get him to change his mind and turn more lenient. But at the same time, as I struggled for the appropriate words, my desperation grew: a journalist's question was transforming into a subject's plea.

I didn't like what was going on around me and what was going on in my head. If Alena felt nauseous, I felt ashamed. If I was going to be honest with myself, what I felt most of all was fear.

Scared, ashamed, embarrassed, before he turned to face me, I stepped back and walked away.

* * *

In my book *The Putin Mystique*, in which I examined the relationship between the Russian people and Vladimir Putin, and how he himself was a product of that relationship, I described the incident as an outsider, with the purpose of conveying how people behaved in the presence of the Russian autocrat.[3] What I omitted – in part because I didn't understand it fully at the time – was my own deep sense of fear and confusion about what exactly I was expecting from a rare interaction with the virtual monarch of a country of which I was a citizen. As a journalist, what I had wanted to do was to ask a simple question: did Putin know that, statistically speaking, this law would lead to thousands of unnecessary deaths? And yet, standing in front of the man, the simplicity of the question, to me, began to sound insulting: how could a person, a statesman of even average intelligence, *not* know this? And if he knew he was enacting a law condemning thousands of Russian orphans to death for the sake of retaliating against the United States, and if I knew that he knew this, then what I was about to say was not a question at all. It was a condemnation, a protest, a provocation – anything to expose the callous, petty maliciousness of the law, and, quite possibly, of Putin himself. To me, in the context we were all in, to ask the question meant to cease being a journalist and to become a dissenter – to defy the president to his face, to enter into a polemic and to call him out for his short-sighted malice. That I was not prepared to do.

Was it because I chickened out, intimidated by the array of bigwigs and black-suited bodyguards flanking the little gray man? Maybe. What effect would my words really have? Would they get me fired? Would they spell trouble for my colleagues? Would I be able to continue to put food on the table and give my own child the lifestyle I had never had? Given that I worked for state media, Putin's government might see me not just as an oppositionist, but as a traitor – and the stakes were much higher for domestic journalists than for those who worked for foreign media. Would we have to flee the country? Would my daughter have to pack a suitcase and say goodbye to her grandmother and her friends? As I began to see it, the bell jar surrounding the Russian autocrat warped and extinguished any normal outcomes from a simple human interaction. As my mind raced to calculate the risk, I realized I could see nothing good that could come out of what I was about to say to him, and only a hundred bad things.

I certainly would have been setting myself against the Russian state personified, and going beyond simply voicing my disagreement about a law. Depending on how Putin responded, it is possible I would have been sacked, although these were days in which one could still voice a degree of qualified dissent, even to his face. However, one way or the other, my fate (and that of my family) would no longer be in my own hands. Would my bosses or my bosses' bosses be mortified, and angrily want me gone? Just as dangerously, would some more outspoken dissidents publicly hail my "protest," which would likely make the authorities feel they had to retaliate and treat me as such?

And for what? The law's moral and practical shortcomings had already been exposed and critiqued; it was not as if Putin was going to change his mind. Was the question really worth asking? Was it that of a journalist hoping for copy, or just that of an outraged citizen speaking her mind? Because that was the point: I was not a rebel, not a dissident, not an oppositionist, I was merely a citizen who sometimes approved of what her government was doing and sometimes did not. One who neither broke laws, nor felt the need to. At that moment, I did not want to protest, challenge, or defy. And I wanted to retain the right of a citizen rather than a subject, to have an independent opinion about what the monarch was doing, rather than unthinkingly internalize the increasingly paranoid, nationalist, and intolerant line of the times. But, in these narcissistic days in the West when all it seems to take is a social media account to claim a crusade of some sort, this is worth stressing: it takes a lot more than having a dissenting opinion to be a dissident. To *be* one is to set yourself directly against the state, to issue a challenge and accept the worst it can do in response. Whether covertly, as a matter of one's internal conscience, or overtly, as an active protester and organizer, it means taking on a consistent pledge to dissent, condemn, or defy. To fight, in other words, a battle you yourself are unlikely to win. It was a fight that I was not prepared then – and if I am honest, have not intended since – to take on.

What is a dissident? What is a rebel?

During Putin's tenure, virtually anyone who has criticized him or his policies has been branded a dissident by Western reporters, with all sorts of implications, and this was one of the reasons I was so adamant to hold on to my own impartiality. Take, for example, the journalist Oleg Kashin, who in 2012 was elected a member of the Opposition Coordination Council, which was trying to build a unified front against Putin's third term in office. Yet, as for a lot of Russian oppositionists and dissenters, the word *dissident* is a very specific concept that he believed did not apply to him. "In my opinion, a dissident is someone who devotes all of himself to confronting the authorities," he told me by text in 2017, from Geneva, not quite exile, not quite emigration – something temporary, in between. "We have much fewer such heroes than representatives of the moderate front, who in one way or another work for the state, succeed, but at the same time consider themselves bearers of absolute moral righteousness."[4]

Kashin had every reason to call out the holier-than-thou pseudo-dissidents with a disproportionate sense of their own importance. In 2010, he was a journalist for the newspaper *Kommersant*, writing about the slew of political protest movements that had sprouted, from the young Communists to the National Bolshevik Party. He was an acerbic reporter, and minced no words when blogging about his detractors. In one of his blog posts, he called the governor of the Pskov region, Andrei Turchak, "shitty." It nearly cost him his life. That year, two assailants, whom Kashin believes were hired by Turchak, confronted him in the dark near the entrance to his apartment, bearing a bouquet of flowers as a distraction. Then they beat him with metal rods and left him to die. He survived with a broken jaw, a fractured skull, and a partially amputated pinkie. He was a writer, after all, and so they went after his hands.

But even so, he maintained that Putin's Russia, at that time at least, was a place where criticism remained possible. It was personally offending someone that put you in danger. "If you offend a person, well, in the prison worldview, that person has to get revenge or else his friends won't understand. It is like gangsters in power."[5] This was not so much about going against the system, but about the system being unable to protect those who found themselves at the mercy of such personalized power. And that was one reason why the kind of dissident movement that the Soviet Union saw in the 1960s didn't really apply anymore.

"The reality of Putinism," Kashin told me years later after his attack, "meant that you didn't necessarily have to put yourself against the whole system to disagree with things that the Kremlin or your local officials were doing." Did he consider himself a dissident? "The word 'dissident' is tied up with a specific time and specific people, and using it seriously now is tactless, especially when you talk about yourself – it sounds like 'Sakharov and I,'" he added, name-checking one of the greats of the dissident movement, who spent most of the 1980s in internal exile, even though he had won a Nobel Prize for physics and was considered one of the fathers of the Soviet atom bomb.[6]

That reality was the main reason why I, standing in front of Putin, found myself resisting two polar opposites: either the need to submit as a subject, or the need to defy as a rebel. It was not black and white. There was a new category: a citizen who could simply disagree. The state was still dangerous, still repressive, but for the first time in Russian history, there was a whole variety of ways that citizens or subjects or oppositionists could interact with the autocrat – and with each other. It was a world in which both what Alena and I had done were equally possible: neither was she denounced for her confrontation, nor was I ostracized by dissenters for my timidity.

In 2012 and 2013, tens of thousands of young people, raised on two decades of relative affluence and political stability, were actively defying their autocratic government. In the process, they were defying a depressingly Russophobic notion: that Russians were somehow prone to submission and "learned helplessness," that they lacked agency and the will to change. Never mind that all of Russian history is a story of dissent and rebellion. Yet what was happening in those years was something different: they weren't just protesting, or confronting Putin – that, as Alena rightly insisted, was by far not the most important part – they were also building legal initiatives around local interests, and using the laws of their country to reclaim agency. The new, independent TV channel Dozhd, which launched in 2010 and became the first to cover the protest rallies in real time both on television and online, became a reflection of that agency, and its possibility. Its slogan, "the optimistic channel," implied that the actions and voices of this new generation mattered, that Russia had a future, and that they were claiming it. Step by little step, they were assembling the tiny bricks that eventually, generations down the line, could use to build an institutional democracy. Even as many braced for the looming autocratic revanche that would descend a few years later, an unheard-of pluralism coexisted with Putin's autocracy.

In December 2012, it often baffled me to think that I lived in Moscow and worked for a Kremlin-funded English-language newspaper, even as I wrote articles describing the Kremlin as an oppressive, corrupt authoritarian government. I covered protest rallies, held two citizenships, and traveled abroad freely. Nothing was taboo. Liberals, nationalists, Putin's fans, and his vehement foes would break bread together and share alcohol over the same table, despite vicious spats online: a kind of intellectual tolerance and inclusivity that didn't seem to fit with the ominous stories of state repression that I found myself writing. The dissidents and rebels of earlier times had faced often more conventionally repressive regimes, where the stakes were higher and more immediate: the hangman's noose, the Gulag, the Soviet psychiatric hospital. At the time, Putin was relying on more subtle forms of repression, maintaining a manipulative illusion of democracy. The result was that we could still believe we had choices and reasons for hope. The line between rebel and conformist became increasingly blurred as people suddenly found themselves with a whole slew of options: running for local council, opposing a highway through a forest, or something as simple as creating an apartment cooperative to ensure that local authorities renovated their plumbing on time.

The twilight of democracy

Alena had become politically active during a pivotal time in Russia. Until 2008, the independent, non-systemic political opposition – in other words, the opposition not represented in Russia's parliament – largely consisted of pro-Western, pro-business liberal politicians, such as the Yabloko party or the Union of Right Forces. Their main agenda centered on democratic reform, and, thus, on Putin's backtracking and his efforts to stifle it. While these were serious issues, it meant these parties had little support outside of the educated, relatively wealthier cosmopolitan centers. The majority of the population, still recovering from the shocks of the 1990s, a time of widespread economic hardship and political chaos, were more concerned with survival than they were with human rights and democratic reforms as such. According to opinion polls at the time, issues such as poverty and corruption ranked highest among their concerns, but these were not the issues on which the liberal oppositionists as yet chose to focus. When Putin turned up the pressure on oligarch-funded independent media after becoming president in 2000, these movements further lost touch with potential supporters in the regions and among the less wealthy. By 2003, they were being pushed out of parliament entirely thanks not only to the Kremlin's manipulation of the media and the electoral system, but also to their simple lack of connection with popular Russian concerns.

Meanwhile, opposition parties that did have powerful regional networks and support – notably the Communist Party and the nationalist far-right Liberal Democratic Party of Russia – managed to retain a significant parliamentary presence, but the Kremlin tamed them through a combination of electoral, political, and media manipulation. By 2008, when Putin was due to step down as president, they essentially represented a token opposition, a facsimile of democratic politics engineered by his deputy chief of staff, the theatrical gray cardinal Vladislav Surkov. They might get headlines for some carefully calibrated rhetorical stands on populist causes, but in practice most of these parties drafted and voted on legislation as instructed by the Presidential Administration.

Thus, with no true democratic alternatives or checks and balances, it was widely expected that Putin would amend the constitutional ban on more than two consecutive presidential terms and remain in power. Instead, he did something that was as unusual for a democratically elected leader as an authoritarian one: he threw his endorsement and his administrative resource behind his prime minister, then a pro-Western liberal Dmitry Medvedev, and himself switched places with him. Medvedev, under Putin's watchful eye, was given relatively free rein to launch a limited liberalization campaign to improve the economy and tackle corruption.

This began to create a new paradox. On the one hand, the Kremlin was now vocally engaged with a core issue at the heart of Russia's democratic challenges: corruption and lack of rule of law. Much effort and publicity was being devoted to innovation and modernization. On the other hand, Medvedev was constrained in his reforms. Real power was ultimately still in Putin's hands, and his injunction to Medvedev was clear: tackle corruption all you want, as long as it doesn't infringe upon my interests or those of my vast circle of vassals. The new liberalization campaign exposed deep economic inequalities, a byproduct of corruption itself. The World Bank's Poverty and Inequality Platform, for example, measures the disparity between rich and poor households in a country using something called the Gini Index. It had been 37.1 when Putin came to power in 2000, well below the United States, or even the United Kingdom.[7] By 2008, it was 41.6, higher than either of them, or, indeed, any other European country.

The more corruption was talked about on central television channels, the more this encouraged independent politicians to take up the issue, normalizing a new form of activism at the grass-roots level: that of economic and infrastructural interests. Politics, in other words, was becoming no longer just about grand narratives of democracy or Communism, or necessarily fighting the leviathan of state power and oppression. Activism and independent politics still remained difficult and deeply dangerous, but new possibilities emerged for interest groups and human rights campaigners – environmentalists, feminists, trade unionists – to effect change on the local level and create meaningful networks. This fledgling work was still difficult and precarious enough that many activists eventually turned against the Kremlin as they recognized that it was Putin himself who was standing in the way of true reform. For instance, police officer Alexei Dymovsky, fired in 2010 for blowing the whistle on corruption in his precinct, gained a nationwide following after addressing his concerns to Putin directly in videos he then posted on the internet.[8] His cause was even taken up in parliament, and such cases began to normalize what in the past had been something only a handful of dissenters willing to risk their lives would do: standing up for their interests, even if it meant standing up to the Kremlin. It no longer seemed quite so futile, quite so inevitably leading to prison or worse. The fact that such abuses continued to happen only galvanized this fledgling civil society, and a growing proportion of the population with it. More options and fewer consequences meant that pockets of civic action emerged in which activists robustly espoused various causes that were neither opposed to, nor supporting, the regime. Issues from school curricula to the siting of municipal waste dumps could and did spark passionate activism as independent political movements advocated and fought for their interests, sometimes clashing with the Kremlin when it tried to constrain them, and sometimes clashing with each other.

When Putin and Medvedev jointly announced they would be switching places again in September 2011, they wound up both dashing hopes for true democratic reform while simultaneously exposing Putin as the architect of a phenomenally potent lie. The parliamentary elections that December were hardly more rigged than recent ballots that preceded them, but Russians had come to expect more from their government and such lies were no longer acceptable. Tens of thousands took to the streets, first in Moscow and St. Petersburg, then in cities across the country, in protests on a scale unseen since the breakup of the Soviet Union. Demonstrators turning up at Bolotnaya – the Moscow square just across the bridge from the

Kremlin where people spontaneously gathered – came from a plethora of political movements. Nationalist war re-enactors marched under the same banner as monarchists, Communists, and liberals; officers of the airborne troops sang ditties decrying corruption and the stolen vote; junior civil servants chanted slogans against the very government for which they worked. These were no longer just the marginalized pro-Western (and usually relatively affluent) liberals who criticized the government for its shoddy human rights record. The Kremlin cracked down hard, brutally breaking up protest rallies and handing down jail sentences of several years to some of the activists. However, it surprisingly let the protests continue and avoided jailing its most outspoken leaders, such as Alexei Navalny, Ilya Yashin, and Boris Nemtsov (who, incidentally, would die in jail in 2024, be imprisoned in 2022, and murdered in 2015, respectively). This bait-and-switch approach was designed to split the opposition, but also to avoid the kind of repressive overreaction that could backfire and lead to revolt within the elites themselves. In the process, paradoxically, it normalized dissent yet further. Even parliamentarians such as Gennady Gudkov and Ilya Ponomaryov openly joined the anti-Kremlin protests and used their voices in the State Duma to challenge the government.

And so, a curious situation arose: precision repressions and electoral manipulation persisted and gradually increased, trying to prevent civil society from growing further. Yet there still remained a narrow space in which political activism could flourish, and those who pursued it gained invaluable legal and political experience. Putin, re-elected president in March 2012, continued having meetings with various members of the opposition as part of the Valdai discussion club to try to demonstrate that Russia remained a pluralistic society, even as his parliament passed ever more restrictive laws and the unspoken "red lines" over what was politically acceptable and what was not continued to be tightened.[9]

Political activists, intimidated by the mounting repressions from challenging the Kremlin wholesale, turned their activism towards local work, beginning to bridge the gap between the population and local, regional, and even federal government. In 2019, for example, when authorities in Yekaterinburg decided to build a church on a central city square, residents petitioned and demonstrated to have a park instead. It was just one of such successful demonstrations across the country that year.[10]

For roughly a decade, this twilight persisted between unprecedented pluralism and civic activism, on the one hand, and duplicitous government manipulation and repression, on the other. It was not until 2022 that the accumulation of foreign agent laws and a new spate of draconian restrictions targeting anti-war activists plunged Russia into full authoritarianism.

But it was in that environment of relative freedom that Alena Popova confronted Vladimir Putin, while I walked away – and each of us continued our work.

That was then. I am now writing this in a time so grim that even contacting Russian activists back home gives me pause lest I inadvertently put them in danger. In hindsight, I can't help but question my own recollections of a period not more than a decade ago. How was any of it possible? Was it a mirage? And why did it end? Why did the cycle of thaw and repression that we had thought we were breaking out of descend upon us again? The liberalism the autocrat had unleashed had awoken something that threatened him personally – but why?

The man who would not be named

Everything was angular about him: his brilliant Hollywood smile, the choppy movements of his hands as he spoke, the Western mannerisms he had picked up abroad at Yale. But it was the smile that really stood out in that sleepy southern Russian town.

Alexei Navalny didn't know me, probably didn't trust me as a representative of the state media, but his smile was a signal of intentional trust, if not sincerity. It was the intentional trust that came from the confidence of his own rational agency, the belief that his country's laws were for him and for the people, and not for those in power, and, most of all, the belief in solutions. The belief that tomorrow did not have to be like yesterday, and that all Russians, of every race and class, could work together to build a "beautiful Russia of the future."[11]

* * *

It was spring 2012, just a month after Putin had been re-elected president, despite the biggest anti-Kremlin demonstrations Russia had seen in two decades. Restarting his presidency on such a shaky footing, Putin turned to a primitive form of patriotism to bolster his power: the hatred of all that was foreign, new, and uncustomary. During the protests against Putin's re-election, Navalny had emerged as one of the most charismatic leaders of the opposition, not least because he had something new to offer. Unlike many of the previous liberal activists, Navalny's criticism of the Kremlin wasn't just about democratic values, but instead predominantly about the rule of law, without which democratic values cannot thrive. A lawyer who had studied at Yale, he had gained notoriety as an anti-corruption blogger and vocally began exposing a disease that had plagued Russian administrations for centuries, a disease that many pro-Western liberals argued was the very essence of Russia: graft. But in doing so, Navalny – who had early in his political career flirted with nationalism – accomplished something revolutionary: instead of simply opposing the government and its repressive laws, he weaponized the legal system against the Kremlin. If Putin had campaigned with promises to impose a "dictatorship of the law" in 2000, then Navalny subverted the Kremlin's own promise against itself. He exposed how Putin was breaking his own laws. In doing so, he enabled a fledgling opposition movement to do something it had arguably never had a chance to do in all of Russian history: to reclaim the country's laws from its corrupt and tyrannical government officials, at least to a degree, and for a while.

The protests against the Kremlin in the winter and spring of 2011–12 posed an unprecedented threat to the regime's legitimacy and so, too, did the emergence of such a charismatic figure as Navalny, someone who, like Putin a decade earlier, seemed to speak to ordinary Russians outside the cosmopolitan bubble. Demonstrators turning up for his rallies were no longer distinctly pro-Western: hearing me and a colleague speaking in English in front of a camera, a demonstrator called us "American pigs." And if in the past Russian flags were virtually unseen in opposition protests, suddenly they were everywhere. Instead, these protests hit the Kremlin's greatest vulnerability: corruption. This was, after all, an issue that united all strata of society. From the truck driver forced to pay off a traffic cop after an imaginary speeding infraction, to the army officer expected to "thank" his superior officer for a positive annual report, or simply the citizen seeing his or her taxes going on padded vanity projects that never actually got built, everyone had their own experiences.

Putin responded with vigor – but also calculation. He pronounced the protests a provocation by the US Department of State, and claimed the activists lacked genuine public support but were rather whipped up by foreign powers.[12] (Alas, he was helped in this by the well-meaning but politically inept efforts of US Ambassador Michael McFaul, who sought to "help" Russian civil society by holding highly publicized meetings with them.) He fired his first deputy chief of staff Vladislav Surkov and replaced him with the heavier-handed Vyacheslav Volodin. Surkov, who trained to be a theater director in his youth, had been the man behind the earlier style of political control, creating a democratic façade to make people think their views mattered. Volodin was more interested in building a "patriotic alliance" against the liberals, courting the working class and leaning heavily on the Russian Orthodox Church to promote traditional Russian values. The state launched a targeted repression campaign against members of the opposition meant to portray them as Western lackeys, passing a series of draconian laws that penalized anyone receiving money from abroad and jailing a select few on trumped-up charges.

At the same time, Putin continued to allow the opposition to gather and protest, while promising to establish dialogue with them.[13] This served two purposes: it hit back at the allegations that the Kremlin was repressive and intolerant of dissent, but it also allowed it to portray Navalny and his supporters as foreign, alien. While the liberal opposition was demonized, nationalists or protesters with specific economic grievances were allowed to march and gather. Preventing attempts to build cross-class and cross-party alliances was a priority. Indeed, the government also organized "spontaneous" pro-Kremlin counter-demonstrations to which civil servants and factory workers were bussed in. Altogether, these moves splintered an opposition which was already struggling to maintain cohesion. Leaders bickered among themselves over who had become a "Kremlin collaborator" by agreeing to hold protests wherever City Hall allowed them, rather than wherever and whenever they wanted – even though this meant encouraging people to risk arrest. Some of the more liberal politicians even tried to "cancel" Navalny for some of his earlier nationalist views, years before cancel culture was even a thing in the United States. The liberal Yabloko party expelled Navalny over his participation in the nationalist Russia March in 2007, and continued to exclude him from their ticket even as he gained popularity in 2011.[14] From the Kremlin's standpoint, the more reason each of the political movements that initially turned up on Bolotnaya Square had to blame America, gay rootless cosmopolitans, or each other for Russia's ills, the less energy would be directed against the regime. Navalny was maligned on national television, but for a whole decade the Kremlin avoided jailing him outright. Right up until it didn't.

* * *

On January 17, 2021, after recovering in a German clinic from a nearly fatal poisoning at the hands of the Federal Security Service, Alexei Navalny boarded a Moscow-bound flight. This was despite the fact that the Russian authorities had launched yet another questionable criminal investigation against him, this time all but promising him a steep prison sentence. In doing so, he broke again with a powerful tradition – one that, indeed, the Kremlin sought to perpetuate – of dissidents in exile. If he was going to change Russia, then he felt it was ill-fitting for a leader to sit in comfort and safety in the West, while calling on ordinary citizens to risk their lives as his foot soldiers.

Navalny probably knew exactly what was about to happen to him, but he projected an unfazed confidence in his abilities and, indeed, in his safety, as though by believing in a rules-based Russia where the laws served to protect the country's citizens he could somehow will it into being. "I'm sure everything will be absolutely great," he told a throng of journalists who accompanied him on his flight. "What? Arrested upon arrival? Me? That's impossible. What should I be afraid of in Russia? What bad can happen to me in Russia?"[15] said the man who had just months ago survived a poisoning and faced mounted criminal cases on trumped-up charges. It was hard to tell whether this was bravado or dark humour. Upon landing, just minutes before police detained him at the border control booth and led him away, he remained defiant: "I am not afraid. I'll feel normal going through passport control and I'll go home because I know I'm right."[16]

* * *

I would like to say, looking back at that period, that never in Russia's history was the dance of the rebel and the tsar so free, so intricate, so fraught with potential as in the aughts and 2010s. But a sober look at the country's history belies that notion – contrary to the toxic ideas about a slavish population unable (or, worse yet, unwilling) to resist state tyranny, Russia's whole history is one long dance of resistance. It is, in that regard, not that different from the histories of Western nations, where it took centuries of competition, rebellion, and even civil war between state power and various estates to forge the kind of institutional democracies we see today. Russian history was always fraught with that potential, and yet the dances tended to be cyclical, oscillating back and forth violently between revolution and repression. What remains unclear is the present – and therefore the future. Is Russia currently mired in a revanchist revolutionary moment that often precedes the birth of true nationhood? Or is it, instead, in a period of stagnation that will leave, in its wake, another thaw? Or is it experiencing both?

And what will determine which outcome will prevail? The temptation is always to focus on the powers that be. After all, they have the men, the guns, the knouts, the censors, and the prisons. Yet real agency lies with the rebels, the dissidents, and the choices they make – and we have seen the extent to which, even in this relatively short historical period, their actions have influenced and shaped the government itself. What distinguished Navalny and the wider movement which both created him and which he so effectively championed was precisely that it began to reach out across the divides between affluent and impoverished, liberals and patriots, metropolitans and heartlanders. He and his team produced slick online videos revealing and lampooning the corruption of Russia's leaders that drew viewers in their millions. More to the point, he increasingly used the corruption issue as a way to try to build a genuinely national constituency for reform, even reaching out to those who would close down his rallies and drag away his supporters, and highlight the degree to which a Russian police officer's lot was often not a happy one, either. This deliberate attempt to build solidarity, to bridge the gap between dissident minority and unhappy majority, was what was so dangerous for the Kremlin and, as we shall see, so unusual in the context of Russian history. Too often, after all, the dissidents' dances were not open to the masses whom they claimed to represent. Russia has often been ruled by a repressive regime – but a distant, inefficient, or distracted one. In practice, Russians have often had considerable agency, whether to flee, to conform, or to rebel. For all the notions of Russia as a collectivist society, the challenges lay in *collective* agency as opposed to individual agency. Time and again, as we shall see in the coming chapters, the fragile bonds of collective agency – the negotiation of common interests that tied human to human, the beginnings of nationhood – were severed either by the calamity of minority-led rebellions, or by the repression of the fragile, ever-fearful tsar.

2

The Traitor and the Tsar

The fragile autocrat

It was an eternally awkward situation, an elephant that trailed Vladimir Putin into every room he entered. The name of Alexei Navalny, the leading light of Russia's non-systemic opposition, a man who had managed to bring together Russians in a way no other politician had managed to do (except, perhaps, for Putin in the early days of his power), was on the lips of at least one reporter at every presidential press conference. Are you afraid of Navalny? Why was Navalny being barred from elections if he doesn't pose a threat? Why was he poisoned? Each time, the president – having gone to great lengths to shield himself from the prospect of debating with or ever even appearing in the same space as Navalny – bent over backwards just to avoid uttering his name. "The authorities are not afraid of anyone," he said in 2018, pretending Navalny didn't exist. "The character you mentioned" was not the only person barred from standing in recent elections, he said on another occasion, deflecting onto his favorite topic of rigged elections in the United States. By 2021, Navalny was just "one of the citizens of the Russian Federation who has been found guilty by a court of law and is in prison."[1]

Nearly 500 years earlier, another autocrat peculiarly preoccupied with the legitimacy of his rule chose a different approach. They were distinctly different personalities, Vladimir and Ivan, in that the former feared to even mention his nemesis's name, while the latter entered into an epistolary debate with an errant vassal who hardly warranted such zealous attention. But they were each of them in a similar predicament, feeling that they faced an existential threat from a mere dissident who would hardly pose a challenge to a truly strong sovereign: Alexei Navalny and Prince Andrei Kurbsky, one of Russia's latest dissidents and arguably its first, respectively, highlighted the weakness even of the apparently most powerful regimes.

* * *

"To the Tsar . . . who now, for our sins, has the conscience of a leper, which you will not find even amongst the godless,"[2] wrote a disgraced general to his ruler. "What evil and persecution have I not suffered from you! But I cannot now recount the various misfortunes at your hands."

Andrei Kurbsky had once been one of Tsar Ivan IV's most loyal servants, fighting and winning battles in the war against his western neighbors. Now, having defected to hostile Lithuania, he suddenly launched a vitriolic campaign against the monarch who became known as Ivan the Terrible, chronicling – or fabricating – abuses and esteeming him below a "simple lowly soldier,"[3] denouncing the tsar's "widely broadcast and blaring writing . . . belched out of uncontrollable anger with poisonous words."[4] What had happened?

Prince Kurbsky has often been called Russia's first dissident. But the reasons for his sudden decision to flee to Lithuania, and, particularly, his subsequent smear campaign against Ivan the Terrible, remain somewhat of a mystery. Born of an ancient princely family with unimpeachable loyalty to the throne, Kurbsky had been a steadfast supporter of Ivan's despite his closeness to certain boyars, aristocrats, who came to oppose the tsar. After a series of victories against Lithuania and Livonia, the general was appointed governor of a good chunk of Livonian territory. Then, in 1562, Kurbsky, commanding a 15,000-strong army, was defeated by a mere 4,000 Lithuanian troops near the town of Nevel. Soon after, Lithuanian King Sigismund Augustus offered him riches, estates, and courtly favor were he to defect. The prince seems to have taken little convincing: he parted with his wife and children (leaving them vulnerable to exile or execution; they were certainly imprisoned, but their final fate is unknown) and took up his erstwhile enemy's offer in 1564, receiving the town of Kovel as a fiefdom. There is no evidence of threats against Kurbsky, or any indication of displeasure from his tsar, prior to his decision.

Instead, it seems, a series of actions undertaken by the tsar himself turned Kurbsky into one of his most outspoken foes, obsessed with bringing down the Russian ruler. Before his disgrace, Kurbsky had been an influential prince at a time when Russia's estates – the nobility, the peasantry, and the townspeople, the newly unified state's fledgling middle class – were coming into their own and all, in their own ways, gaining greater power, or at least a stronger sense of their own identity and interests. Many within the aristocracy in particular appreciated the need for modernization, and, when Ivan was crowned tsar in 1547 at the age of 17, they saw in the young, idealistic, and impressionable Ivan a reformist monarch. In the 1550s, Prince Alexei Fedorovich Adashev and the priest Silvester from the Blagoveshchensk Cathedral in the Kremlin spearheaded efforts to create what would become known as the Chosen Council. By that point, Russia already had the roots of a parliament – the Zemski Sobor, or Assembly of the Land – and the Chosen Council was meant to become something of a cabinet, a close-knit group of leading priests and princes advising the tsar.[5] Kurbsky was close to Adashev and Silvester, and the priest was especially passionate about imposing legal constraints on the tsar to ensure a more "just and kind" reign.[6]

He also fiercely supported their reform efforts, and would himself become a member of the Chosen Council.[7]

The early years of Ivan's reign saw the foundations of the institutions of the state in what had hitherto been a thoroughly personalistic realm. The intention was to strengthen the tsarist order, allowing it to govern more efficiently and raise the taxes needed for the wars he would be waging, but in the process, even if in the name of greater state control, it inevitably also brought that state closer to society. Ivan's Banditry Office, for example, was the first, however limited, serious attempt to address the widespread rural criminality which was such a concern for the peasantry, just as the Petitions Office – under Adashev – accepted and acted on direct requests to the tsar from even the most wretched of his subjects. Ivan founded the Moscow Print Yard, the first domestic printing house. His *Sudebnik* of 1550 was the first authoritative and standardized law code in Russia. It even increased the rights of the peasantry, banning their forced enserfment and granting peasant communities greater degrees of self-government. The *Stoglav* ("Hundred Chapter") text that emerged from a 1551 synod (which included Silvester) addressed not only doctrinal questions but also corruption and abuse within the Church. These were in no way signs that Ivan was willing to accept the notion of serious constraints on his authority – he was no closet constitutionalist. These were all measures intended to strengthen the monarchy and the state. Yet running through all these early reforms was an understanding that institutions provided a means to connect monarch, aristocracy, gentry, and commoners, and that even if the tsar held power by the will of God, he exercised it with the consent of the ruled.

This would have been an important step forward in the evolution of Russian governance – had it lasted. In 1554, Adashev led a diplomatic mission to Livonia, as part of Ivan's efforts to gain access to ports on the Baltic Sea. These areas were controlled by the Livonian Order, a branch of the crusading

Teutonic Knights, who were blocking access to Russian merchants eager to trade with the West. Hesitant to wage war, Ivan first resorted to political pressure and tried to get the Order to resume paying tribute for territories they had taken from Russian princes two centuries earlier. Despite promises on the Livonian side, ultimately Adashev's mission failed, and Ivan launched a military campaign against the Order in 1557. Adashev, historians believe, opposed the war, and Ivan dismissed him from court in 1560, and Silvester soon after.[8] Besides, the war, and the financial burdens it created, was resented by many boyars, and their evident dissatisfaction clearly alarmed and angered the volatile and ever-paranoid Ivan, who sought new means of buttressing his rule.

The collapse of the Chosen Council was a culmination of a brewing domestic political crisis. But something had changed within the ruler himself: not only did he see the reforms as a failure, he somehow felt personally betrayed. Like so many autocrats before and since, he understood the need to listen to society and elites alike, but resented it when they told him what he did not want to hear. Faced with growing challenges from an increasingly powerful boyar class which had felt emboldened by the reforms, Ivan felt cornered. For protection, he turned instead to younger, ambitious, and aggressive members of the service gentry, families which were granted land in exchange for service, and launched a campaign of repression of his real or imagined enemies. In 1565, to blackmail the boyars into accepting his will as a supreme and unlimited governing force, he left Moscow for the village of Alexandrova Sloboda and "abdicated" his throne. In reality, what the abdication meant was the separation of Russian lands into the *oprichnina* – Ivan's personal realm – and the *zemshchina*, that of the princes, appointing to the latter a nominal ruler, his crony Simeon Bekbulatovich. In practice, the protectors of Ivan's realm, the *oprichniki*, had unlimited rein to plunder and confiscate the lands of the *zemshchina* if the owner was but suspected of treason – which Ivan's henchmen gleefully abused to their advantage.

Kurbsky's defection in April 1564 predated the launch of Ivan's infamous terror by some eight months, which, given that he was at the time in good standing with the tsar, has perplexed some historians. Ian Grey, for instance, characterizes Kurbsky as a selfish opportunist of "weak loyalties."[9] Yet Kurbsky had maintained close contact with and remained dedicated to the tsar after the dismissal of Adashev and Silvester, despite being close to them as well. However, their dismissals, as well as Ivan's increasingly arbitrary accusations of treason against other boyars, very likely made clear to any insider the repressions that were to come. As a friend of Adashev and Silvester who, despite his professed loyalty to the tsar, shared their views on the need for legal limits to his power, Kurbsky must have guessed that sooner or later Ivan would see him as a traitor too, simply for disagreeing with him, and that it was a matter of time before his black-robed horsemen, with severed dogs' heads and brooms at their sides (symbolizing that they were the tsar's hounds, who would sweep away any treachery), would come for him, his family, and his lands.

What is more interesting, however, is the fact that, judging by their correspondence, Ivan seemed to regard Kurbsky – a mere prince who fled the terror of a sovereign who claimed the power of God on earth – as something of an equal. This was a man who managed to subordinate the nobility to an extent that no Western monarch at the time could, reversing centuries of Russian development, all in the course of just seven years. (That is how long Ivan's reign of terror lasted.) It was not just that he reviled Kurbsky as "rotten in soul and body," having committed "a dog's treason" and given him "colic of misfortune, colic of insult, colic of annoyance and reproach!" It was also that he clearly felt the need somehow to refute Kurbsky's claim that he had "locked up the Russian kingdom and the free nature of man, as if in a hellish stronghold," and to convince him that he was doing the right thing and did indeed hold "autocracy, by the will of God."[10]

If Ivan was indeed as powerful as he professed, then why did he feel the need to respond to a runaway prince with a series of hysterical diatribes? Why was Ivan the Terrible so vulnerable as to be threatened by Andrei Kurbsky in the first place?

The autocrat stands alone

There are a number of explanations for Ivan's sense of vulnerability – but all of them highlight that the monarch was only as strong as the society he sought to govern. The alienation of ruler and ruled, and the alienation between the estates of the ruled, undermined the very basis of the monarchy.

One school of thought, the most popular, blames the terror on Ivan's growing paranoia, brought on by the death of his wife, Anastasia, as well as his general emotional instability, whether by nature or nurture. But this explanation ignores the growing influence of figures such as Adashev and Kurbsky, and, indeed, the vast leaps made in the development of Russian society itself. By the second half of the sixteenth century, contrary to some subsequent myths of a dark land populated by a backward, slavish people, Muscovy was a burgeoning, even prosperous country, with the beginnings of a national parliament, the Assembly of the Land; institutional limitations on the tsar; robust trade with Europe; and even trial by jury. While historians such as Richard Pipes would describe early Russia as wholly agrarian and point to the lack of a viable urban merchant class as a factor in the despotism of its tsars and emperors, a closer look at the contemporary evidence suggests Muscovy's socioeconomic development was not so far behind, and in some cases exceeded, that of central Europe. In 1520, residents in the northern border town of Narva, which is now in modern-day Estonia, noted with some anxiety the rapid urbanization they were seeing around them: "Soon there will be no one in Russia to take the plow any longer, for all are running to the cities and becoming merchants."[11] The Soviet historian Alexander Yanov writes: "Both elites [the new bureaucratic apparatus and the hereditary aristocracy] learned the art of interacting in the decision-making process. The political functioning of the traditional ('patrimonial') aristocracy, which by reason of its hereditary status was independent of the state, thus represented a strong social limitation on power."[12]

Yanov, in his 1981 study *The Origins of Autocracy*, marvels with dismay at the sudden turn towards repression taken by Ivan following his earlier reforms and his state-building. According to him, Russian history is not one long descent into tyranny, but rather an oscillation between European-style absolutism – periods of relatively liberal reform and attempts at integration with the West – and oriental despotism. A great number of factors play into this dance, but ultimately there is no single neat driver.

Yanov was long retired by the second decade of the twenty-first century when another Russian ruler who, while committed during his first two terms to state-building and fostering democratic institutions, gradually succumbed to paranoia, launched a war of aggression against his neighbor, and suddenly instigated the deepest repressions Russia has seen since Soviet times. Emotional instability and paranoia can only go so far in explaining a phenomenon to which so many Russian autocrats ultimately fall prey. Instead, if there is a pattern, it is this: much like in any Western country, social classes build up and develop their representative institutions, forming the foundations of a legal rational state, then begin challenging the ruler – often the same one who sought to foster these institutions in the first place. The ruler, fearing the challenge, fights back with such force as to obliterate these institutions. In the case of Ivan, the civic destruction wrought by his terror plunged the country back decades, if not centuries. In the case of Joseph Stalin, the Great Terror managed to achieve phenomenal industrial progress, but negated the very spirit of the social reforms that were meant to lie at the heart of the Communist ideology imposed by the Bolsheviks. In the case of Vladimir Putin, he was able to tolerate an increasingly robust civil society and political opposition – until he wasn't.

In all of these cases, the same question arises: why does Russian civil society – the nobility's institutions in the time of Ivan, the oppositionist class that emerged in Russia after 2012 – fail to withstand the ruler's repressions and allow itself to be obliterated, silenced, or exiled by what is in effect a surprisingly vulnerable autocrat?

Going back to the decisive events of the 1560s, an increasingly insecure autocrat, seeing no chance to guarantee his dynasty, exploited the divisions between emerging social classes, pitting one against the other to weaken the aristocracy and clothe himself in an armor of dread. According to Yanov, one factor behind establishing the *oprichnina* was not just the need to instigate political repression, but to seize more land, which was at a premium, in order to continue to expand and buy off the emerging service gentry – that very class of soldiers and bureaucrats that had recently emerged as part of a centralized state apparatus. By allowing the *oprichniki* to take over the territories of the boyars, Ivan was, to use an anachronistic term, waging a class war, playing an institution which was disproportionately recruited from the gentry against the established aristocracy.

As Yanov himself notes, left to their own devices, the service gentry and the old patrimonial aristocracy would likely have eventually negotiated some kind of political deal that would have created institutional checks and balances both on each other, and on the tsar himself, who ultimately depended on them to govern his country for him. But this equilibrium was destroyed as the sovereign aligned himself with a new, ambitious gentry class that, as a result, found more in common with the tsar than it did with other social classes.

Something about the structure of Russian society made it easier to establish stronger vertical ties than horizontal ones. In other words, despite the socioeconomic growth of the fifteenth and sixteenth centuries, an alienation persisted between the various classes of society, and between the ruler and the ruled. While the monarch would align himself with this or that section of society, it was almost always to buttress himself against another class from which he felt a threat emerging – usually either the ruling aristocracy or the rich liberal class. Just as Ivan would enlist the new service gentry as his *oprichniki*, Peter the Great used the foreign-speaking aristocracy to modernize the "backward" merchant class a century and a half later, obliterating Russian national consciousness in the process; Lenin aligned with the "working class" – in reality, agrarian migrants to the cities – to overthrow the monarchy and wipe out the aristocracy; Boris Yeltsin turned to a new pro-Western business class to break the nationalist–Communist opposition (undermining fledgling democratic institutions that sought to represent the interests of the disenfranchised); and finally Putin mobilized the nationalists and Communists to tame the liberals, wiping out all opposition in the process. In each of these periods, the country suffered from a persistent alienation of the state from its people, of the people from each other, and, worst of all, of the people from themselves.

The escape of the rebel

First there was the word. The name for the Slavic tribes that would eventually form the Russian ethnos comes from *slovo*, the word, and these earlier tribes would call themselves *Slovene* or *Sloviane*, those who speak, as opposed to *Nemtsy*, the mute, those who do not speak or who cannot be understood. During the time of the Roman Empire, these tribes inhabited an area of Central Europe that stretched from what is modern-day Poland to Slovenia. Following the fall of Rome in the West and beginning in the fourth century, these tribes began to split into three branches: the Western Slavs, the Southern Slavs, and the Eastern Slavs. "Little is known of Slav prehistory," Pipes rather dismissively writes. "All that can be said with reasonable certainty is that the early Slavs were nomadic cattle grazers organized into clans and tribes, and that they had neither political nor military forms of organization."[13]

There are two contradictions within this very sentence. If little is known, how can we be confident that the Slavs had no political forms of organization? But more importantly, how can one assert that there were no political forms of organization, having just said that these nomadic cattle grazers organized into clans and tribes? The Alpine Slavs – one of the tribes that stayed in Central Europe – formed their own independent state in present-day Austria as early as 626 after their own duke, Valuk, formed an alliance with the Frankish king Samo. Clearly, some form of organization existed, given that there are records of these very clans and tribes.

Pipes, writing in the second half of the twentieth century, was not the author of the notion of Russians as incapable of self-organization and self-governance. The myth of the Russian people as civilizationally backward, prone to conformism and complicity with tyrannical leaders, and incapable, unlike their Western counterparts, of organizing and building a government that represents them was not invented by liberal Russian émigrés or well-meaning Western scholars, although they eagerly embraced it. Nor was it the work of foreign travelers to Russia such as the nineteenth-century aristocrat the Marquis de Custine, who traveled to St. Petersburg, marveled at its unparalleled splendour and tyranny, and furthered the stereotype of Russian despotism in the West in his book *La Russie en 1839*. Instead, the very first author of this notion – albeit,

inadvertently – is the unknown eleventh-century monk
who began compiling the first history of Russia, the *Primary
Chronicle*, or *Tale of Bygone Years*.

> The tributaries of the Varangians drove them back beyond the
> sea and, refusing them further tribute, set out to govern them-
> selves. There was no law among them, but tribe rose against
> tribe. Discord thus ensued among them, and they began to
> war one against another. They said to themselves, "Let us
> seek a prince who may rule over us and judge us according
> to the Law." They accordingly went overseas to the Varangian
> Rus': these particular Varangians were known as Rus', just as
> some are called Swedes, and others Normans, English, and
> Gotlanders, for they were thus named. The Chuds, the Slavs,
> the Krivichians, and the Ves' then said to the people of Rus',
> "Our land is great and rich, but there is no order in it. Come to
> rule and reign over us." They thus selected three brothers, with
> their kinsfolk, who took with them all the Russes and migrated.
> The oldest, Rurik, located himself in Novgorod; the second,
> Sineus, at Beloozero; and the third, Truvor, in Izborsk.[14]

The idea of there being "no law among" the people remained
a persistent strand among the Rurikid princes – and, later,
tsars, or *caesars* – as they sought to justify their divine rule
using the Byzantine model of the sovereign as vicar of God.
But it was born out of an inherent alienation, both ethnic and
cultural, between the rulers and the ruled. In many ways, the
Rus' Scandinavian princes who came to rule these lands, the
so-called Varangians, were colonizers of the Slavs, who would
eventually take on the same name. In other words, the Russian
people were, from the start, colonized by their own government. This is by no means a unique phenomenon and, indeed,
the Varangian princes soon assimilated into the Slavic ethnos
and culture. But on the territory that would become Russia, the
princes faced considerable challenges in setting up institutions

that would connect them with their subjects on their own terms. The *veche*, the ad hoc assembly of all free men within a town or city, was in practice typically dominated by the rich and powerful but could also be unpredictable and unruly. Sometimes, a prince could appeal to it for support, but it could just as easily turn against him. When one Prince Yaroslav fell foul of the people of Novgorod in 1270, for example, the *veche* essentially deposed him, saying: "[P]rince, go away, we do not want you. Or else we shall come, all of Novgorod, to drive you out."[15] Even the Orthodox Church, for all that it would later be regarded as the epitome of Russia, was initially imposed and failed fully to integrate with local custom, even while pagan gods became saints: Veles, protector of the herd, became St. Vlasiy, and so forth. In this way, "it was in no sense a native product," writes Frederick Conybeare, a scholar of the history of Russian religious dissent, in the same way that, for instance, the Armenian Church fused with the pagan habits of the people.[16] This alienation bred a chronic tension not so much between the Russian tsar and the masses, but between the Russian tsar and the landed aristocracy, the boyars. No wonder that in archaic popular revolts, the peasants would appeal to the "good tsar" against the "bad boyars" – a conceit which the tsar happily exploited.

There is little mystery to this alienation, just a conflation of a variety of objective factors. Pipes outlined the factors behind this predisposition to alienation, and they were primarily geographic and climatic. The very land of the Rus' was defined by long distances between cities, deep forests that made rivers the main arteries of communication, harsh winters, and, most importantly, soils that, with the exception of modern-day Ukraine, could not provide the kind of crop yields that would in due course allow Western European peasants the leisure to become craftsmen and city builders and the surpluses to generate mercantile middle classes.[17] Taken by themselves, none of these factors are unique, and at different times they affected state-building in Western Europe, even where foreign invaders in effect established themselves as local elites and rulers (such as the Normans in Britain). But taken together, they posed chronic challenges to forging the kind of natural ties between the government and the people that define a strong state.

Take, first of all, the impact of harsh climate and soil on socioeconomic relations within the peasant commune. The subsistence economy of the Russian peasantry imposed extremely rigid behavioral norms on the members of family and commune: to compensate for the difficulty of their circumstances, *all* of the members of the commune had to commit enormous labor to yield a profit. Oppression, writes the historian Christine Worobec, evolved over centuries as a survival strategy.

> The precariousness of subsistence agriculture, and the peas-
> antry's burdensome obligations to family, community, and
> state reinforced rigid and oppressive power relations within the
> village. Russian peasants developed a set of behavioral norms
> and a moral code to buttress the status quo. They feared and
> punished severely delinquent activity that threatened the col-
> lective interest and community solidarity by challenging the
> subordination of woman to man, child to parent, young to old,
> and weak to strong.[18]

But in the very beginning, the constraints of this survival strat-egy, coupled with the challenges of communication between ethnically and culturally different peasants and their ruling princes, ensured a sort of isolation between the emerging classes. In the tenth century, writes historian Jerome Blum, "the landed aristocracy maintained a separate identity as an autochthonous elite, independent of the favour and bounty of the ruling princes."[19]

Early on, a fascinating paradox emerges that has persisted throughout Russian history: the oppressive nature of social bonds within the commune, coupled with the atomization of insulated groups, castes, and classes with a deep distrust of outsiders, created the need for *escape*. The will towards unbridled liberty – to sever completely the oppressive bonds to fellow humans whether as part of a spiritual quest, or as the ultimate act of defiance against conformity – emerged as a uniquely Russian coping strategy. In what historian John Maynard termed "flittage," the individual peasant was allowed an escape card from the oppressive norms of the commune, so long as he also forwent its protections and advantages.[20] "The peasant from the Kievan era on into the fifteenth century had the right to come and go as he pleased," wrote Blum,

> so long as he had not indentured himself. He could choose where he wanted to live, and he could move from one place to another whenever he wanted. He was attached neither to the commune of which he might be a member, nor to the lord on whose land he was living, nor to the prince in whose realm he happened to reside.[21]

Here was the nascent Russian rebel, whether a runaway peasant, or a Cossack fleeing to build an intentional community on the periphery just to escape the stifling constraints of commune and land, or what is perhaps a prototype for the Russian rebel: the holy fool, a hermit who rejects both the norms and all the comforts of society for the sake of communion with God.

Hailing from Byzantium, the role of these "fools for Christ" was a "tangle of humility under the guise of rebellion and rebellion under the guise of humility," writes the Russian scholar Sergei Ivanov. These *pokhaby* first and foremost challenged those in power. It was no small coincidence, Ivanov writes, that "holy foolery" as a socially acceptable and recognized institution emerged simultaneously with Ivan's brand of autocracy, and served, in the public eye, as a sort of religious constraint

on the tsar's power. Nonetheless, unlike their Byzantine counterparts, *pokhaby* often enjoyed a privileged closeness to the
tsar. The fool for Christ St. Basil – known not just for the iconic
cathedral erected in his honor on Red Square, but also for his
habit of walking around naked and pillaging shops – became
a particular "frenemy" of Ivan the Terrible, who brought him
to court and took his advice seriously.[22] Behind their intimacy
is a common loneliness: both regarded themselves as outside
and above social norms, their exceptionalism ordained by God.

All of these identities were lauded as a necessary *exception* to the harshness and tyranny of life. But the unbridled
nature of that lauded liberty, of the *escape*, had an unintended
consequence: the enormous work of building ties between
communities could be forgone as well. The loneliness, the isolation, the lack of social bonds which, had they been built over
time, could make civil society stronger were the price paid for
the escape to freedom.

* * *

By the time of Ivan the Terrible, many of these obstacles to
building stronger social bonds were being overcome, as Yanov
writes: merchant towns thrived in the north, and, as a result,
peasants were no longer hostages to earth and weather in the
way that they had been in the past. Some were slaves and
many owed labor dues to the local landlord, but they were
not yet serfs, unfree peasants bound to the land. Thanks to
Ivan's early reforms, social estates had the opportunities to
build independent institutions, but instead of regarding them
as potential allies in a state- and nation-building project, Ivan
came to see them as a threat. Ivan, in other words, relied on the
dependence of a powerful social estate simply to survive. When
the boyars became too strong, he turned to a more populist
base, the service gentry; when those gentry who formed the
backbone of the *oprichniki* looked as if they were out of control,
he turned back to the boyars. Although his first major purge of

oprichniki, the execution of up to 200 in Moscow in July 1571, was at the hands of their fellows, when the *oprichnina* was essentially disbanded the next year, power essentially devolved back to the old aristocrats.

The vulnerability of the tsar thus made him particularly sensitive to the moods of his base – the threat to his very existence, in other words, came not so much from external foes as it did from internal *traitors*. Ivan, thus, could simply not abide by Kurbsky's defection: he had to be argued out of it, if possible (and Ivan's replies suggested he was offering Kurbsky a chance to return, even if he wisely did not rely on the tsar's mercy), or else be cast out as a heretic beyond the pale not just of Ivan's realm, but of *truth*. If Ivan had the gall to engage with Kurbsky to try to argue him out of existence, the far more timid Putin may have simply hoped that Navalny would disappear if he didn't say his name. The dissident is dangerous not as an individual – Kurbsky was just one man, after all – but because his existence and his defiance challenge the legitimacy and authority of the monarch and the system. The very fragmentation that allows and encourages the ruler to play off one social group or stratum against another also means that he cannot assemble any kind of national consensus in his support, just as it impedes attempts to establish any common front against state power. The ruler and the rebel are both, ultimately, alone.

* * *

The havoc wrought by Ivan's terror was intensified by the fact that he died leaving no viable heir, too paranoid to prepare a succession. In a fit of rage at his suspected treason, he had killed his oldest and most capable son, Ivan Ivanovich, leaving the pious, unworldly, and ultimately childless Fyodor I to succeed him, a man signally lacking the strength of will and clarity of purpose to hold back the chaos which became known as the Time of Troubles that followed his own death in 1598. Ivan's reign of terror had decimated the aristocracy, but also the institutions he himself had built, all but destroying with them hundreds of years of social progress. The economy collapsed. According to the historian Paul Avrich, foreigners encountered once prosperous Muscovites subsisting on grass, dogs, and cats, as lawlessness reigned on the peripheries.[23] The anarchy that came from the tsar's efforts to impose the living law of his will only furthered the notion that a weak civil society needed a strong ruler, a "good tsar," to rein in the "bad boyars." In the chaos of succession, Boris Godunov, a former *oprichnik* who rose to become a boyar, came to reign first as regent and then as tsar after Fyodor's death. Under his rule, the economic situation grew so dire, and peasants ran from their land in such great numbers, that some landlords resorted to kidnapping peasants from their neighbors to make up the shortfall in the agrarian workforce. To deal with this, starting in 1597, Godunov imposed a series of decrees that outlawed what remaining freedoms peasants had to leave their land. Coupled with the increasing collective responsibility to pay taxes, these decrees essentially tied peasants to the soil, binding them in full serfdom. In other words, to combat unbridled freedom and disorder, the tsar resorted to such stifling oppression that no natural social order had the scope to thrive from the bottom up: only by the knout could the peasant be kept in line.

In the centuries following the Time of Troubles, the idea of Russians' ingrained lawlessness would crop up frequently in the writings of Russian courtiers as they praised their despot. This time, as the new dynasty of the Romanovs sought to Westernize the populace, it was directed at the masses, exploiting the myth of the unruly Russian bear to justify the need for more state control of the people in the name of what it considered progress, stifling agency, independent organization, and civil society in the process. Peter the Great's chancellor for foreign affairs, Count Gavriil Ivanovich Golovkin, claimed that the emperor "by indefatigable labour and leadership led us out of the darkness of nonexistence into being and joined us to the society of political peoples,"[24] but his comments are merely a testament to how far this ubiquitous notion had been internalized, that Russians could not be allowed to manage their own affairs and needed a strong state to save them from themselves. The new tsars were more systematic about strengthening their power, but the myth upon which they leaned – the lawless Russian *muzhik* bent on civil war and strife – had a way of fulfilling itself, again and again and again.

3

The Rebel and the Tsar

March of Justice

"Our soldiers are being killed, and the happy grandpa thinks that everything's fine," said the rebel, euphemistically, as custom had it, decrying the tsar. "But what should the country do, and how shall we win the war, if by some accident, I mean hypothetically, it just so happens that this grandpa is a complete asshole?"[1]

The man to challenge the Kremlin and march a 3,000-strong army on Moscow was hardly the kind of person who would usually be called a dissident. A criminal convicted of violent burglary, he built a transnational empire peddling the skills he developed in prison, leveraging his Kremlin connections, securing choice government contracts, and ultimately forming a secret army to fight the Kremlin's secret wars.

He was a thug, an angry man with "no conscience, and no hobbies," as one Russian official described him,[2] who took to recruiting his mercenaries among fellow criminals and convicts. He cursed like a sailor, and was not above having someone who merely criticized him taken out to a forest and beaten up, if not worse. He had the clients of his business competitors filmed vomiting over their white tablecloths so that he could continue making millions off the cheap, expired products he fed to schoolchildren and soldiers. But he made sure that the oysters in his own restaurants were always fresh.

And yet Yevgeny Prigozhin had become indispensable to the Kremlin. Some would claim that Russia's thuggish tsar simply gravitated to fellow thugs – the two certainly had a shared past, developing a relationship long before the one became a mogul and the other a head of state, and both benefited from a mutual symbiosis. But the two were ultimately brought closer together by bigger tectonic shifts in the Kremlin's contract with the Russian people.

In 2011, Vladimir Putin, having kept the public guessing whether he planned to return to the Kremlin or not for a third presidential term, finally made up his mind and declared he would be running (and presumably winning, given the nature of Russia's rigged electoral system, which he himself had established) in the March 2012 elections. He did not expect that the relatively wealthy, pro-Western liberal class he had hitherto relied on as his base would feel as betrayed as they did, and rise up against him in the biggest protest movement Russia had seen since the collapse of the Soviet Union. As the tsar sometimes does during such pre-revolutionary moments throughout history, when society demands change and various political and economic classes rise in turmoil, he co-opted the revolution in order to survive. But instead of taking criticisms against corruption, cronyism, and rigged elections at face value, he merely pivoted to another base.

As will be discussed later, the same social divisions which had constrained previous generations of dissidents were largely still present. The liberal dissidents too often failed even to try to win support from the blue-collar masses, whether patronizingly assuming they knew best what the wider population wanted and needed, or ignoring them, or even contemptuously discounting them. Once again, the tsar would reach past his elites to form an alliance against them with his people. Putin turned to the blue-collar workers, the pensioners, the members of the military and security community, all groups which tended to lean towards nationalist, conservative, and often deeply anti-Western sentiments. To secure his rule, Putin had to securitize his policies, creating a new narrative that presented him as the national champion, pitted against Western efforts to subvert and dominate the Russian state. "We will die near Moscow, like our brothers died!" Putin shouted in front of a crowd ahead of his election in 2012, quoting the Russian poet Sergei Yesenin about the Battle of Borodino in the Napoleonic War. And now, again surrounded by enemies, "The battle for Russia continues. Victory will be ours!"[3] He moved onto a war footing, initially against everyone and everything perceived as having pro-Western proclivities, and then, later, with covert and then overt aggression in Ukraine. In the process, he pitted the haves against the have-nots, exploiting political grievances and inferiority complexes.

Prigozhin clearly saw himself in the second camp. By then worth tens of millions of dollars, he was hardly a have-not, but as an ex-con who would never be accepted into the high society to which he aspired, he had a chronic chip on his shoulder.[4] The businessman, having made a fortune on government catering contracts, eagerly spearheaded the fight against the privileged liberal intellectuals who had mocked and excluded him. He had the means and the inclination to set up an online troll farm to go against the Kremlin's new enemies: first the domestic opposition, then the US government itself. But it was his creation of a mercenary army that would soon take part in covert Kremlin operations in Ukraine in 2014 that really established his indispensability to the government. The creation of a tame private military company as an instrument for deniable operations abroad had long been on the Kremlin's wish list, and Prigozhin, a businessman close enough to Putin, but not too close, both self-motivated and prepared at the time to remain in the shadows, emerged as the leader of Wagner, what would become a 50,000-strong private army with operations in Ukraine, Syria, and across the African continent.

In 2022, with the full-scale invasion of Ukraine, the Kremlin's reliance on Prigozhin became even more marked. It had initially planned for its military operation to take mere weeks, presuming at best limited resistance. Once it became clear that the Ukrainians were not about the capitulate, and Russia faced a longer and much harder campaign, it found itself desperately in need of well-equipped, well-trained, and well-compensated fighters. It could not rely on its own contractors or conscripts in a war that was so unpopular that the Kremlin had to criminalize even calling it a war. Prigozhin's Wagner was made up of men who were good at what they did, and enjoyed doing it, until they found themselves in a meatgrinder, winning battles at massive cost and taking Ukrainian towns only for the Defense Ministry to take credit while – the Wagner fighters raged – providing them with the minimum funding and ammunition.

Yet what could Prigozhin do about it? By the twenty-first century, the old estates – aristocracy, gentry, middling classes, workers, peasants – were no more. They had been replaced by less obvious and more permeable, but nonetheless still powerful, divides between new ones. Prigozhin was rich and powerful, connected with the movers and shakers of the system, but he was no oligarch, and he was definitely a client, not a friend of the monarch. Call him a minigarch or a mere millionaire, but he was "gentry" to the "boyars" of Putin's inner circle, men like the banker Yuri Kovalchuk, the gas industry baron Igor Sechin, or Defense Minister Sergei Shoigu, a leading light in the president's own United Russia party, and a man who even took him on hiking holidays in his native Siberia. In practice, there was never much question as to whom Putin would back in any confrontation.

What had initially begun as a long-simmering feud between Prigozhin and Shoigu over resources turned into a full-blown armed revolt. On June 23, 2023, Prigozhin's men seized the military headquarters in the southwestern city of Rostov, just across the border from Ukraine, and a Wagner column began a march on Moscow. Its demand – that Shoigu be sacked – was merely the tip of an iceberg. Prigozhin couldn't articulate quite what wider cause his "March of Justice" was about, and had little clear sense of how, exactly, he saw the endgame. Yet by the time a private army of the dispossessed and the despised, one that the Kremlin had fostered to fight its wars on the cheap, had turned on Moscow, it was about much more than ammunition. It was about a kind of truth, a kind of justice, and the very legitimacy of whatever it was for which the tsar was sending thousands of men to die. But without a coherent goal in sight, the revolt was, one could say, "senseless and merciless." It was not inevitable, and yet it was part of a pattern: a weak monarch leaning on private muscle to fight his wars, forgetting, in the process, that mercenaries are not just toy soldiers. They have their own agendas, their own will, their own sense of justice – and the capacity to act upon them.

The soldier's revolt

After all, that has long been the fear of Russia's rulers and elites alike: *bunt*, that savage rising from below. "God forbid," Alexander Pushkin wrote in 1837, "we see a Russian revolt, senseless and merciless,"[5] coining an epitaph that would mythologize the awesome fear that uprisings in Russia evoked both for the people and for the authorities. He was referring specifically to the deserter, grifter, and rabblerouser who mustered one of the biggest rebellions against Romanov rule: Yemelian Pugachev.

In early September 1773, a Urals Cossack named Mikhail Kozhevnikov got a visit from a friend with a strange request. He was asked to harbor a fugitive royal prince in his *khutor*, his homestead, and, indeed, the following night, a thin, black-bearded stranger on horseback wearing a long, shabby camel coat arrived at his doorstep and told an even stranger story. The traveler said that he was none other than Emperor Peter III, the late husband of Empress Catherine the Great, who had been overthrown in a palace coup ten years earlier and was believed to have been killed. His assassination had been a ruse, the stranger claimed. He had been saved by "God and good people," and for the last decade had been on the run in Kiev and Constantinople, gathering like-minded officers and Cossacks who believed that the German-born Catherine the Great was an illegitimate ruler. That fall, he planned to take Yaitsk, stronghold of the Ural Cossacks, capture their leader, the *ataman*, and then proclaim an end to serfdom, work to replace all of Russia's corrupt judges, topple the empress, and find a true Russian prince to ascend the throne.[6]

The story was just that, nothing but a fantasy. Nonetheless, even while operating under a complete fabrication, the movement Yemelian Pugachev spearheaded was genuine and built on legitimate grievances against the state.

The Ural Cossack community had established itself along the river of the same name, then known as Yaik, when a host of Don Cossacks moved there from southern Russia and began intermingling with local tribes at the end of the fourteenth century. Cossacks are a peculiar type of community: both ethnos, in that they consider their identity hereditary, and also social, in that military service defines their way of life.[7] But it wasn't always like this. The origins of Cossack communities are disputed, but at least a large component of them are believed to have come from self-exiled serfs: many of them thieves, criminals, and vagabonds who came together to escape the inhospitable earth, commit to utter freedom, and make their own rules.[8] Those rules were often brutal: according to Alexander Pushkin, who wrote the first definitive history of the Pugachev rebellion, the early Ural Cossack tribes, in their pursuit of independence, often killed their own children and left their wives before every new pillaging expedition. Their *atamans* soon outlawed the practice, but their community structure reflected that fierce commitment to freedom: all men had an equal voice, elected their *atamans* and councils, and voted directly on their own laws and customs. Their freedom had a limit, though. On the wide steppes, they were exposed and vulnerable to nomads to the south and east, the Crimean and other Khanates, and the rising Polish-Lithuanian Commonwealth to the west, so in the early seventeenth century they petitioned the first Romanov tsar, Mikhail Fyodorovich, for patronage and protection. The tsar granted it, in exchange for their muscle, which they gladly provided.[9] What might look like a sort of colonization was in fact more of a public–private venture, of the kind that, 400 years later, Prigozhin would eagerly exploit: the tsar got to expand his territories, while the Cossacks got some form of protection, even as they maintained their willful and martial way of life.

This partnership, however, was uneven and would soon prove untenable. The more Moscow pursued its own agenda of expansion, the more it clashed with the interests of its freedom-loving clients, who were forced to fight in its wars. Peter the Great forcibly overhauled the state's relationship with the Cossacks. His order to subjugate their military units to the War Collegium sparked a rebellion. The Ural Cossacks burned down their camp and planned to flee to nearby Kirgiz lands, but an army sent from St. Petersburg quickly reined them in. Henceforth, the tsar would appoint *atamans* directly.[10]

The irony is that although the Cossacks would acquire an unsavoury reputation as the state's stormtroopers, this new arrangement was also a recipe for continual insurrections. Ivan Bolotnikov at the beginning of the seventeenth century, Bohdan Khmelnytsky some fifty years later, then Stenka Razin and Kondraty Bulavin at the beginning of the eighteenth – all the great rebellions of the age were sparked and led by Cossacks, and all had, at their heart, an angry sense of a social contract broken. Because the tsar was so far away, the Cossacks directed the brunt of their dissent against the *atamans* appointed from the capital, or against Peter's generals, rather than the emperor himself. He was, after all, ever deemed the sacred protector of the people. Rebellions broke out over anything from government levies on salt extraction to attempts to arrest runaway serfs who had sought sanctuary in Cossack communities. However, it was disputes over military service that, long after Peter's death, would trigger one of the most notorious rebellions of the era. During the Russo-Turkish war of 1768 – which would pave the way for Russia's initial annexation of the Crimean Peninsula – Catherine the Great leaned on the Ural Cossacks to provide badly needed recruits.

These revolts were part of a wider resistance to a series of pro-Western reforms pushed through by the new Romanov dynasty. Yet as was often the case, the government's attempts to reshape Russia in line with how it saw the West failed to reckon with the people's unwillingness or inability to bear the costs. In the 1650s, Tsar Alexei sided with Patriarch Nikon over controversial Church reforms aimed at bringing worship practices closer to those of the Eastern Orthodox Church abroad. Others, like Archpriest Avvakum, saw the Jesuit-trained scholars that Nikon brought in from Ukraine as a foreign threat to the very Russian way of life, if not outright heresy. For his resistance, he was repeatedly imprisoned and finally burned alive in his home. The reforms and Avvakum's martyrdom split the Church into the New and Old Believers, and the latter would continue to be persecuted until the twentieth century.

Yet the government's modernizing zeal continued. By the second half of the eighteenth century, Russia's military had been entirely Westernized – a process that began with Peter's brutal reforms and ended with Catherine's final Germanification of the armed forces. Cossacks recruited into the regular army had to submit to shaving their beards and taking orders from foreigners and "heretics," as Catholics were known. It was the last straw for the Cossacks, many of them Old Believers who practiced a more archaic form of Orthodox Christianity. They prized their beards "almost equal to their lives," in the words of the Russian nineteenth-century historian Pyotr Shchebalsky.[11] Because the *atamans* and the dissenting Cossacks were essentially opposed to one another, the protests were generally scattered, lacking leadership, charisma, and a unifying idea. For years, this discontent waited for a leader, and in 1773, it found it. Pugachev was peddling exactly the kind of myth needed to catalyze a rebellion that would challenge the very foundations of state power: the myth of legitimacy.

Wronged

Born to a family of Don Cossacks around 1742, Yemelian Pugachev, in line with the custom of his people, joined military service at the age of 17. Soon after he got married, his unit was sent to Prussia, where he fought in the Seven Years' War, and later divided his time between military assignments and domestic life in southern Russia. In 1769, having obtained the rank of *khorunzhy*, or unit commander, he was deployed to Bendery in Bessarabia to fight in the Russo-Turkish war. The Cossack was fiercely ambitious, in his own words always "wanting to distinguish" himself, so much so that he bragged to his fellow soldiers that his sword was a gift from his godfather, Peter the Great himself.[12] (Neither claim was true.) Pugachev saw himself as destined for greater things, and, having distinguished himself in Prussia, came to see this as his God-given right. This made the injustice with which, as a soldier, he was often treated all the more intolerable. In one incident that clearly made an impression on him, he was whipped for accidentally letting one of his officer's horses run off during a skirmish with the enemy.

But it was in Bendery, stricken with a mysterious illness, that he apparently began to question his service. Pugachev was so "severely ill," he would tell his investigators years later, after his capture, that his "chest and legs rotted," and even when he was temporarily sent home, his condition only got worse.[13] He yearned to be released from service. In 1771, Pugachev traveled to Cherkassk, capital of the Don Cossack Host, asking for a permanent discharge, but was denied. In Taganrog, where he stayed with his sister, he learned that his brother-in-law and his fellow soldiers were similarly disaffected by being treated like common serf-soldiers rather than free-born Cossacks, and that they wanted to desert. One by one, they secretly fled to Terek, in what is modern-day Chechnya.

No matter his skill, his wits, or his bravery, no matter how distinguished he was in battle, once Pugachev himself had taken that step, he was to be forever a fugitive and traitor in the eyes of the state that he had, until then, loyally served. For two years, he traveled the south, dodging the authorities and amassing a loyal following of Cossacks, vagabonds, and former serfs. Initially, he kept his "royal status" a secret, and posed instead as a wealthy merchant promising dissident Cossacks riches if they fled with him to Turkey.

However, by the time he reached Mikhail Kozhevnikov in the Orenburg region, a merchant with Old Believer sympathies, he had devised a plan to reveal himself as Peter III. With the authorities closing in on him, he was forced to act faster than he had intended. Just days after Kozhevnikov saw Pugachev off, he was arrested along with several Cossack accomplices and questioned. On September 17, Pugachev "revealed" himself to the Yaik Cossacks. Because he was himself illiterate, he had an accomplice draft his manifesto: "I, the Sovereign, Peter Fyodorovich, pardon you of all your sins and grant you the river from its source to its mouth, the earth and the grass, and a subsidy of money, lead, powder and grain."[14] The following day, he took his 300 men and marched on Yaitsk.

There, Pugachev's group was met with a loyalist regiment of 500 Cossacks, backed by infantry, and armed with two cannons. Two hundred of those Cossacks were sent forward to parley with Pugachev's forces, but half defected there and then when their commander refused to read Pugachev's message out loud.[15] From then on, the rebellion spread like wildfire, not least because loyalist commanders, their regular forces committed to the war in Turkey, had to rely on Cossacks to fight Cossacks. The *atamans*, appointed by the tsar, tried to resist their split loyalties, but, as "traitors," they were the first to be butchered by Pugachev's forces.

Pugachev laid siege to Yaitsk, but capturing it proved harder than he had anticipated, so he marched on other Yaik fortress towns, capturing them one by one. First to fall was Iletsk, and with each victory his forces grew. So did their gory butchery. Upon taking the fortress of Tatischev, they captured the commander, Grigory Yelagin, and, seeing that he was obese, had him skinned, cut out his fat, and used it to dress their wounds. Yelagin's wife was chopped to pieces, while his daughter was only spared the same fate when Pugachev suddenly decided to take her as a concubine.[16] But even that didn't save her, as Pugachev's men grew suspicious of how close she was getting to their leader. When Pugachev grew tired of her, he handed her back to his men, who shot her and her 7-year-old brother, and left their bodies – still holding each other in fear – to rot in the bushes.[17]

Thanks to a combination of brutality and generous promises, Pugachev's forces grew from 300 vagabonds into a 3,000-strong army within two weeks. In that time, he took seven fortresses and had laid siege to Yaitsk and Orenburg. But it was his ability to find a common language with the discontented local Cossacks and their particular grievances that determined his power. It wasn't just that he was a tsar – or convincingly masqueraded as one – it was that he, unlike the centrally appointed *atamans*, let alone the empress, actually seemed to *listen* to what the peasants and Cossacks had been talking about, had been trying to get across to the authorities. In his words:

> I was in Kiev, in Poland, in Egypt, in Jerusalem, and on the Terek River. From there I went to the Don and then came to you. And I hear that you have been wronged and that all the common folk have been wronged. There is great reason why I am not loved by the gentry: many of them, young men and others of middling years . . . went off into retirement and lived at their will off the peasants in their villages and quite ruined them.

When he went against them, Pugachev continued, "they arrested me and they made up a false tale about me and they forced me to wander over the face of the earth."[18]

In the course of two years, he would lay siege to Orenburg and Kazan, with his forces taking control of the area between the Ural Mountains and the Volga River in the west – a territory roughly the size of half of modern-day Ukraine. In the villages they controlled, the peasants' pent-up fury was unleashed. Egged on by Pugachev's butchers, they "let loose the red rooster," burning down the landlords' mansions and farmhouses. It would take Russian authorities two years to quell the revolt, capture Pugachev, and reinstate control over the territories. But they could only do so after the end of the Russo-Turkish war, at which point regular forces could be redeployed to put down the rebellion. In January 1775, Pugachev was beheaded and then drawn and quartered on Moscow's Bolotnaya Square, where, two centuries later, tens of thousands of Russians would gather for a different, albeit equally unsuccessful, revolt.

The lesser evil

The Russian historian Alexei Ivanov, writing in 2024, soon after Prigozhin's rebellion, questioned the essence of *Pugachevschina*, the phenomenon of the brutal revolt that Pugachev unleashed. Depending on their ideological slant or political allegiance, Russian historians frame it as the wanton violence of a criminal gang, a people's revolt against capitalist oppressors, or a war of independence. However, Ivanov argued that all of these miss the central essence of this revolt. For him, it was about identity, or identities: in each of the areas Pugachev's forces came to control – from the Tatar steppes, to Kirgiz and Bashkir lands, to Cossack *stanitsy* (fortified villages) – the rebellion unleased the pent-up *identities* of these cultures, defined, as they were, by the land on which they lived, and the various economies that this land created.[19] What they all had in common – and what fueled the blood-curdling brutality, the senseless butchery in the name of an abstract concept of justice – was the fury of those who saw themselves as wronged, and who had previously been relatively powerless against those who had done them wrong. But "wronged" is a tricky concept: were the serfs, bought and sold along with the land to which they were attached by tsarist decree, who had to send their sons to war for the rest of their lives (conscription was for life, only reduced to a "mere" twenty-five years in 1793), wronged by the tsar to whom they submitted? Of course, to modern sensibilities, they were, but it takes more than just being poorly treated and oppressed for that acquiescence to transform into potent fury. It takes being lied to, for your story to be ignored, distorted, and erased, and for your perceived oppressor to carry on insisting on the justice of his cause, oblivious to its glaring injustice. It also takes the right kind of leader, one with the ruthless skill to be able to fuse his own grievances with those of his constituency.

Yevgeny Prigozhin was no Yemelian Pugachev. And his Wagnerites were no Cossacks. When Prigozhin's forces marched on Moscow, they seemed constrained by the fear of what their own mutiny could unleash. Prigozhin bombastically claimed that he expected half the army to join his march, but he did not really have a plan, or a vision, or a real *reason* to amass a bigger following for his limited adventure, which was ostensibly just about taking down Defense Minister Shoigu. Once one of the most respected figures in Russia, thanks to the war Shoigu had become widely unpopular, but having him removed and foiling his efforts to bring Wagner to heel was hardly a cause for which many Russians, cowed by the wartime repressions and the paranoia that had come to define the Putin regime, would be willing to fight. To be sure, in Rostov, the Wagnerites were welcomed with flowers, coffee, and pastries, as locals asked them to pose for selfies. Ultimately, though, Prigozhin took a deal offered him by the Kremlin and stood down. "Now the moment has come when blood could be spilled," he said in a statement. "Understanding the responsibility [for the chance] that Russian blood will be spilled on one side, we are turning our columns around and going back to field camps as planned."[20]

What drove Prigozhin and his supporters was their own fury, a fury at the lies Putin and his regime were telling about the war, and the injustice in how it was being waged, and how their willingness to spill their own blood was being abused. This posed a challenge to one of the fundamental aspects of Putin's rule, the way he exploits the willingness of private citizens to buttress his power and wage his wars, only to start treating them as serfs and disavowing them when he no longer needs them. Pugachev and Prigozhin were similar rebels in that they were both loyal agents of the state who turned against it when they felt it had betrayed them, and who gathered to them others who likewise felt abandoned and deceived. Where they differed was in how far they were willing to unleash the fury of their followers. Unlike Pugachev, Prigozhin seems to have feared this system-smashing fury almost as much as

Putin – after all, he was a rich man, with a stake in the status quo, and a business empire built on Kremlin patronage – and hence his willingness to accept a deal without the guarantees that might have prevented the "accident" which saw his plane tumble from the sky just two months later.

Even though the mutiny failed and Prigozhin stood down, Putin found himself considerably weakened by it and, especially, by the last-minute deal he was forced to make. Instead of trying to brush the disaster under the rug and focusing on unity and resolve alone, he took pains to underscore the catastrophic nature of the near-averted disaster. Had Russia's enemies succeeded, "our society would split, would drown in the blood of civil strife," he said, before calling much of the Wagner forces "patriots," and promising them sanctuary as a reward for turning back from the brink of civil war.[21] The Russian president, having brought up *smuta* – the civil strife during the Time of Troubles that plagued Russia for decades after the death of Ivan the Terrible – promised not to punish anyone for bringing the country to its brink. This was, of course, to buy time, as whether Putin had always planned this or, as is entirely possible, changed his mind later, Prigozhin was soon to die in what was all but certainly an assassination.

In the aftermath of the failed rebellion, there was a mix of frustration and relief in Moscow. So strong is the awareness of how bad things could become in the event of regime collapse that there is an inevitable desire to get back to business as usual. But the irony was that time and again Putin's strongest card has perversely been the perceived weakness of the state he has built: that, without him, the country faces total government collapse, *smuta*, and civil war. This has helped ensure his survival and compensated for his frequent decisional paralysis.

This didn't start with Putin. Throughout history, the tsar embracing his own fragility in the face of a senseless and chaotic revolt – warning his subjects of the catastrophic alternative to his power – has often been the best strategy to put down a rising. For the majority of people, the tsar's brutality and oppression are constrained, familiar, and predictable – but the brutality of Pugachev's Cossacks? Of the Wagnerites, many of whom were violent convicts given a gun and a license to kill? Of the unknown quantity who are reformers and revolutionaries? (After all, from Lenin's Bolsheviks to the young free-marketeers of the 1990s, convinced a crash transition to the market was what the economy needed, they have often seemed to leave misery and chaos in their wake.) Of young, angry men convinced that they have been wronged? Even – and especially – if they are right?

The very fragility of Russia, and the perverse vulnerability of its state, is at once a cause and an effect of society's challenges in building bonds not simply within but between estates and communities. It creates opportunities for those able to appeal to people who have become outsiders in their own homeland. Prigozhin was supported by his mercenaries and his ex-cons, men who felt little stake in existing society, and was cheered on by the so-called "turbo-patriot" nationalist fringe. Pugachev's rebellion drew not just on *odnodvortsy* ("single homesteaders") who felt marginalized and impoverished by the changing status of the Cossacks, but also Old Believers and many non-Russian subjects of the empire. There were nomadic Bashkirs, angry that Russian colonists were settling on their grazing land, and Tatars, who resisted the imposition of conscription and the poll tax. There were shamanic Mordvins and pagan Udmurts, seeking an end to intrusive attempts to convert them to Orthodox Christianity.

Yet the corollary is precisely that this kind of rebel is feared, for he represents the dark and mindless fury lurking in the forest, just outside the fire's light, just over the next ridgeline, and on the wrong side of town. Whether it was Catherine facing down the *Pugachevshchina*, or Putin presenting himself as averting another *smuta*, or, as we turn to in the next chapter, a martinet like Tsar Nicholas I becoming the "Gendarme of Europe," resisting liberal revolution not just in Russia but across the Continent, Russia's rulers have, perversely, relied on the rebels to give them relevance and meaning. When the rebels are outsiders – whether socially marginalized or inspired by alien, foreign ideologies – and when state and society are not strong enough to be able to negotiate with them, incorporating their beliefs and addressing their interests, then they can only be destroyed. Louis XIV of France famously had the motto *Ultima Ratio Regum*, "the last argument of kings," cast on his cannons. The last argument of Russia's tsars – and general secretaries and presidents – was instead, perhaps, that they were the lesser evil, the devil you know.

4

The Revolt of the Elites

"The best part of society"

A hundred thousand of them gathered, with snowflakes sticking to their eyelashes, blowing into their gloved hands for warmth, on the same square where, 237 years earlier, Yemelian Pugachev had been beheaded, drawn, and quartered for leading a revolt against Empress Catherine the Great. Standing peacefully, they protested for their right to basic dignity, free and fair elections, and reforms limiting the powers of a leader who had manipulated both the law and his own electorate to return to the presidency. For the weather they braved and the white ribbons that they brandished as symbols of peaceful protest and transparency,[1] the demonstrations were dubbed the Snow Revolution. It felt impossible not to get swept up by the rightness of their message of hope for change, and the nobility of their methods.

It was February 4, 2012, and about 160,000 of the "best . . . most productive part of Russian society," in the words of Vladislav Surkov, the architect of Russia's democratic façade, were "demanding respect."[2] They gathered on Moscow's Bolotnaya Square, in a protest movement that was quickly gathering momentum following disputed parliamentary elections the previous December. The rallies first numbered hundreds, then thousands, and then tens of thousands as Russians from a variety of political movements and social strata demonstrated in Moscow and St. Petersburg before the new year. Despite their variety, they were unified by a simple demand: that their government stop lying to them. It was not hard to sympathize with Surkov's characterization. There was something familiar in their faces: these were your cool urbanite friends, creative intellectuals who wore quirky clothes, drank specialty coffee at the new cafés sprouting up around the city, posted memes on your social media network, the ones who traveled regularly to Europe and began to see their own country as potentially no different. They were the ones who had broken entirely with the claustrophobic social constraints of the previous generation, and who were, while not necessarily rich, affluent enough to travel as well as consume, to believe in their own agency and that, ultimately, the laws of the democratic country that Russia aspired to be should work for them, and not against them.

Indeed, a meter or so away from me among the crowd in front of the stage, listening to Alexei Navalny and other speakers, bundled up like the rest of us in an oversized parka to brave the −20 Celsius frost, stood the former minister of finance. He was a staunch fiscal liberal and a man so close to Vladimir Putin that, for all his opposition sympathies, he remained virtually untouchable, even after he stopped being the tsar's confidant. Alexei Kudrin would not talk to journalists, and so when I approached him, trying to get him to open up, I merely gushed at how important it was for a public figure like him to join the protests, and asked if I could give him a hug. It didn't work, but he smiled sheepishly and cautiously leaned into my half-embrace.

He was not the only one among the elite who had joined the protest. That December, socialite Ksenia Sobchak, the daughter of Putin's mentor Anatoly Sobchak and influential senator Liudmila Narusova, had taken to the stage to proclaim, despite some initial boos, that "I have something to lose, but nevertheless I am here."[3] Standing huddled in the crowds that snowy February day was billionaire Mikhail Prokhorov, a liberal oligarch who was allowed to run (if not win) against Putin in the upcoming presidential elections. He represented many of the protesters' demands and, indeed, planned to make Kudrin his prime minister if he became president. And while the spirit of the protests was vehemently against Putin, demonstrators tended to share a commitment to lawful reform, rather than lawless revolution.[4] As the rallies grew more tense, and protesters faced off against phalanxes of riot police, they brazenly tied white ribbons to the latter's plastic shields and chanted in unison, "the police are with the people."

Despite the presence of celebrities and millionaires, despite the spirit of hope, there was little the movement could do meaningfully to challenge Vladimir Putin's re-election, except stand vigilant and try to minimize vote rigging at the polls. Although Alexei Navalny had emerged as the most charismatic and potentially unifying voice of these demonstrations, their main speakers were a motley assortment of established, albeit unpopular, political parties and unregistered political movements, including republicans, anarchists, monarchists, and everything in between, not least nationalists.

Earlier, Kudrin had offered to act as a potential mediator between the protesters and the authorities,[5] but months down the line it was becoming clear that he would not be able to maintain his credibility in both camps. As a fiscal liberal and an adherent of democratic institutions, he was wildly unpopular among most Russians, who held him responsible for the 1990s reforms that left them impoverished and disenfranchised.

Mediation, in any case, required not just a single clear message from the protesters, but also the Kremlin's willingness to listen. After Putin's re-election that March with a (contested)

64.35 percent share of the vote giving him a first-round win – Prokhorov came third, after the Communist candidate, with just over 8% – the Kremlin began to abandon its initial inclination for dialogue and unleashed a crackdown. Rallies turned violent as riot police began acting increasingly aggressively, kettling protesters, provoking clashes, and dragging those who tried to resist to jail, even when the Moscow mayor's office had approved the gatherings. As the stakes rose, and rallies became less peaceful and more dangerous, the movement's demands lost their relevance, and morale began to sink. Surkov, demoted in stature and sent to oversee the tech innovation sector in Medvedev's cabinet over his veiled support for the liberal movement, paid lip service to dialogue so long as it was without political substance. "Innovation in general means strengthening or creating institutions that can tap the potential of this most productive part of society, the productive minority," he told journalists in 2013 when they pressed him about his earlier enthusiasm for what had now turned into a "minority" and been relegated to the tech sphere.[6] As for Kudrin, by that summer, after Putin's inauguration, he would be saying "the protest is not that widespread, so government officials are wondering whether dialogue is needed." He added that "I understand that for such a dialogue, the opposition must consolidate in something – on some platform, with some leaders. I think this will happen, so at some point this dialogue will become more possible."[7] In other words, someday, but not today.

Within a year, the revolt of the elites had dissipated, producing neither the reforms nor the dialogue for which they had hoped. If anything, all that the Snow Revolution seemed to achieve was a gradual return, over the course of the next ten years, of a Soviet-style dictatorship.

There are a number of parallels between the Snow Revolution and the Decembrist Revolt of 1825. There are a great deal of differences, too, but from the start, they had three fundamental factors in common. First, both began amid foment in the elites that was the direct result of the government's liberalization. Second, they triggered in the ruler an existential fear for his survival – the incoming tsar in the first case, and the returning president in the second. And, third, and most tragic, these revolts both in effect put an end to the ongoing liberalization that the government had been on course to implement, making the leader feel that he had to choose between continued reforms and his personal life and livelihood.

Liberalization betrayed

Fully 187 years earlier, it was a windy December morning. Snowflakes were swirling around the officers and settling, still intact, upon their drawn swords, cold as their new emperor's eyes. What might seem to be a very different protest was drawing to its bloody conclusion before it had even properly begun.

For Lieutenant Colonel Sergei Muravyov-Apostol and his brothers Matvei and Ippolit, there was something irreconcilable about the practices the officers began to see in their regiments compared to the lifestyle to which he and his peers were used.

In April 1820, a new colonel, Fyodor Schwartz, had been appointed commander of the Semyonovsky Lifeguard Regiment, a relatively liberal unit, where corporal punishment had been abolished. As a newcomer, he tried first to adhere to the norms of his new collective, but soon grew frustrated. It may have been because of his own inadequacies, but it would under any circumstances have been difficult to reconcile the culture of this elite regiment, drawn heavily from the sons of the nobility, with the increasingly draconian demands of imperial military discipline. To establish order, at least as he saw it, he turned to vindictiveness and abuse: forcing "soldiers to spit in each other's faces; teaching them, for his own entertainment in his hall, a variety of tortures: [like forcing them] to stand motionless for hours, their legs tied in splints, getting stabbed with forks." In the words of Sergei's brother and co-conspirator Matvei Muravyov-Apostol, "he ruined them."[8]

And when Alexander I, who had been thought to be a liberal, the tsar on whom Muravyov and others had pinned so many hopes, decided brutally to suppress the mutiny that erupted against Schwartz and disband the whole regiment rather than to listen to the soldiers' complaints, it represented something of a turning point. If they wanted change, the officers would have to take matters into their own hands.

It had become evident that across Russia, both soldiers and serfs were being treated as less than human. For Muravyov-Apostol, as well as a growing number of well-born young officers, this was becoming increasingly hard to bear. Having spent most of his childhood in France, he not only spoke French as his first language, but also communicated in it as the semi-official language of the imperial court and the aristocracy. By the turn of the nineteenth century, a hundred years of Westernizing reforms, first introduced by Peter the Great and his German-speaking court and foreign military and technical experts, then by Catherine and her Enlightenment-inspired Francophilia, had fostered an elite in which many officers spoke Russian so poorly that they found it difficult to communicate not just with the peasants who tilled the land that they owned, but also with their own rank-and-file soldiers. Those who ruled Russians, and those Russians themselves, literally spoke a different language.

For Muravyov-Apostol, Tsar Alexander I initially embodied the ideals of a Russia not only Westernizing, but also becoming an equal power in a European community of nations. Emerging from war with Napoleon as a leader of the victors, Alexander spoke in the courts of Vienna and Paris as a progressive and a reformer. Russian liberal officers were delighted and inspired when, following the Congress of Vienna in 1815, he granted the vassal state Kingdom of Poland a constitution. There was hope among them that he would extend his liberal inclinations domestically. After all, there had already been some movement towards gradually abolishing serfdom when, in 1803, Alexander had issued a largely symbolic decree allowing landowners to free their serfs and, under certain conditions, to endow them with land.[9] But like many Russian rulers, from Peter to Putin, enamoured of Western prosperity and modernity, but ultimately unwilling to accept the liberties that made them possible, Alexander soon came to believe that freedom had to take second place to the practical challenges of managing such a vast, multifaceted society. "Liberty," Alexander once said, "should be confined within just limits. And the limits of liberty are the principles of order."[10]

A diligent student and an ambitious officer eager to prove himself on the battlefield, Muravyov-Apostol watched as the emperor rode in to Paris after the defeat of Napoleon, and fought in battles that made his country a formidable European power. Yet he returned home to practices so barbaric that it was hard to imagine that these two countries – that of the French-speaking court that defeated Napolean and aspired to Enlightenment values, and that of the lower-rank officers who frequently whipped soldiers and serfs with rods and knouts to the point where the bones in their backs were left exposed – were one and the same.

After 1815, Alexander seemed to have grown disillusioned with his own liberalizing rhetoric. The efforts towards order trumped those towards freedom and enlightenment and, exhausted by the Napoleonic wars and by the burdens of autocracy, he turned to mysticism and melancholia. "I know that most people in government must be changed, and you are right that evil comes from the choices of both senior and lower officials," the tsar lamented to one of his generals. "But where can I get them? I can't even choose 52 governors, but thousands are needed. . . . The army, the civilian part, everything is not the way I want it, but what to do? I can't do everything myself, there are no assistants."[11]

The reactionary views of his former minister of war, Count Alexei Arakcheyev, became increasingly appealing to Alexander, and he ordered him to implement an idea he had been entertaining of establishing "military settlements," essentially colonies of soldiers who both served as reservists and tilled the land. The wars had established Russia as a European power, but had drained its military and financial reserves. This measure was intended to allow Alexander to maintain the capacity to field more troops without increasing government spending. What was even more appealing to him, though, was that these plantations would give him a network of garrisons, instruments of control across the countryside.[12] Arakcheyev – a militaristic micromanager so cruel that he required his female serfs to bear a child each year – approached his task with such zeal that he failed, in the process, to take into account the actual production capabilities of the human beings he sought to mold into soldiers, let alone the agricultural conditions particular to the Russian climate. Like most of the government's innovations at the time, military agricultural colonies were copied from Prussian practices in principle, but not in practice. Misconceived and mismanaged, they became notorious for their barbaric cruelty, dysfunction, and periodic revolts. Those "settlers" who failed to meet their unrealistic harvest quotas – or balked at submitting to some of the most undignified requirements, like having one's beard shaved – faced flogging or exile. The biggest of these insurrections, in 1819, was put down by Arakcheyev himself, who had seventy men beaten with metal rods, with a number of them dying on the spot.[13]

Far from the liberal reforms that the officer corps had anticipated as they returned from their brief occupation of France, it was such practices which spread throughout the military. The "best parts of Russian society" grew bitterly disillusioned with Alexander, and with autocracy in general.[14] "It often happened that soldiers killed the first person they met, preferring hard labor [as a convicted murderer] to the life of a soldier," Muravyov-Apostol would later write of the conditions he witnessed and that he tried to change. "We were persecuted for not pushing people to such extremes."[15]

Upon returning from the West, Muravyov-Apostol and a number of high-ranking aristocrats began creating secret societies committed to true liberal reform. One of the first such groups, the Semyonov Artel, initially came together more like a drinking club – as a chance for a dozen or so officers from the Semyonovsky Regiment who had returned home from France to have supper together and shoot the breeze. "After dinner, some played chess, others read foreign newspapers loudly and followed events in Europe – such a pastime was decidedly an innovation," recalls Ivan Yakushkin, one of the founders of the club, later to be one of the more militant Decembrists.[16]

Their talk always seemed to return to the same thing: the hope they had felt having fought in the war, and their shattered expectations upon coming home, when peasant-soldiers who had suffered through the grueling deprivations of engagements such as the Battle of Borodino returned to the grueling deprivations of serfdom. Alexander, upon hearing of a such a club in the Semyonovsky Regiment, felt quite understandably threatened that young, elite officers were reading the Western press and discussing new ideas. He had the club banned because it "displeased" him.[17]

Muravyov-Apostol and his peers later set up the Union of Salvation in 1816, with a charter that committed their organization to ending serfdom and making Russia a constitutional monarchy. This would eventually become the Southern Society – one of two that ultimately took up arms against the new tsar. As Alexander's reforms stagnated and as reactionary repressions mounted, these turned into hotbeds of debate about how to restructure Russian society. Most were committed to lawful, peaceful means, but as always happens in such circles, a more aggressive minority emerged, led by Yakushkin, that insisted such methods could never bring the change that was necessary: assassinating the tsar was the only option. Without the means to do so, the option was ultimately discarded and even forbidden, but once the notion of regicide had been implanted in the collective imagination of the liberal opposition, the prospect could never be fully eradicated, and grew all the more tempting thanks to its proscription.

Years later, the revolutionary thinker Alexander Herzen would recall the treatment that serfs and soldiers were subjected to at the hands of members of his own class, and which had made a deep impression on him as a child: his father, punishing a peasant for falling short on his tribute by ordering his beard shaven, and the peasant, in tears, groveling and begging that he was willing to pay a hundred silver coins just to be spared the indignity.[18] As with any pre-revolutionary environment, though, there is a threshold after which habitual mistreatment becomes existential injustice. For Herzen, that line lay in how the various classes identified themselves vis-à-vis each other, and their respective responsibilities.

> In the old days there was, as there is now in Turkey, a patriarchal, dynastic love between landowners and servants. Nowadays the zealous Rus' servants devoted to the family and tribe of their masters are no more. And this is understandable. The landowner does not believe in his power, does not think that he will be responsible for his people at the terrible judgment day of Christ, but uses them for his own benefit. The servant does not believe in his subordination and endures the violence not as divine punishment, not as a trial, but simply because he is defenseless.[19]

In an increasingly secular society, the habitual suffering of the lower orders had gradually been stripped of its ethical framework. Now it took place out of habit, and the aristocrat who wielded his power no longer believed in his own justifications, responsibilities, or righteousness. As such, what was once a brutal, albeit understandable, reflection of the divine order of things had degenerated into little more than tyranny and abuse for its own sake, and the more the one practiced it and the other submitted to it, the more intolerable it became. For those who would soon come to be called the Decembrists, however, recognition of the intolerable injustice of their predicament and the desire to overturn the oppressive order came not from those who were suffering the mistreatment, but those who felt complicit in it: the very aristocrats closest to the tsar.

But a revolt needs a trigger, whether an overreaction on the part of the oppressor, or, on the contrary, a moment of opportunity. For the Decembrists, that moment was to be found in a brief power vacuum in December 1825.

"They can't even hang us properly"

In the pitch-black early morning hours of November 27, 1825, 28-year-old Grand Duke Nikolai Pavlovich stood reeling in the imperial chapel. A dutiful, deeply pious man who had just learned of his older brother Alexander's death, hardly before he could process what had happened and what it would mean for his life, he dropped to his knees before the altar and swore allegiance to his brother Konstantin Pavlovich as Emperor Constantine I, and demanded that everyone in the chapel, from his family to the highest dignitaries in the country, did the same.

What was, for most of the witnesses, a seemingly straightforward gesture concealed, for the grand duke, an existential urgency. He suspected what others did not, and it clearly tormented him: that his beloved brother, his adored Tsar Alexander, had several years earlier left a secret manifesto proclaiming him, and not his brother Konstantin, the heir apparent. After all, Konstantin had married a Polish Catholic countess and the price for Alexander's approval for this union was his secret exclusion from the succession. Nikolai Pavlovich was also aware of one of the reasons why Alexander had passed away not in St. Petersburg, but in the far-away southern frontier town of Taganrog: the tsar had reason to believe that "ruinous free-thinking and liberalism will flood, or, indeed, is already flooding, our armies," and he already suspected the senior command officers of the south.[20] In other words, the tsar had passed leaving his heir apparent cut out of the succession, and his real heir facing a brewing insurgency that questioned the very legitimacy of the throne.

Nikolai Pavlovich was terrified. His father, Tsar Paul I, had been assassinated when he was 5, and this was a specter that would haunt him all his life. Now, he would have to toe that line between fear and duty, knowing, ultimately, that not just the fate of millions of people, but his very life, hung in the balance. In addition to Alexander's ambiguous manifesto, it was becoming increasingly clear that Konstantin Pavlovich, long reluctant to be tsar, was in no hurry to either take the throne, or formally and above all publicly abdicate it in favor of his younger brother. The grand duke knew exactly the precarity of his position: given that officers in the southern army were plotting to take advantage of the power vacuum, he would have to take the crown without waiting for the formal abdication of his brother, thus risking his legitimacy as the future tsar being questioned.

Meanwhile, for the liberal secret societies among officers serving all across Russia, the window of opportunity was closing. The Northern Society, less militant partisans of a constitutional monarchy, remained at odds with the Southern Society, whose members believed that only an overthrow of the monarchy and an ensuing dictatorship – much like in France – could establish the republic that they saw as the future of

Russia. But the fragility of the succession presented an opportunity which would not come again in any of their lifetimes. Nikolai Pavlovich and the revolutionaries found themselves in a race, with both the grand duke and the plotters hoping to survive the looming coronation. The rebels decided to act on the morning of December 14, the very day when the country, its officers, and dignitaries would swear an oath to the new tsar, Nicholas I.

"Better to be taken on [St. Petersburg's] Senate Square than in bed," one of the rebels, Nikolai Besstuzhev, recalled of the deliberations that had gone on all night. "Better for others to discover what we have died for, than for them to be surprised when we suddenly disappear from society and no one will know where or for what we perished."[21]

Similar deliberations were taking place at the Winter Palace. At about 1 in the morning, Nicholas presented the State Council with a manifesto about his accession to the throne. The oath was scheduled for 9 a.m., and the new tsar went to spend what was left of that night with his wife.[22] "Perhaps by this evening neither of us will be among the living," he said to his aide de camp, General Alexander von Benkendorf, "but at least we will die fulfilling our duty."[23]

By the time some 3,000 soldiers and officers of the Moscow Life Guards Regiment, 2nd battalion of the Grenadier Regiment, and sailors of the Guards Marine Crew gathered on that wintry morning on Senate Square, it was no longer about reforms, or constitutions, or a Beautiful Russia of the Future. It was a struggle for power. To draw support from the soldiers and the masses, the insurgents exploited the ambiguity of Constantine's position to paint Nicholas's accession to the throne as illegitimate. "Long live Constantine, and his wife, Constitution!" soldiers chanted, having been convinced by some of the conspiring officers struggling to explain to them what a constitution was that it was simply the wife of the true emperor. It was a tenuous rationale, and probably initially intended as a joke, but it stuck, and, more to the point, it worked.[24]

With word that three loyalist senior officers had been killed after attempting to stop the Moscow Life Guards Regiment, Nicholas moved fast to defend the Winter Palace. The First Battalion of the Preobrazhensky Guard was mustered, and he would lead it himself to confront the insurgents. Unlike another cold-eyed autocrat who would prefer, two centuries later, to hole himself up in a fortress rather than face his people, Nicholas decided to address the insurgents directly, putting himself right into the line of fire. To the civilian onlookers, he spoke plainly: "Do me the favor to return home. You have nothing to do here."[25] At one point, the only thing that protected the young tsar from the rebel troops of the rebel Grenadier Guards was that they didn't recognize him and passed him by.

Even so, Nicholas dithered. Aware of the stakes, he at first tried everything to avoid bloodshed. He sent his representative, Count Mikhail Miloradovich, to negotiate with the rebels, but the general, who of all the court had taken the insurgents the most seriously, was killed, one of the first loyalist casualties in the revolt. Even after, Nicholas was reluctant to open fire, and twice countermanded his own orders to shoot. The rebels did not disperse, though, and finally the tsar ordered his soldiers to fire on them. Nicholas drove them from Senate Square with grapeshot, then when some of them tried to regroup on the frozen Neva River, his cannons shattered the ice beneath their feet. The uprising in St. Petersburg was dispersed.

But it was at this moment that the new tsar had to show unwavering and vengeful power. With the Pugachev rebellion still relatively fresh in their memories, the royal family were not so much afraid of the aristocracy as of the increasing likelihood that the revolutionary spirit could infect the masses. The grapeshot was fired, as Nicholas would later write in his diaries, "so that [the rebellion] doesn't spread to the mob," or, as his wife put it, to the "vile rabble." Defending his right to the throne became paramount, but so did creating a narrative that downplayed the threat that the tsar was facing from the masses. The insurgent officers needed to be unmasked as "monsters" rather than errant boys, let alone martyrs. All this came from a legitimate fear: Nicholas was convinced that he had survived that day only by a miracle of God.[26]

Indeed, the arrests had begun on the eve of the revolt itself, as Nicholas's loyalists struck also against the leadership of the Southern Society. A second rebellion in Chernigov, led by Muravyov-Apostol himself, who had ended up as second in command of the Chernigov Regiment of Foot after the Semyonovsky Regiment had been disbanded, initially succeeded in capturing the city, but was likewise quickly put down. A wave of arrests that began in November continued through March. The leaders were captured and their trials began.

At dawn on June 13, 1826, Sergei Muravyov-Apostol and four other leaders of the revolt were due to be hanged, their execution commuted from quartering. The rope around Muravyov-Apostol's neck broke, and he fell to the ground, breaking his leg. His last words, before he was hanged again, this time successfully, were, "Poor Russia! They can't even hang us properly."[27]

Years later, Alexander Herzen would recall the following morning:

Having celebrated the execution, Nicholas made his ceremonial entry into Moscow. I saw him here for the first time; he rode on horseback next to the carriage in which the dowager empress and the young empress were sitting. He was handsome, but his beauty was cold; there is no face that reveals a person's character as mercilessly as his face. The forehead, quickly running back, the lower jaw, developed at the expense of the skull, expressed an unyielding will and weak thought, more cruelty than sensuality. But the main thing is the eyes, without any warmth, without any mercy, the eyes of winter.[28]

The predictable reaction

I stared down at the small puddle of blood on Bolotnaya Square, as a warm May wind swirled the remaining dust and debris where just an hour earlier the riot police had suddenly charged on the protesters and dispersed them. It was May 6, 2012. A few meters away, a tiny metal android figurine keychain glinted in the sun, and I picked it up. It had a white ribbon tied to it; one of the protesters must have lost it in the scuffle. That little memento would remain with me on my desk for the next ten years, until, on March 7, 2022, as I hurriedly packed all I could fit into two suitcases, I decided to leave that little memory of the Snow Revolution in my Moscow apartment, where it belonged.

I felt like I had known all along that it would end with that little puddle of blood. Having just completed a book about Vladimir Putin, when I saw those protesters first marching, the hope that I shared mixed with a gut-wrenching sense that this would never work, that simply by turning up in such large numbers these young rebels, confident in their safety simply because they were too young to know otherwise, would unleash the Kremlin's centuries-old fury. A fury that, like an ancient volcano, could lie dormant for decades. A fury that, like a scared, drunk old man, could lash out violently at its noisy children when it awoke in terror. I had been recently reading too much history, and saw nothing but bloodshed and more oppression at the other end of people's revolts, whether in Russia or elsewhere. When an eager left-wing European journalist spent a day with me wandering the city, hoping to get an exciting soundbite on what was going on, at one point I blurted out in irritation, "revolutions bore me."

Back then, I didn't quite know how things would go from there, but a growing sense of dread began for me that day, the day of Putin's inauguration. That was when, after months of tolerating the protests and hinting at the potential for dialogue, the authorities began to crack down in earnest. The March of Millions that day ended with over 400 arrests and criminal charges for thirty people – and that puddle of blood.[29] Individual persecutions were followed by a series of ever more constrictive laws. Even relatively urbane Kremlin insiders like press spokesman Dmitry Peskov seemed caught up in panicked bloodlust. In the State Duma, he demanded that, "for hurting a riot policeman, the protesters' livers should be smeared on the asphalt."[30]

It was like a gradual, creeping hardline coup, but a coup being orchestrated by the country's ruler. That evening, I had to try to explain to my 5-year-old daughter where I had been and why people were protesting, how voters were accusing Putin of stealing their vote. Because vote in Russian – *golos* – is the same word for voice, my daughter looked up at me, horrified, asking if Putin, like some ghoul out of Mordor, was literally *stealing* people's *voices.* I assured her that was not the case. It wasn't just for her peace of mind: such demonic hyperbole, increasingly popular in the oppositionist press, only strengthened the Kremlin's terrible and terrifying aura, helping it stifle any agency on the part of civil society. But it was that day that I began to wonder – having started a family in Moscow with a firm belief in Russia's future – whether I really wanted my child growing up afraid of what she could and couldn't say in public.

Putin, obsessed with history, had a portrait of Nicholas I hung in his antechamber and reveled in the widespread comparisons between him and the monarch, often alluding to his autocratic predecessor as "extraordinary."[31] Although the Snow Revolution was far less violent than the Decembrist revolt, and Putin's own position far more secure than the tsar's, the Russian president may have felt himself stared down by the ghost of history, cornered into overreacting by the specter of the past, failing to see any number of alternative options that were offered by the present.

Having ascended the throne on the blood of a suppressed revolt, one with which many members of his own aristocracy could not help but sympathize, Tsar Nicholas I had to abandon plans for reform, including addressing the question of serfdom. Instead, he set up a system devoted to securing the regime – and his own safety – through mounting censorship, repression, and an ideology of reaction. Contrary to some of the austere and merciless depictions of Nicholas, most notably those of Herzen and other Decembrist sympathizers, the autocratic apparatus he came to set up was more a product of necessity than a long-term vision or design. According to the historian W. Bruce Lincoln, one reason why Nicholas personally questioned the leaders of the Decembrist revolt was to learn more about what it was in Russia that they were trying to change.[32] He convened a number of secret commissions trying to find a way to abolish serfdom, which he fully acknowledged was not just an outdated economic model for an empire trying to compete as a peer with the European powers, but also a moral failure. "There is no doubt that serfdom in its present position is evil," he would write, "but trying to extinguish it now would be a matter of even more disastrous evil."[33]

And so the security needs of the moment overtook Nicholas's agenda, and would shape it for a generation. Far from learning from the deficiencies of governance that the insurgents sought to correct, the tsar delayed addressing them, fostering, in the long term, an even more radical, uncompromising opposition to autocracy. As a result, when his successor, Alexander II, did attempt to bring about more comprehensive reform, including emancipating the serfs, he would end up assassinated for his troubles. The very inability of would-be reformers to build a coalition of support too powerful for the tsar – or the president – to ignore meant that their only option was to challenge the state directly. The officers of 1825 used what they had: their soldiers. The marchers of 2012 tried to use what was at their disposal: the law, the media, the ballot box. Yet respective monarchs feared them, ironically enough, too much to listen to them. It takes confidence to be willing to introduce change, doubly so when that change is brought to the table by your opposition, let alone when they are not the kind of grubby outsiders who flocked to Pugachev's banner, but the educated, the affluent, the very people who had benefited from the status quo. Nicholas was personally brave, but in those turbulent and uncertain times following Alexander's death, he felt he could not take such a risk, not just for his own sake but for his very dynasty's. In Putin's Kremlin, there were both hardliners and adherents of compromise. But Putin himself ultimately abandoned the possibility of compromise with those who were, after all, protesting the very process which had returned him to power. Either way, this was reaction driven by fear and perceived weakness. The Decembrist revolt and its aftermath ensured that the next generations of nineteenth-century rebels and dissidents, at least, would see the only route to progress being through violence and revolution.

5

The Will of the People

The haves and the have-nots

"We're here to help the people of Astrakhan take back their vote," Alexei Navalny said to me with a disarming grin I had never seen on the face of a Russian politician, and for a moment, I was smitten by his optimism.[1]

It was unseasonably warm in Astrakhan on April 14, 2012 – a balmy 24 Celsius, but a heatwave was on the way with temperatures in the 30s by the following week, after the Moscow protesters had left the city. This warm southern town on the mouth of the Volga River, an hour's drive to the Caspian Sea, was hardly the first place one would think of to stage a revolution, though it had had its share of dissent. In 1670, the first wave of Cossack rebellions, led by Stepan Razin, spread to the city, which became one of his strongholds until it was retaken by government forces the next year. But what kind of unrest could possibly ruffle the relative affluence of peak Putinism in this provincial town, with the trade and riches of the Caspian at its feet?

An increasing disparity between the haves and the have-nots, and an ongoing hunger strike, was beckoning the cosmopolitan dissenters from Moscow. After Putin's re-election in March, the White Ribbon movement struggled to maintain momentum. But its leaders were determined to leverage a key strength of the Snow Revolution: that the protests, while challenging Putin in spirit, were not so much about him as they were about free elections and the rule of law. Having touted these principles for years, Putin's government was now facing a movement that demanded they act according to their stated principles. This was not just about Putin's re-election, but about vote rigging across the country. Yet if Putin, who had effectively quashed any political competition among established parties, scarcely even needed to falsify the ballot to get re-elected, the same could not be said for the regional parliamentary and mayoral elections. This was the second time the leftist parliamentarian Oleg Shein had run for mayor of Astrakhan and lost, with the incumbent mobilizing particularly thuggish activists against a rival who, while coming in second, managed to garner an impressive 29 percent of the vote despite all the rigging. But this time, Shein's luck had changed: his party, the nominally oppositionist A Just Russia, had gained sixty-four seats in the State Duma the previous December, making them the third largest party behind the Communists and United Russia. Several of its deputies were using their new clout not only to support the White Ribbon movement, but also to stand up for their own party members. After coming in second in the March 4 ballot, Shein, citing mass electoral fraud, refused to recognize the vote as legitimate, and began a hunger strike in protest. It was a new opportunity for A Just Russia to demonstrate that it was a genuine political force. But even more importantly, it was an opportunity for the urban, creative class that had protested all winter in Moscow and St. Petersburg to take their movement to the people.

The best and the brightest of the White Ribbon movement booked trains and bought plane tickets, while others hitched rides with like-minded activists, and they all headed south, to spread their message among the masses. Alexei Navalny, who had that winter coined "the Party of Crooks and Thieves" as a phenomenally apt epitaph for United Russia, had begun taking the first steps in bridging the gap between the affluent oppositionists in the capital and the rest of the country facing the brunt of Putinist corruption. "The Astrakhan bandits, who by franchise have become 'members of the United Russia party,' consider themselves the only source of power, not the residents of Astrakhan who supported Shein in the elections," he wrote on April 9.

> Take your white ribbons, tents, hipster posters and whatever else you have, and go. In Astrakhan it is +24, and a train ticket costs 1,500 rubles. Our entire protest movement is not worth much if we cannot move the protest to where it is needed and where it is expected. Protesters are not needed now on Red Square, not on Bolotnaya and not on Sakharov. [They are needed] in the city of Astrakhan, on 8 Sovetskaya Street.[2]

By the time I arrived at Sovetskaya Street, where Oleg Shein's local office was based, it was, indeed, a hipster party in the best Moscow tradition. On a tree-lined boulevard in the center of the city, the Moscow activists held camp: they played music, some talked to journalists, while the socialite Ksenia Sobchak rapped with singer Vasya Oblomov, deriding outgoing president Dmitry Medvedev for failing to stand up for democracy and the Russian people. The younger activists engaged in the kind of free-spirited theatrics to which tent camps and protest lend themselves, particularly in good weather: draping themselves in white sheets, they started dancing erratically to electronic music.

Navalny was joined by two of A Just Russia's most outspoken members, Ilya Ponomaryov and Dmitry Gudkov, who had been among the leaders of the White Ribbon movement in the capital and wanted to bolster the party's outreach in the regions by supporting Shein. But by then, it was Navalny who was the star of the show – everybody wanted a piece of him, everybody, that is, who had traveled from up north to take part in the latest hipster rave, and I was no different.

"We are here to take back our vote," he told me then. "These are our laws, and this is our country. The Party of Crooks and Thieves is breaking our laws. We don't need the government's permission to use our laws to exercise our rights."[3]

It was a powerful message. Just the previous month, I had registered as a presidential election observer at a ballot station in a tiny Moscow-region village. Deep into the night, after twelve hours of witnessing the most blatant carousel voting, ballot box stuffing, and obfuscation by everyone from the young head of the local voting committee to the middle-aged women tasked with counting the votes, I asked one of them, trying to hold back my frustration so that I could hopefully understand the bureaucrats' motivations, "why are you doing this?"

"Because this is how we've always done things," the woman said to me calmly, hardly taking her eyes off the list of votes, penciling in the "right" numbers in the column under the name V. V. Putin.[4]

Navalny and the other newly minted opposition leaders were taking their message to people who were still doing things the way they'd always done them. It was for them, for the locals, and for their empowerment that they had left Moscow and brought their protests to Astrakhan's warm, dusty streets. As the column of youngsters, headed by Ponomaryov with his loudspeaker, marched down the boulevard, I saw some of those older locals in whose name these protesters came out. Leaning over their balconies, these middle-aged women started shouting at us. "Go back home, and leave us in peace. Nobody wants you here."

It would take some time for Navalny to hone his messaging skills and actually accomplish what had, for centuries, been one of the biggest challenges for Russian dissidents of all camps: learning to speak the same language as their people. That afternoon in Astrakhan, I tried to imagine what we all, with our ribbons and posters and trendy clothes, looked like to those middle-aged women on their balconies, schoolteachers and factory workers surviving on a couple of hundred dollars a month, exhausted after picking up their children from kindergarten, and hoping for a quiet weekend fishing, or getting their vegetable garden plots ready for the summer. My conversations with some of the locals confirmed as much: who are these privileged, patronizing snobs who think they know what we need, coming to our town and disrupting our weekend just because they're rich and bored enough to rock the boat without a thought for how it will affect the rest of us? And why are we to believe them when they say that this time their revolution is actually going to better our lives, rather than leave us poorer?

"Like a saddle on a cow"

Sometime in the spring and summer of 1874, peasants living in villages along the Volga began to notice strange things happening in their midst. Travelers appeared, dressed in odd ragged clothing but with the soft white hands of the privileged; they spoke Russian, or something like Russian, but had trouble understanding common phrases; they talked of hardship but struggled to accomplish simple tasks, like harnessing a horse. Sometimes, they would beg for a place to sleep and a cup of milk, which, for the peasants, was a particular nuisance.

Take one Nikolai Konstantinovich Bukh. The son of a wealthy state official from Kaluga, Bukh was studying to be a surgeon at the prestigious Medical Academy of St. Petersburg, and in his spare time voraciously reading the fashionable émigré anarchist thinker Mikhail Bakunin. "Our people clearly need help," the veteran revolutionary wrote in his home in Zurich in 1873. "They are in such a desperate situation that it costs nothing to raise up a village in revolt. But although any rebellion, no matter how unsuccessful it may be, is always useful, single revolts are not enough. We urgently need to raise all the villages."[5]

Bakunin's words couldn't have but made a deep impression on Bukh and a whole new generation of ambitious young men and women in Russia who had the money to live well enough and yet, in the restrictive climate of a government increasingly wary of its own intellectuals, fewer prospects to make themselves useful citizens. When Bakunin's self-styled emissary Sergei Nechayev, writing from his apartment in Zurich, penned his *Catechism of a Revolutionary*, he radicalized many of them even further: "A revolutionary is a doomed man. He has no interests of his own, no affairs, no feelings, no affection, no property, not even a name. Everything in him is absorbed by a single exclusive interest, a single thought, a single passion – revolution."[6]

Somewhere in the coffeehouses of Paris, Zurich, and London, between encouraging French and German workers to rise up against their exploiters and debating Hegelian philosophy, Bakunin and adepts like Nechayev developed the bright idea of creating socialist cells in Russia to foment discord and overthrow the tsarist regime. Ideas are beautiful things; there is a special exhilaration about reading Karl Marx over a fine Bordeaux – and especially debating with the great man himself in a Parisian café – caught up in the moment of creating a whole hypothetical utopia in contrast to the dirty, miserable, dysfunctional reality that you actually inhabit. In their transnational epistolary debates, there emerged radicals like Nechayev and moderates like Pyotr Lavrov, who tried to adapt Nechayev's uncompromising demands to the complex conditions in the field. But in the end, their work and their lives, whatever tactics they adopted, were devoted to the abstract.

Not the dirt on the ground, not the grime in the wrinkles of the hands of the peasants they tried to court, not the prosaic chores of plowing the field, chopping wood, hauling hay, and making ends meet. All this was romanticized in their journals, but their reality could never match the intoxication of the ultimate abstraction: revolution.

Bukh, like many fellow activists who took up the calls to "go to the people" and inspire them to rebel, learned this the hard way when he went to proselytize in the village of Poshekhonye in the spring of 1874. "The peasant costume suited me like a saddle on a cow, arousing suspicion in everyone I met," he would recall. In one instance, an old woman who offered him a bed for the night, in an apparently deliberate attempt to play a prank, used old flea-ridden furs to teach the young activist what it was really like to live their lives. He would spend the next year and a half trying to get rid of the parasites.[7]

"We tried to carefully hide our origins from the peasants: we abandoned our noble documents and instead stocked up with forged peasant passports," recalled the revolutionary Vladimir Debagoriy-Mokrievich.

> European costumes were replaced with common people's caftans . . . it even got to the point that in clashes with people, we pretended to be illiterate. Going to the people and dreaming of merging with the masses . . . we made our first journey almost in rags. We ourselves looked at the rags with sympathy, and it seemed to us that the people would also greet us with sympathy.[8]

Contrary to their assumptions, they often ended up finding that poor people don't always trust other poor people. In real life, as opposed to the uplifting magazine stories the privileged and leisurely write for others like themselves, the poor often have to struggle against those who, driven by need, will steal or deceive their peers to get what they want. The poor, much like anyone else, while wanting to eradicate the injustice of their lot, also tend to prefer that the natural order of their lives – their homesteads, the way they raise their children, and how they put bread on the table – is not too disrupted in the crusade for justice that bored rich kids from big cities claim to be pursuing in the people's name.

There is a problem in getting at the real impressions that these well-meaning students and zealots made on the peasants they tried to inspire. The peasants were overwhelmingly illiterate and did not leave behind much of their recollections, and it is hard to trust the narratives of those who so poorly misconstrued their target audience in the first place. The accounts of the *narodniki* – the affluent, protest-minded young intellectuals who took up the fashionable trend of "going to the people" – oscillate between an idealistic notion of the *muzhik*, the peasant, as a pure, ascetic, hard-working pillar of the aristocracy's privilege, and a violent, unpredictable, hard-drinking, and vulgar brute too uneducated to understand the emancipatory ideals these intellectuals tried to preach. These notions persist to this day, deeply ingrained in how some Russian dissidents see their own people, although there is nothing uniquely Russian about their liberal guilt. In their struggle to find a unifying pattern, to devise a system of governance that could at once elevate and rein in these multitudes, they often failed to see them as individuals, let alone as having their own interests and ideals. Treating and judging a whole nation like a single person, to be redeemed or persecuted, depending on his or her compatibility with the ideals they were trying to impose, they furthered the alienation they came to overcome.

The aristocratic *narodnik* Sergei Stepnyak-Kravchinsky tried to puncture some of these notions among his comrades with a particular poetry, challenging novices who feared (usually rightly) that the peasants would not take kindly to outsiders, though he still ended up falling, inadvertently, into the other essentializing trope. "Those . . . who had already gone through the same torments of doubt and fear," he recalled,

> told them with delight that this fearsome *narod* is kind, simple, and trusting like a child, that they meet their friends not only without any suspicion, but with open arms and open hearts; that their speeches were listened to with the deepest sympathy; that everyone, old and young, at the end of a long day of work, gathered around them in some dark, smoky hut, where, in the faint light of a torch, they talked to them about socialism or read something from the books that they brought.[9]

This beautiful passage – and perhaps the lexical peculiarities of the Russian language, in that the all-encompassing *narod*, or people, is a singular noun connoting a homogeneous mass – was designed to communicate with other revolutionaries, rather than with actual members of the *narod* itself.

By contrast, the *narodnik* Nikolai Sergeyev was disappointed by what he found in Astrakhan when he traveled there in 1876, dressed in a canvas shirt and carrying a fake passport. Hoping to encounter the rebellious spirit of Stepan Razin and Yemelian Pugachev, he found instead drunken revelers

> deaf to our preaching; they were not prepared to listen to our speeches about their bitter lot and the means to improve it. . . . There were many drunken men and women who shouted furiously and sang obscene songs, and the youth spoke very freely with women, every now and then squealing and screaming shrilly from under the guys who leaned on them during the fuss. Looking at the appearance of my so-called "comrades," in this Volga rabble, I thought: these are the descendants of those people with whom Stenka Razin once began to destroy Russia, threatening to reach Moscow and take revenge against the oppressors of the people.[10]

Just like the tsar whom they hoped to overthrow in the name of the people, these budding revolutionaries, when facing living, breathing members of this *narod*, balked in fear – because it was a force that, once unleashed, answered to nothing but itself. But the revolution could not wait. If the *narod* could not be rallied to its end, then the priests of the revolution needed to find other means.

In the wild

The Russian word *volya* is a curious one, in that it has two meanings. The first translates into the noun form of *will*, and there the two words share a common Indo-European root *welh*, which means to choose or to want. The second is more interesting, in that it means freedom. It is distinct from the other Russian word for freedom, *svoboda*, in that it connotes something far more intense and unbridled. A wolf that has been released from captivity, for instance, could be said to be *na svobode*, free, but it is more correct to describe it as *na vole*, in the wild. Narodnaya Volya, the People's Will party of the *narodniki* as it eventually came to call itself, fused both of those meanings into one – hearkening back to the boundless release of the ancient peasant breaking from the shackles of all social bonds.

* * *

One would have thought that, with the pent-up political energy accumulating under the restraints of Nicholas I, his death in 1855 would have heralded a new top-down liberalization wave, one in which his son, Alexander II, would engage the growing community of Westernizing intellectuals and reformists. Indeed, contemporary hagiographies painted the new tsar in this way, and his 1861 manifesto freeing the serfs established him as the Tsar-Liberator. But the reality, as always, was more complicated, and would give rise to the phenomenal political contradictions and persistent alienation that would characterize his rule vis-à-vis the reformist sectors of society.

Raised as a military man by his father, Alexander II was no natural reformer, but was, instead, forced rapidly to push through complex changes that had been long overdue. The 1853–6 Crimean War made these particularly glaring, not least because the failure to reform the agrarian base was hampering industrial development, and thus Russia's efforts at modernizing its dated armed forces.[11] Peasant uprisings intensified throughout the war, with many serfs expecting that they would be rewarded with freedom for their sacrifices. Whereas Nicholas's commissions tasked with working out plans for emancipation consisted largely of liberal-minded statesmen, Alexander's committees, which were having to work with much greater urgency, included conservative landowners who feared penury if they had to hand over so much of their land for nothing. The resulting Emancipation Manifesto was a compromise in which one of the key challenges – how exactly newly freed serfs could reclaim any land at all – was buried under bureaucratic complexities and led to all kinds of unexpected costs that few former serfs could afford. To "redeem" their land, peasants had to pay their former masters fees for the next forty-nine years.

Reformist thinkers were at first ecstatic that the tsar had mustered the political will to finally push through the momentous emancipation. When Alexander issued the Emancipation Manifesto, the revolutionary Alexander Herzen wrote in his magazine, *The Bell*, that "his name now stands higher than his predecessors," and christened him "the Liberator."[12] But the confusion and complexity of the land ownership issue for the serfs immediately sparked unrest. Two months later, a literate peasant in the village of Bezdny named Anton Petrov apparently misread the Manifesto, adding a footnote claiming that a number of serfs had already been freed in 1858, and convincing

villagers that they were thus entitled to all the land and bread
in the hands of the estate lords. As many as 5,000 peasants,
many from neighboring villages, came together in Bezdny,
demanding what they believed was rightfully theirs. General
Alexander Apraksin, charged by the tsar with putting down
the unrest, claimed that Petrov had been paid by some of the
wealthier peasants deliberately to misrepresent the Manifesto.
If this was the case, it clashes profoundly with the exoticizing
tropes of some of the *narodniki*, who painted the peasants as
earnest, pure, and naïve. But likewise it falls into an equally
essentializing trope that the Russian government has deployed
for centuries: that the disadvantaged were perfectly capable of
looking out for their own interests, deceiving the state for profit
or out of malice, egged on by grifters or foreign enemies. The
truth, as always, likely lies somewhere in between: the arcane
language of the Manifesto lent itself to genuine misinterpreta-
tion, one that certain opportunists were sure to exploit.

Be that as it may, what happened next was nothing short
of a disaster. General Apraksin looked straight at the crowd
and said, "I feel sorry for you lads, but I must and will shoot;
those who feel innocent, leave." But the peasants continued
to chant, *volya, volya,* and would not disperse, so Apraksin
ordered his soldiers to open fire on an unarmed crowd, killing
fifty-one and wounding many more. When Apraksin's report
was presented to the Tsar-Liberator, Alexander penned a curt
resolution at the end: "I cannot but approve of the actions of
Citizen Apraksin; however tragic, there was nothing else left to
be done."[13]

Herzen and many of the reform-minded intellectuals realized just how thin and unsuccessful the "liberalization" actually
was. That spring and summer, newly freed peasants rose in
revolts around the country when they realized that, having
received their freedom, they were deprived of their land, and
forced to fend for themselves. The Bezdny uprising triggered
a cycle of arrests, deaths, more uprisings, and more arrests,

radicalizing a new generation of intellectuals in the process. Students and professors at the University of Kazan joined their cause, leading to yet further arrests, and Herzen's tune in *The Bell* changed dramatically. "The people have been deceived by the Tsar," his colleague Nikolai Ogarev wrote that spring.[14]

The profound sense of disappointment and betrayal that these events engendered spurred students to action, and thus the first *narodniki* circles were formed. The imperial authorities responded to the student protests by clamping down with particularly draconian regulations that summer, leading to the mass expulsion of the more outspoken students and their professors, and then to the temporary closure of universities in Moscow, St. Petersburg, and Kazan. This exodus simply filled the ranks of the first revolutionary cells and *narodnik* circles, encouraged by revolutionary thinkers like Herzen, who first sounded the battle-cry in late 1861:

> So where can you young men go, locked out from the sciences? Shall I tell you where? Then listen, for the darkness won't keep you from hearing: from all sides of our vast homeland, from the Don and the Urals, from the Volga and Dnieper, a groan is swelling, a murmur is rising – the first roar of the sea wave, which boils, fraught with storms, after a terribly tiring calm. To the people! to the people! – this is your place, exiles of science ... you will not become clerks, but warriors, not rootless mercenaries, but warriors of the Russian people![15]

The initial ventures into the countryside throughout the 1860s focused more on education than radicalization, with the first *narodniki* piously hoping that these tools would help empower the peasants inadvertently disenfranchised by their "emancipation." But a lack of success meant that their leaders increasingly took up more aggressive and ambitious agendas. If the first *narodnik* wave was more about enlightenment, the second, starting in the 1870s, was about the urgent need for revolution. But that, too, failed to resonate with the majority of the peasantry – some of whom were the first to turn the proselytizing tourists in to the authorities.

By this point, the increasingly radicalized dissenters could no longer hold back from the agenda of revolution that they had spun into a categorical imperative. With peaceful means no longer working, many of them believed it was time to kill the tsar – Liberator or not. Unlike the previous generation of Decembrists, who saw regicide as a last resort and tried, at first, open confrontation as befitted their officers' honor, the new insurgents adopted terror as the most effective method of achieving their immediate goals.

The Zemlya i Volya (Land and Liberty) movement, re-emerging as a radical party in the latter half of the 1870s, gave rise in 1879 to an even more violent offshoot, Narodnaya Volya, People's Liberty, or People's Will. One of the Executive Committee's first decrees that summer was sentencing Tsar Alexander II to death for his repressions against Zemlya i Volya members who had already staged violent, albeit unsuccessful, assassination attempts. As the attacks increased, the tsar was hounded into seclusion, forced to set up a Supreme Commission for the Maintenance of State Order and Public Peace, headed by Count Mikhail Loris-Melikov, who was granted near total power in Alexander's stead. Narodnaya Volya's campaign of terror only intensified, with a revolutionary, acting independently of his party, taking a shot at the count just a week after his appointment. Loris-Melikov's government retaliated ruthlessly: terrorists were hanged almost immediately after conviction. But the count took other measures as well. He saw continued and accelerated reform as the only way to weaken the party's popularity and made several appeals to the public in hopes of promoting dialogue and ensuring that some of his leniency towards the younger radicals would help rehabilitate them. It didn't. The count's abolition of Tsar Nicholas's dreaded secret police, the Third

Section of His Imperial Majesty's Own Chancellery, couldn't have come at a worse time, and the assassination attempts continued unabated. And yet, if ever there was a chance for true and lasting reform, it was under Loris-Melikov's government: by 1881, he had even drafted a constitution that, if it had had time to be adopted, would have become the first such document in Russia's history.

In December 1880, the plotters began planning a multi-pronged attack on the tsar, involving a mine placed in a tunnel, four bombs to be thrown at his carriage, and, if that failed, a close-proximity shooting or a stabbing. In February, they moved to act. Ignaty Grinevitsky was one of four men selected to throw a bomb on the fateful day on March 1. The night before, he wrote:

> Alexander II must die. . . . He will die, and with him, we, his enemies, his executioners, shall die too. . . . How many more sacrifices will our unhappy country ask of its sons before it is liberated? . . . It is my lot to die young, I shall not see our victory, I shall not live one day, one hour in the bright season of our triumph, but I believe that with my death I shall do all that it is my duty to do, and no one in the world can demand more of me.[16]

The attack was a success. The first bomb thrown merely wounded the tsar, but the second, thrown by Grinevitsky himself, proved fatal. He died hours later, in the Winter Palace. Of course, all the reforms in progress were halted, and the constitution that he was due to proclaim that very day was, tragically and ironically, no more.

The legacy of the populist nihilists was cemented: the assassination proved a success, in their eyes, at least. While not bringing down the dynasty, it had demonstrated that, in their tactics, if not in their strategy, the terrorists were a potent force, and their methods must be continued. Exactly six years after the assassination, a new set of Narodnaya Volya assassins attempted a new attack. The plot was foiled, the conspirators arrested, and five of them were hanged. One of the men hanged on May 8, 1887, at what had by then become a rather routine execution, was a graduate of the St. Petersburg Imperial University by the name of Alexander Ilyich Ulyanov. His younger brother Vladimir was later to become rather more widely known under his revolutionary codename: Lenin.

Only connect

A couple of months before the events in Astrakhan, a curious meme emerged in protest circles: a girl with an open, somewhat confused face, nestled in a faux fur parka, saying proudly, "We started dressing more better." The girl was named Svetlana Kuritsyna, and on December 6, 2011, just as the Snow Revolution was starting, she had traveled from her home city of Ivanovo to take part in a pro-Kremlin counter-protest. A journalist had cornered her and asked why she supported Putin and the United Russia party, and she smiled and beamed at the opportunity to be on camera.[17] Overnight, her awkward response became a symbol of everything the protest class seemed to be fighting against, for the superficiality of her values, her bad grammar, and the inherent *provinciality* that it represented in the eyes of many of the affluent, educated protesters.

Sveta from Ivanovo was a student from a struggling family who had joined a pro-Kremlin youth organization to help get an education and a career. The trouble was that the sneering and patronizing response from the metropolitan liberals – and their leaders would only start to reckon with this problem much later, after the damage had been done – looked like a critique not of Putinism, but of all the impoverished, hard-working, aspirational Svetas in the country, their families, their whole communities. Even though the Snow Revolution had begun to bridge many gaps and included many movements and classes, at its intellectual core many of its most active spokespeople couldn't shake the ancient snobbery against their own people. The Sveta incident made it look as if the "protest class" wanted nothing to do with the actual people in whose name it claimed to be protesting.

The Kremlin, of course, pounced on the opportunity to deepen this schism as it sought to isolate the protesting class. Sveta was rewarded by getting her own prime-time talk show on national television,[18] as state-controlled channels began to transform their domestic political narrative – which had been a variation of neoliberalism – to court the common man and woman, the factory workers, kindergarten teachers, miners, and tank manufacturers, sometimes paying them to protest, but at others times funneling money to their own social organizations.

It worked, and in a way the Russian government did what it had done for centuries as its go-to survival tactic: leaned on the common people for its legitimacy by magnifying and exploiting their grievances, yet putting the blame on a self-interested upper class. The very state which had poured money into making Moscow a glittering symbol of the new, modern Russia, and which had educated, fêted, and employed its educated new class, now demonized them, presenting itself as the people's protector against this effete, condescending, and out-of-touch common enemy. When Igor Kholmanskikh, a foreman at the UralVagonZavod tank plant in the smokestack city of Nizhny Tagil, publicly offered to bring some of his "lads" to Moscow and sort out "those loafers who are always grumbling," the strategy had its poster boy.[19]

Putinism, however, was unique in that the gray chameleon at the head of state power, who liked expensive faux marble and gold-plated swimming pools in the imperial palaces he built by syphoning off public funds, never seemed to fully buy in to the populist ideologies he deployed. He was himself alienated both from the working class from which he hailed and the oligarchy to which he aspired. The reaction of the people – those who were too busy earning a living to protest – was understandable as they looked at these youngsters who hadn't an inkling of what their lives were like. They were not the fools the government and opposition both took them to be. They trusted neither, but the government, at least, would throw them a few crumbs once in a while. When the locals do rise up, it's "so the [government] finally hear us and see how we live," I was told by a local factory worker from the single-industry town of Pikalyovo, where Putin flew in to quell a workers' protest over wage arrears in 2009. "It's all for show, their [the government's] behavior," said a local driver of Putin's performance there. "But what's the point of rocking the boat and making it worse? At least we got our salaries."[20]

* * *

The challenges of the 2012 protesting class in the regions mirrored those of the *narodniki* in that both came face to face with the alienation between the cosmopolitans and the agrarians, the rich and the poor, the educated and the uneducated. The *narodniki* had to traverse such a profound chasm – linguistic, cultural, and social, not to mention the oppression of the authorities – that many gave up on the tedious negotiations that are the building blocks of common social bonds, the pathways towards a common national identity. Instead they turned to radicalism. In 2012, that chasm was no longer as deep: the protesters' countrymen were literate and had the relative means to buy the same smartphones and connect to the same social media channels that the dissenters used to spread their messages. They were also educated enough to question and think independently about some of those messages. But the divide continued to pose hurdles, bolstered as it was by a deeply ingrained, essentializing snobbery among many Russian intellectuals who continued to view the majority of their coun-trymen as imperial subjects with the mentality of slaves, rather than the citizens that many of them had already become. This divide pushed some protesters towards more radical rhetoric, if not action, which the Kremlin authorities ruthlessly cracked down on, essentially shutting down the protest movement.

And yet it also pushed countless others to continue towards their goals through more modest, less radical means. That day in Astrakhan, even more inspiring than my interaction with Navalny was a conversation I had with a young man; I'll call him Mikhail. Just released from the police station where he had been detained for unauthorized protest, he was standing among his fellow activists in the city square, beaming with pride, a dog-eared pamphlet in his hand. On closer inspection, it turned out to be the Constitution of the Russian Federation. He had spent that entire morning, he told me, sitting around with cops, quoting from the booklet, and talking about rule of law.

"You know, they came to like me in the end," he said. "We joked, I told them how this is all supposed to work, and they agreed with me!"[21]

Was it the constitution, his political skills, his adeptness at spreading the message? Or was it that he just seemed like a nice straight-forward guy, talking to other straight-forward guys as equals rather than as dupes to be enlightened, as a way to pass the time as the paperwork was being sorted? I had spent a long time by then interviewing pro-Kremlin protest-ers and working-class Russians from the provinces, and, as a journalist from Moscow, was frequently made aware of how difficult it was not to sound condescending to people who had few reasons to trust you. The more you sympathize, the more you risk patronizing; the more you disagree, the more you risk sounding preachy. Mikhail didn't seem to preach, condescend, or exoticize. He was just able to connect, on an equal footing, with a common purpose, but not necessarily an agenda. And in the process, he was just one person planting the seeds of something that, in a generation's time, will hopefully bear fruit.

Few rebels and revolutionaries have that kind of patience, though. That gap between classes and estates that historically made building alliances so difficult – and mutual misunderstanding and exasperation so easy – would persuade some of the idealists and ideologues who wanted to change Russia that patience was the wrong way to approach their task. The early rebellions had sought to harness the power of the dispossessed and disorganized have-nots, and they had been crushed by the state. Then the elites had had their shot, only to be crushed in turn, lacking the muscle to force change on regimes too frightened to allow any compromise. When the late nineteenth-century rebels reached out to the people, they were scorned, the masses proving unwilling to listen to those who regarded themselves as there to save them from their ignorance and poverty. Maybe, the rebels came to believe, it was time for them to seize whatever opportunities arose when the state was weak and distracted and, once they had power, educate society and instil in it the "right" interests, by force, if necessary. By then, it had become a fight with the government, rather than a project to better the people's lot. The masses could, after all, later be told that this was what they had wanted all along, or at least should have wanted, had they but known. The rebels were, they could tell themselves, simply anticipating the will of the people.

6

The Rebel as Tsar

The "peasants" and their muscle

"Make way," the man drawled, slinging his Kalashnikov over his shoulder after waving it in my general direction, as he and three others pushed through the makeshift security check. Ruddy, dusty faces – miners, mechanics, or factory workers who looked much older than they actually were – in different states of inebriation, smelling of cheap smoke and partially metabolized alcohol, scurried with an overwhelming sense of newly acquired importance past hastily assembled barricades consisting of trash, tires, boards, and barbed wire towards the broken entrance of the Regional Administration Building. The separatists had now made it their stronghold.

The rest of Donetsk was in bloom: tulips and lilacs blossomed in the manicured central parks where parents strolled with their baby carriages, and life, generally, went on. It was May 2014, the third month of the "Russian Spring," several weeks after an assortment of these violent, volatile men, led by local politicians and businessmen who, aside from their own ideals and political aspirations, smelled the lucrative opportunity of cozying up to Russian state coffers, had stormed and captured government administration buildings in the eastern Ukrainian cities of Donetsk, Luhansk, and Kharkiv. Inspired by Russia's annexation of Crimea that February, they declared independence from Ukraine and hoped that Moscow would come to their aid. In some ways – and as I write this I am aware of how difficult it will be for many Ukrainians and their Western supporters to hear this, in light of Russia's brutal war against the country – the 2014 Revolution of Dignity in Kyiv earlier that winter, when pro-Western protesters hoping for closer ties to Europe and an end to endemic state corruption toppled the government of Kremlin ally Viktor Yanukovych, bore many of the hallmarks of a quintessentially Russian revolt. Faced with an entrenched, corrupt, and violently repressive government, and finding it hard to bridge social, cultural, and economic gaps with a great deal of their countrymen in the predominantly Russian-speaking east – many of whom opposed closer economic integration with Europe because they feared it would jeopardize their close ties with Russia – some of the Kyiv demonstrators and their nationalist supporters in Ukraine's parliament, the Rada, turned to radical, even violent, means.[1] Demonstrators of the ultranationalist, anti-Semitic Svoboda party, for instance, and the Right Sector movement emerged as some of the most active members of the violence on Maidan, Kyiv's Independence Square, that winter.[2] But just as the nationalist radicals did not have the absolute support of the otherwise larger, and more peaceful, pro-EU/anti-Yanukovych movement, this wider movement was also at odds with some in Ukraine's eastern regions. Counter-protests started to take place in the east, with political groups there reaching out to Russia for help, and with the Kremlin beginning to eye a potential geopolitical opportunity to further split and weaken Ukraine. After the Euromaidan demonstrations succeeded, the new victorious leaders in Kyiv and their supporters ignored those unhappy with their policies – such as government restrictions on the use of the Russian language – and, indeed, with the very means through which they took power. "We should have been reaching out to people in Donetsk from the very start, and we asked for delegations from Kyiv to start a dialogue," a Ukrainian advisor to Donetsk governor Serhiy Taruta told me in the spring of 2014. "But Kyiv refused; they weren't interested in dialogue."[3]

Many of the pro-Western activists in Kyiv whom I spoke to were even less conciliatory. "What is the point of talking to them?" an intellectual in Kyiv who supported her new government asked me the following year, talking about her countrymen in the east. Deploying a pejorative term used for those presumed still to be stuck in an old Soviet mindset, she said, "they are all primitive *sovok* peasants. They don't understand anything, it's just not in their DNA."[4] And in Crimea, a pro-Kyiv activist said to me, "We will kill [the Russian-backed local protesters]. And the rest will just go back to Russia."[5] It was telling, too, that progressive supporters of the Revolution of Dignity took up the word *vatnik* – a cotton-filled jacket used to stay warm by the poorest in Russia's remote regions, and by prisoners of the Gulag – as a derogatory term for backward pro-Russian "patriots." As the linguist Gasan Guseinov summarized, "A *vatnik* is a piece of clothing for poor, disadvantaged people who have nothing. . . . It denotes a primitive man who is unable to rebel against those who have oppressed him all his life. This is a very offensive word."[6] It had first been used by Russian cosmopolitan protesters in 2011–12 against Russians who supported the Kremlin, but in the Ukrainian conflict, it took on all the connotations of class and cultural hatred. Much like the American "deplorables" who voted for Donald Trump, they were vilified, the message went, simply for being poor.

So who were these so-called *vatniks*? In many ways, the pro-Russian insurgency in eastern Ukraine emerged as an answer to the Revolution of Dignity, and tried to ape it for its own ends.

The budding pro-Russian counter-revolutionaries in the east, many raised on heroic tales of Bolshevik resistance in the Civil War a century earlier, represented a small and radical minority of a wider movement in the region. That wider movement was wary of the new Kyiv government and its members wanted greater autonomy to safeguard their interests, but they didn't necessarily want to secede, and they certainly didn't want to start a separatist armed conflict.[7] But with armed nationalist activists roaming the streets of Odessa and some of the cities in the east, threatening violence to silence proponents of decentralization (and subsequently using it, lethally, to ensure that the new government toed their line),[8] their cause was hijacked by their separatist radicals, who also roamed the same streets, so that it was hard to tell who was who. They called the other side *ukropy*, or dill, because it sounded a little like Ukrainian, and glorified the Russian Army that would one day come to liberate them.[9] Buttressed by nationalists from Russia, it was the radicals who wanted to copy Kyiv's success, but now under their own banners. On April 6, 2014, 2,000 protesters stormed the building of the Regional State Administration, and their leaders proclaimed a new, independent republic.

Donetsk was now their town. In the name of a distinct Russian identity, these separatist insurgents, joined by enthusiastic volunteers, rogue security officers, and veterans from Russia, had taken up arms against the new pro-Western government in Kyiv, which itself was the result of a people's revolution earlier that winter, one that centered on a distinct Ukrainian identity. "If they can take government buildings," insurgents would tell me, "then so can we." After initially trying to resist, many in the local police and military either joined their cause, enlisted into the loyalist volunteer battalions backed by Ukraine's National Guard, or, for the most part, kept their heads down, waiting for the powers that be to fight it out. That week in Mariupol, I saw two dead policemen lying in the dust next to a burning tank, their bodies barely covered by a tarp – killed by the Ukrainian

National Guard when some in their precinct caved to demands
of a pro-Russian protest rally to open their arsenal to them.
They served as a good reminder of what can happen when local
law enforcement feels itself trapped between confused, con-
flicting loyalties. On the one hand was a vocal contingent of
aggrieved residents of your own hometown, supported by the
powerful, and seemingly sympathetic, Kremlin. On the other,
there was a new government in the capital of your country,
brought into power by a popular, albeit violent, revolution,
increasingly and vocally hostile to the language, identity, and
culture of your friends, family, and neighbors.

"Why all the brute force?" I asked one of the separatist
gunmen in Donetsk. "Why do you need the guns?"

"Don't you see?" the drunk man, we'll call him Ivan, retorted.
"It's to protect us from the Ukrainian Nazis from Kyiv. Right
Sector, Svoboda, they're all over the place. They hate us and
they want to destroy us."

He was not entirely wrong. Days earlier, I had spoken to
activists from Right Sector, a paramilitary Ukrainian nationalist movement that had been front and center in the street
fighting in Kyiv that toppled the old government. They confirmed Ivan's sentiment: they did, indeed, hate him and wanted
to destroy him, the nationalist activist said, because their cause
was the only right and true one, while his was built on Kremlin
fabrications and lies, rather than real grievances.[10] The full
story, of course, was that the Ukrainian nationalists feared
their pro-Russian counterparts because their patron in the
Kremlin had just used them to annex a chunk of Ukrainian territory. But likewise, many Russian-speakers in the east feared
the Ukrainian nationalists due to their aggressive, vitriolic
rhetoric. Citizens of a single country, they were alienated from
each other, and unable to find a common, national interest to
overcome their respective grievances. (It would, ironically, be
in part thanks to Putin's invasion eight years later that Ukraine
would fully coalesce around its new national identity.)

At the time, no one really understood who these self-styled separatists were – and neither, I suspect, did they. Ukraine insisted that these were Russian invaders – special forces or soldiers whom Moscow had "covertly" deployed. But I had seen Moscow's covert soldiers in Crimea: quiet, efficient, and disciplined, they looked like they knew exactly what they were doing. These men, by contrast, swaggering and undisciplined, were local Russian-speaking, Russian-identifying Ukrainian citizens, aggrieved by what they saw as Kyiv's increasing contempt of them and their ways, a contempt that long predated the annexation of Crimea. They wanted what they thought was justice and freedom, but in what form, exactly? Within Ukraine still, but with renewed guarantees of their language and autonomy? For Donetsk to proclaim independence and live as Russian protectorate? To join Russia?

Moscow, for its part, was telling them to stand down, even while doing nothing to prevent – and even encouraging – the inward flow of volunteers and adventurers. That April, a former FSB (Federal Security Service) officer and war re-enactor named Igor Girkin, with the nom de guerre Strelkov, defied his Kremlin-backed handlers and led a group of fifty-two men across the Ukrainian border to join up with Ukrainian insurgents and set up a stronghold in Slovyansk. He had played a pivotal role in mustering volunteer support for the seizure of Crimea in February, but he and his supporters strongly believed that taking Crimea was not enough. The Kremlin dithered on how much it actually wanted to commit to the nationalists it had unleashed for the purpose of what it thought would be a quick geopolitical move to wrest Crimea from Ukraine. It had wanted to take Crimea, a strategic base of its Black Sea Fleet and a part of Russia until it was transferred to Ukraine for largely administrative reasons in 1954. It did not really want the polluted, industrial Donbas (Donetsk Basin) region. Yet having ignited genuine, yet dormant, yearnings for some kind of "Russian identity" amongst some within the predominantly

Russian-speaking population of eastern Ukraine, the Kremlin would have a hard time extinguishing these without risking its own credibility. "We just want for everything to go back to the way it was in the Soviet Union," one of the pro-Russian protesters in Donetsk told me that May. The first order of business, it seemed, was to defend themselves against the "Ukrainian Nazis" and take power. Surely, they reasoned, they could figure everything else out later, and if Moscow saw their determination and success, it would send its troops to protect them.[11]

The Kremlin, as it turned out, utterly miscalculated the appeal its own designs had for the local Russian-speakers in Ukraine, perhaps mistaking the volume of the militant minority for genuine support. The people of the Donbas wanted justice, sure, just not necessarily the Kremlin's justice. Putin would miscalculate again, in 2022, when he decided, based on reports from his own security services as they desperately competed to tell their boss what they thought he wanted to hear, that Kyiv would fall within weeks. But by then it was too late: no one wanted to remember what those voiceless Russian-speaking "peasants," too "slavish" to organize a proper, civilized opposition, wanted in the first place – which may not have been Kyiv, but nor was it Moscow.

With power in eastern Ukraine lying in the gutter, waiting for someone to come along and pick it up, the lawlessness that I saw in Donetsk, Mariupol, and Odessa in the spring of 2014 conjured images of a revolution long past, one as dark, bloody, and meaningless as any Russian revolt. This, I thought, looking into these men's terrifying faces, is what it must have been like to behold the Bolshevik fighters storming the Winter Palace in 1917. Not the glory and triumph of a successful revolution, not the red banners and lofty slogans of liberation later mythologized in film and propaganda posters, but chaos, dirt, trash, cheap cigarette smoke, and fear; empty hours waiting around tables stacked with dirty cans of leftover scraps and empty bottles, punctuated by sudden bouts of excitement, by armed men scurrying here and there, shouting, drinking, fighting. The violent counter-revolutionaries of Donetsk were but a radical minority, a vanguard riled up by stronger forces on a quest driven by ideas they projected onto the masses, individuals so alienated from those masses that they believed, mistakenly, that their cause and the people's will was one and the same, the only true and righteous one, pure from the fabrications and lies, compromises and distortions concocted by cynics in the war rooms of their enemies.

Power lies in the gutter

Long before the rebel had turned into the tsar, he, a relatively affluent descendant of former serfs who had, over generations, risen through the imperial state service to acquire the status of gentry, knew exactly what the working class of his country wanted and how it would achieve it. It was, after all, a scientific truth that he had studiously deduced from decades of reading the great social scientists and historians of Europe, Karl Marx and Georg Hegel, and traversing socialist circles in the West. "The most uneducated, the most backward strata of the working class, who had naively trusted the Tsar ... the working class received a great lesson in civil war," wrote Vladimir Ilyich Lenin, from his comfortable exile in Geneva. "The revolution is spreading."[12]

Lenin was writing this in 1905, soon after Bloody Sunday, when tsarist troops fired upon and dispersed a demonstration of peaceful protesters, killing more than a hundred and sparking a nationwide wave of strikes and peasant protests. It would, of course, take another twelve years and a world war for the imperial government to collapse. During that time, Lenin watched a society that was perfectly capable of radically transforming itself without his help. As he waited for the chance for him and his acolytes to impose their will upon over 160 million people, he was already convinced that only armed revolt and civil war, in which millions of those would be slaughtered, could achieve the kind of state that the "backward" working class deserved, if only they were not too "backward" to understand it. "Only an armed people can be a real stronghold of national freedom," he continued in his pamphlet (one largely aimed at dissident elements in the socialist movement, who advocated for less radical means). "The immediate arming of the workers and of all the citizens . . . this is the practical basis." The final goal for this armed, radicalized working class, a goal that would inevitably materialize if only they carried out their mission according to the science, his science, was "ridding mankind of all exploitation."[13] By force.

His chance would come in the months after the disruption of war and the activities of newly emerged local councils, or *soviets*, forced the abdication of Tsar Nicholas II. They began to rule in tandem with the Provisional Government, in an awkward period of "Dual Power" that did nothing to end the war, feed the masses, or resolve the political crises. Negotiating an agreement with Germany, eager to weaken a nation with which it was at war, Lenin traveled secretly by train into Russia and plotted his coup. In the disarray, hunger, and lawlessness, it was not hard to convince starving, confused soldiers of his vision, and then impose it on the rest of a starving, confused populace. But once Lenin succeeded in his one chief mission – winning the fight – he was faced with the prospect of holding on to power and building his new idyll. That, however, was another story – the story of his chief acolyte, the cunning, ruthless thug named Iosif Dzhugashvili.

* * *

Everything about him exuded cold, hard logic and determination, from the mastery of the visible defects of his body, to his stilted, mechanical speech. No matter that his distinct syntax was just as much a product of speaking in a non-native language, of having an accent so strong he felt uncomfortable speaking publicly. Instead, he honed his sentences to the point of such linear, mathematical precision that they left no room for doubt, even – or especially – when the very premise of his assertion was ambiguous. He seemed to speak, move, and act with an unequivocal commitment to his own vision of the future, as if it was a static, empirically proven fact. Everything that needed to be sacrificed in its name went into that meatgrinder: fingers, limbs, millions of human bodies, logic, facts, even the very writings of the thinkers – and his mentor himself – who inspired his dogmatic ideology. What resulted was not a society ordered according to the laws of the revolution, though, but an inchoate, bloody mess that nevertheless boasted one of the most powerful militaries in the world.

"What pushed you to become an oppositionist?" the German writer Emil Ludwig asked the man by then known as Joseph Stalin in December 1931. "Perhaps it was your mistreatment at the hands of your parents?"

"No," said Stalin, who, as a small child, had thrown a knife at his drunken father, notorious in their small Georgian village for his violent outbursts against his wife and child.[14] "My parents were uneducated people, but they treated me quite well. But quite another thing is the Orthodox theological seminary, where I studied then. Out of protest against the abusive regime and the Jesuit methods that existed in the seminary, I was ready to become, and actually became, a revolutionary, a supporter of Marxism as a truly revolutionary teaching."

"But," countered Ludwig, an experienced interviewer of great men and their illusions, "don't you recognize the positive qualities of the Jesuits?"

"Yes, they are systematic and persistent in working to achieve bad goals," replied Stalin, who had burgled, bombed, lied, and murdered for the needs of the revolution. "But their main method is surveillance, espionage, getting into the soul, bullying – what could be positive about this?"

For Ludwig – a German well versed in Karl Marx and Western socialist thought – the main point of contention was the role of the individual in history. Didn't Marx downplay the role of heroic individuals in history? Stalin had it all figured out, though, twisting the words of his scholars to build up a scientific truth that was entirely his own: "These were vulgarizers of Marxism. Marxism has never denied the role of heroes. On the contrary, it recognizes this role as significant."[15]

This notionally collectivist ideology would indeed usher in a return to an era of untrammeled and personalistic autocratic power, exerted with all the capabilities of the twentieth century: Ivan the Terrible with telephone, railways, the radio, and barbed wire. The irony is that this was not power in the hands of an hereditary monarch, or even an elected president, but a former rebel, who would justify his authoritarian tyranny with the language of egalitarianism and liberty.

The 1930s heralded the most severe bout of repression in Russian history. In 1937–8 alone, the peak of the Great Terror, nearly 800,000 people were executed in prison or killed in the Gulag camp system.[16] But it is misleading to limit the Great Terror to just two years of Soviet history – even if that was the height of Stalin's political repressions, when the sedans of the secret police, nicknamed "black crows," clogged Moscow's streets for their nightly arrests. The scholar Steven Rosefielde estimates that from 1930 to 1938, 8.7 million died in forced collectivization and the resulting famine, and then another 1.1 million during the Great Terror.[17] Deaths were not limited to prison or camp executions – famine and the violence of collectivization and industrialization claimed even more lives. Indeed, the Terror began with the founding of the Soviet Union, and it was not merely an accidental excess. It was, both for Stalin and for his mentor, Lenin, by design: first to take power, then to hold on to it, as they eliminated their class enemies. "The court must not eliminate terror," Lenin wrote in 1922 after the end of the first spasm of state terror that ended with the Civil War. "To promise this would be self-deception. It must justify and legitimize it in principle, clearly, without falsehood and without embellishment." Only then, he argued, could revolutionary ideas be legally applied.[18]

It is hard to find a more mythologized phenomenon in history than the 1917 Soviet revolution and the ensuing terror, one more prone to projection of the historian's ideological leanings and distortion in favor of a political argument. Socialists to this day struggle with the period, trying at times to differentiate Stalinism from Leninism in hopes of salvaging something of a political ideology so badly tarnished by the Soviet experiment. Many argue, citing Marx himself, that Russia, with its lack of democratic experience, wasn't yet prepared for a socialist revolution, implying that under other circumstances, Russia could have sustained a successful form of socialism. The dissident Communist Roy Medvedev argued for an indictment of Stalin the individual, urging a reckoning with his crimes so that the unprecedented progress made by the Soviet government could be better valued and continued. Western revisionists like Stephen Cohen, in his compelling biography of moderate Bolshevik Nikolai Bukharin, have demonstrated that there were any number of alternatives to Stalinism throughout the early Soviet period.[19] By contrast, critics of Communism and American neoliberals like Richard Pipes indict the ideology itself.[20] The Terror, this school of thought holds, was continuous and a direct and inevitable function of the ideology of Communism.

There is a great deal of truth on both sides, but as the one tries to rehabilitate Soviet socialism while the other tries to prosecute it, what gets lost in debate is that the brutality of the Soviet regime was much more about the alienation of state power from the people whom it ruled than about any ideology it chose to adopt. There is a third school of thought:

of a certain path dependency in Russian political culture and its history, whereby historical decisions long past all but wipe out the possibility of democracy.[21] This is a compelling explanation, particularly in current times, and especially for many Russians themselves, who, to cope with the trauma of recurring tyranny, fall into a kind of self-hating depression. They find themselves denouncing their own people and culture wholesale, refusing to believe that anything good can come out of that entity called "Russia." I myself, when younger and more depressed, occasionally fell under the spell of this explanation, until I became dissatisfied with its essentialist and problematic nature: it ultimately strips people of agency and reduces them to automatons of history. To persuade people that they have no choice but to march to a predestined future because it has so been ordained by historical science or by the prophet of your choosing is ultimately the tool of despots and not historians. It also, ultimately, means to ignore your own agency and free will, and to accept that nothing you do matters. So, I'm afraid there's no simple explanation for the question I'm about to pose, and nor should there be: why did a group of rebels fighting for liberation from the tsarist regime in the name of freedom come to establish a second *oprichnina*?

"Why are you rioting?"

Vladimir Lenin had always been a blur to me growing up: an icon of a bearded man with kind eyes whom I was supposed to love, until he was replaced in an American Southern Baptist Sunday school by a similar icon called Jesus. I was born in 1980 and so am old enough to remember having to sing songs and color posters in kindergarten on all the Soviet holidays. All that was supposed to have been made anathema for me when I emigrated to the United States in 1987, but the sum of my experiences (maybe the fact that, unlike most Russian

émigrés, I grew up poor in places that would later become
Donald Trump country) instilled in me a deep distrust of both
countries' competing iconostases, and the ideologies each
sought to bolster by pillorying the other. Yet even as a small
child in Moscow, I remember being perplexed by the sheer
concentration of Leninist iconography, and confused by the
mythology of the October Revolution, a story that everyone
around me claimed made perfect, irrevocable sense when it
made absolutely none to me. "Why is it always Lenin this and
Lenin that?" I asked my grandmother while we were walking in
the street one day. I must have been about 5 or 6. "Why does
everyone like him so much and he's such a big deal?" My grandmother went pale, kneeled down beside me as she looked me in
the face, and told me never to say anything like that again. I felt
ashamed, as if I had said something rude or personally offensive. It took me years to realize she was merely scared – scared
of a government that was so scared of her that it had to turn its
founding father into an embalmed pharaoh, the priests of his
cult peering fiercely into your soul to ensure its purity.

* * *

At first, the younger brother didn't seem to want anything to
do with the revolutionary's political career. A quiet, pedantic,
studious boy, Vladimir Ulyanov hardly spoke, let alone spoke
out. Whether out of academic ambition or to differentiate
himself from his more outgoing brother, he almost deliberately
kept his head down. "[A] 'reticent' and 'unsociable' youth who
'neither in school nor out of it gave his superiors or teachers by
a single word or deed any cause to form of him an unfavorable
opinion," wrote Fyodor Kerensky,[22] the head of the Simbirsk
gymnasium where Ulyanov studied until the age of 17. "One
cannot say that he was loved; rather, he was appreciated," a
classmate would describe.[23]

Whether it was the execution of Alexander Ulyanov in May
1887 or a new cohort of rebellious peers at the Kazan University

where Vladimir had enrolled that summer that led to his first political awakening remains a mystery. All of a sudden, on December 4, 1887, the pedant found himself at the vanguard of a student protest against new, ever more restrictive university regulations, and even the installation of a political minder in their midst. At least that was how Soviet propagandists painted his role, as one of its initiators. The reality is far murkier. Details of the protest – what exactly was said and done, and by whom – are rather scarce, replaced instead by hagiographies and polemical analysis of what it meant, films with compelling titles like *The First Bastille*, and ornate paintings of a young man leading a gaggle of students down a stairway to confront two clearly intimidated, aging bearded men. According to official Soviet legend, as he was being taken to prison that night by court bailiffs, one of them asked the youth, "Why are you rioting, young man? There's a wall in front of you!" To which the young Lenin defiantly replied: "A wall, but a rotten one. Poke it, and it will fall."[24]

The circumstances of his arrest and expulsion from university are disputed, however, so that exchange, like so many things about Lenin's youth, should be regarded as apocryphal. According to contemporary professors and students, and local historians who tried to recreate those fateful events, the boys weren't arrested: 39 out of 300 were merely temporarily detained for a brief "prophylactic chat." Ulyanov wasn't their leader, merely a passive participant, a person of interest largely because of the recent execution of his terrorist brother.[25]

Following his expulsion, police questioning revealed that in the fall leading up to the protest, Ulyanov had joined a *narodnik* cell with ties to "anti-government circles" in St. Petersburg.[26] Whether he indeed took an active role in the protest, or was merely propelled by the events around him to its forefront, it is clear that his university career was over. With the universities of Moscow and St. Petersburg closed to him due to his brother's activities, and now exiled to the small village of Kokushkino, whether he wanted to or not, Ulyanov was forever linked with the organization that eventually led to his brother's death: Narodnaya Volya.

Stuck in Kokushkino, Ulyanov spent a year reading, first the foreign press, then Russian revolutionary intellectuals, until he discovered Georg Hegel, and, finally, through the dialectical process, Karl Marx. His cousin, Nikolai Veretennikov, would describe that he had a way with the local peasants and that they liked him.[27] This was a skill that would prove critical for a future leader to present a message that, whatever it was at its core, turned out to have a lasting, phenomenal resonance that continues to this day. Be that as it may, he was self-taught, largely in the silent, abstract confines of his thoughts and his reading. It is hard to imagine that, even in his rustic home, he took much part in the practicalities of rural life: cooking, heating the cottage, working in the field. It has been noted that Ulyanov was not much of a handyman, and had to rely on others to run his household.[28]

Later returning to Kazan and Samara, he grew closer with the activists of Narodnaya Volya. By this point, in 1890, the movement had grown frustrated with its efforts to gain a substantial following among the peasantry; the population at large was hardly impressed by their assassination of the only Russian tsar to push through a modicum of liberal reform. Ulyanov began to show a passion and talent for polemics, arguing fiercely in *narodnik* circles, particularly with more liberal activists, about the role of the individual leader. While insisting that "the people" were the true movers of history, by 1894 he had come to the conclusion that "the Russian worker, rising at the head of all democratic elements, will overthrow absolutism and lead the Russian proletariat (along with the proletariat of all countries) on the straight road of open political struggle to a victorious Communist revolution."[29] This was in a country in which the peasantry comprised over 80 percent of the population and the working class was but miniscule,[30] but Ulyanov,

like many of his increasingly disappointed cohorts, was growing impatient.

Ultimately, to square this circle, the path to the revolution
lay in the vanguardist approach, because it was useless to wait
until these clueless, backwards masses rose up themselves. The
Marxists, Ulyanov argued in 1901, the year he took on the
pseudonym Lenin, had to form a political party to become
the *vanguard* of the people's revolution: "Why do the Russian
workers still manifest little revolutionary activity in response
to the brutal treatment of the people . . . ? We must blame
ourselves. . . . Class political consciousness can be brought
to the workers only from without; that is, only from outside
the economic struggle, from outside the sphere of relations
between workers and employers."[31] The more Lenin tried to
avoid blaming the people, the more he patronized them, the
less he regarded them as political actors in their own right.
His heart may have "beat with ardent love for all toilers, for
all of the oppressed," as his wife, Nadezhda Krupskaya, would
later eulogize,[32] but one can't help but wonder if the aggressive impatience hinted at in these lines concealed that which
thirty years later turned into the meatgrinder of the Civil
War and the Red Terror: a deep-seated contempt for his own
people.

"Everything is possible!"

Just four years after Lenin wrote those lines, the Russian
people did, in fact, begin to rise up against their government,
just not quite in the way he had outlined in his pamphlets,
and certainly not led by his party's vanguard. Gradually, in
chaotic spurts and stages, with rapid progress interspersed
by periods of stagnation and revanche, for the first time in
Russian history, its society was building its own form of rules-
based democracy, with representation, freedom of thought

and debate, and budding institutions with the mandate to rule a country instead of individuals ordained by God or tradition.

At the turn of the twentieth century, the monarchy was plagued by two fundamental problems. On the one hand, the country was industrializing rapidly, possibly too rapidly for its society properly to metabolize. The emancipation of the serfs liberated some 23 million people into the open market, but also placed enormous constraints upon them. Peasant communes – not individuals – were granted land which they could neither sell nor give away, while each individual had to pay a redemption fee to the commune until the land had been paid off. In the end, everyone got a smaller allotment of land than that which they would farm before the emancipation. The injustices that came with this limited freedom fed the socialist movements that sprouted around the time, but they also forced many of the peasants into towns and cities, creating a new labor force as they struggled to pay off their redemption fees. In the two decades after emancipation, from 1861 to 1879, the number of factories nearly doubled, while their output grew exponentially, from 7.9 to 51.9 million rubles.[33] By the end of the nineteenth century, the urban population had grown from 7 million before emancipation to 28 million people.[34] This created a paradox of sorts: a rapidly growing proletariat in a society still overwhelmingly agrarian, and unprecedented economic growth amid rampant poverty. Finance Minister Count Sergei Witte said that for the Russian worker, "raised on the frugal habits of rural life. . . . Low wages appeared as a fortunate gift to Russian enterprise."[35]

On the other hand, the Romanov dynasty, and the monarchy as a whole, was suffering from a crisis of confidence and, in hindsight, could be said to have been in the process of a gradual implosion. The assassination of Alexander II not only put a stop to many of his reforms, but also triggered a conservative revanchism in his traumatized son, Alexander III. The new tsar sought to keep the recently liberated peasants

in communes to ensure that they remained politically conservative and to stem the mounting tide of protest. Rather than
instilling communal and patriotic values, though, such measures only exacerbated their poverty. (Human beings rarely
value community and social bonds when they are forced upon
them from the outside, as the Communists would later learn
for themselves.) Violent riots increased as starving peasants
turned on their landlords, while urban workers, risking life
and limb, organized illegal strikes. The government found itself
lurching frantically between tightening the screws and giving
local communities some freedoms when it was simply unequal
to the mounting problems on the ground, such as during the
famine of 1891–2. The ascent of Alexander's son, Nicholas II,
in 1894, in some ways led to an apotheosis of impotence: a
weak Russian government, ruled by a man himself deemed
weak by many of his contemporaries, who had a habit of abdi-
cating in spirit long before his formal abdication in February
1917.

The Revolution of 1905 was a result of the expensive and
humiliating defeat in the 1904–5 Russo-Japanese War, as well
as a response to Bloody Sunday, but was more fundamentally
an attempt by local communities to take matters into their
own hands and demand that the government fix these irreconcilable problems or step aside and let them deal with them
themselves. This was the first time that workers organized governing councils, or *soviets*, at their factories. It would see the
emergence of the formidable revolutionary Leon Trotsky, one
of the leaders of the Russian Social Democratic Labor Party.
Trotsky was a socialist activist who spent decades agitating,
organizing, and dodging the secret police, but had recently
split both with the Mensheviks (the party's more moderate
majority) and the more radical Bolsheviks, led at the time by
Lenin. While the uprisings that year would neither overthrow
the tsarist regime nor cause it to commit to sustained reform,
they did force the autocrat into reactive mode. Having to

choose between becoming a dictator – a task for which he was hardly prepared – and accepting a constitution, Nicholas caved and issued the October Manifesto, careful not to call it a constitution, even if it was just that in anything but name: it proclaimed the creation of a parliament, the State Duma, which had the power to approve bills issued by the tsar and his appointed government. Though the tsar's court remained the center of power, the Manifesto introduced unprecedented democratic freedoms and led to a parliament in which the Kadet (Constitutional Democrat) Party faced off against the Trudovik (or Labor) Party, not about the need for reform, but how about radical it was going to be.[36] So radical was the proposed legislative body, in fact, that Nicholas would dissolve parliament that summer, but the experience would set a precedent. More importantly, it bolstered the institution of prime minister, and paved the way for one of Russia's most forward-looking statesmen, Pyotr Stolypin.

Nicholas's retention of the title of autocrat, however, ensured that the mounting contradictions and tensions within the power of the monarchy, and especially how it was perceived by its people, only grew. One step forward, two steps back, he oscillated between institutional reform and reaction, and ultimately found himself sleepwalking into World War I in 1914.

By January 1917, with the government embroiled in an horrific war that was more about its duties to an alliance of empires than it was about Russia's own interests, domestic contradictions converged and ultimately overpowered a monarch who was both intrinsically weak and exhausted by the turmoil into which history had plunged him. On the morning of February 23, 1917, 7,000 hungry, underpaid female textile workers took to the streets of St. Petersburg, now Petrograd. Each day, the mob swelled until it numbered a quarter of a million, and the Petrograd garrison with its machine guns and armored cars joined them. The capital's authorities were paralyzed as the protesting workers opened prisons and called the inaugural session of Russia's first grass-roots democratic representative body: the Soviet of Workers' and Soldiers' Deputies. Days later, Nicholas abdicated, and power was handed over to the State Duma Provisional Committee, a temporary body charged with maintaining law and order that soon became the Provisional Government. Because of the power and influence of the Soviet of Workers and Soldiers' Deputies, Russia became in effect ruled by two bodies, in a state of *dvoevlastiye* ("Dual Power"). The Soviet, in practice, had the power to curb any of the Provisional Government's decrees, but each was unable to govern effectively.

The collapse of the monarchy and the suddenly enormous powers of the grass-roots *soviets* almost overnight unleashed centuries of pent-up energy and rage. An unbridled will to freedom that awed and terrified Western nations, who had seen their own people's revolutions the century before, swept through Russia, overturning everything in its path. "Everyone is overcome by a recognition that a miracle has occurred, and, consequently, that more miracles will follow," wrote the mystic poet Alexander Blok. "Freedom is extraordinarily majestic! Everything is possible!"[37] Those writing the first draft of history saw the chaos as both exhilarating and ominous. "Across the entire country, an unending, disorderly rally went on day and night," wrote tram-conductor-turned-writer Konstantin Paustovsky.

> Gatherings of people raged in city squares, at monuments and chlorine-smelling train stations, in factories, in villages, in bazaars, in every courtyard and on every staircase of a more or less populated house. Oaths, appeals, denunciations, oratorical fervor – all this would suddenly drown in frantic cries of "Down with!" or in an enthusiastic hoarse "Hurray!" These screams rolled like cobblestone thunder across the street intersections.[38]

But the plethora of debates, the conceptual interrogation and revision of each and every institution, paralyzed the functioning of those very institutions – themselves still too new and fragile to have much weight. Russia was still engaged in a war it was unable to sustain, and the Provisional Government was still faced with the task of either signing a truce to end it, or mustering the resources necessary to continue fighting. It chose something in between, trying to rally the masses for war in the name of the new revolution. Emerging as the leader of the Provisional Government was Alexander Kerensky (incidentally the son of the head of the Simbirsk gymnasium who spoke of the pedantic student Vladimir Ulyanov), a brilliant, passionate orator, but one who seemed to lack the ruthlessness needed for those chaotic times. "It is difficult for a cow to run fast. Kerensky was prime minister," the revolutionary poet Vladimir Mayakovsky coined in an untranslatable rhyming epitaph. It proved so effective in conveying both the absurdities of the time and also the prime minister's singular incapacity for the role of war leader that it came to encapsulate his legacy for the next century.[39] In his speeches, Kerensky painted the war as a necessity for the revolution, believing that the Russia of the future could not survive territorial losses in the case of defeat. "Let the freest army . . . in the world prove that there is strength and not weakness in Liberty," he proclaimed.[40]

But the soldiers' freedom mattered little if they were starving. Faced with death from both sides – the bayonets of the enemy, on the one hand, if they advanced, the firing squads of their own generals, on the other, if they did not – peasant soldiers defected in the tens of thousands, desperately trying to make their way home to their huts and their families. They now had an additional incentive. The revolution provided them with an opportunity so long denied after the emancipation of the serfs: the chance to claim their land for themselves.[41]

Once again in Russia's history, it was these desperate, aggrieved, traumatized, terrified armed hordes who proved to be the random factor. But this time, in the anarchy of the summer of 1917, from an orgy of freedom rose a demand for order, discipline, and justice, precisely the things the new, democratic institutions of the time were as yet too weak to provide. Russian history has seen a whole assortment of different kinds of rebels, dissenters, rioters, and protesters. Some take to the streets, seeking an end to the injustices they face, demanding that those who rule them muster the courage to act. They are the aggrieved, the seekers of justice who still call out state power. Others are individualist opportunists who take advantage of the chaos to vent their own rage, plunder for their own gain, or both, even if they genuinely buy into the revolutionary moment's demand for justice. Then there is a third kind of rebel: in some ways the mirror image of the despot he has been conditioned to fight, he is ruthless, obsessed with power, and willing to destroy anything in his path to achieve it. At the heart of his fury lies an unadulterated conviction in his own righteousness; a morally absolutist imperative of the path to justice, a belief that he is privy to a scientific truth that will order a society that is, on its own, incapable of order. Alas, when democratic institutions are weak or non-existent, it is the third type of rebel to which society is most vulnerable. Sometimes history calls on a reforming tsar to take up the mantle of despot, and sometimes it is the rebel.

For Vladimir Lenin, just recently back from exile, the masses of aggrieved peasant soldiers proved to be the perfect vanguard for his revolution. "The present task must be an armed uprising in Petrograd and Moscow, the seizure of power and the overthrow of government," he proclaimed in September, after his Bolshevik faction of the Social Democratic Party won a majority of seats in the *soviets* of Moscow, Petrograd, and other key Russian cities.[42] On October 25, with the Bolsheviks having most of the soldiers in Petrograd on their side, Lenin and his forces – now known as the Red Guards – took control of key government facilities, communication centers, and military headquarters. That night, they marched on the Winter Palace itself and quickly toppled the Provisional Government. Just a few thousand loyalist cadets and soldiers at first tried to resist this 40,000-strong force, but they were swiftly defeated. In the confusion that ensued, it was up to the leaders to define what had happened. Lenin and Trotsky proclaimed an end to the Provisional Government and the victory of the All-Russian Congress of Soviets.

A whole new country, the Soviet Union, was born. But for Lenin and some of his more ruthless disciples like Stalin, democracy was an ideal that had to take second place to the pragmatic needs of the moment – and their own role as the vanguard of the true revolution. Lenin and his cohorts closed down the first representative body which was elected (because the ungrateful and ignorant masses had failed to vote in a Bolshevik majority) and over the following years of chaos and civil war turned supposedly democratic institutions into mere rubber stamps.

In power, then, the Bolsheviks found themselves perpetuating a curious and persistent pattern of Russian history: a tsar by turns wiping out an existing aristocracy, as Ivan the Terrible had done, and replacing it with one subjugated to the court, like Peter the Great with his Table of Ranks, which effectively merged them with the civil service. In the process, the new regime creates its own "vanguard" cherry-picked from the aggrieved class of the tsar's choosing. In the doctrine of Marxism-Leninism, the Bolsheviks had an ideology that could unleash the pent-up fury of the Russian people to destroy not just the aristocracy, but also the dynasty behind them. Yet what would fill their place? A new aristocracy, of Party officials, informants, ideologues, and secret policemen, all more tightly controlled by the new monarch than Ivan or Peter could ever have dreamed of. By the time Vladimir Ulyanov realized the monster he had created and tried to stop Stalin's growing power, as the fearsome avatar of this new elite, it was too late:

he was dying of a series of strokes, and the rebel was already becoming the tsar.

By coup, not consensus

> At the western corner of the Palace lay a big armoured car with a red flag flying from it, newly lettered in red paint: "S.R.S.D." [Soviet of Workers' and Soldiers' Deputies]; all the guns trained toward St. Isaac's. A barricade had been heaped up across the mouth of Novaya Ulitza – boxes, barrels, an old bed-spring, a wagon. A pile of lumber barred the end of the Moika quay. Short logs from a neighbouring wood-pile were being built up along the front of the building to form breastworks.[43]

The American journalist John Reed described the chaos and exhilaration of October 25 and the storming of the Winter Palace, across Admiralty Square from St. Isaac's Cathedral. His work became immortalized in part because those revolutionaries succeeded: the men and women who established this new regime were victorious, even if their leaders would soon subvert their creation into the very opposite of what it was supposed to be. In many ways, those who supported the Bolsheviks would lose in the long term, simply handing their fates to a new cast of exploiters, even as they won the day.

Much the same could be said of the revolutionaries I saw in Donetsk and Mariupol once they had begun looking to a foreign country for leadership and support. The Kremlin had no real interest in what they wanted, but ultimately was not willing to abandon them either, cynically seeing an opportunity to use them to put pressure on a Kyiv that, it felt, needed to be brought to heel. By the end of May 2014, Moscow had sent in a new assortment of "volunteers" – most now regular Russian troops and intelligence officers – not only to prevent loyalist forces from suppressing this inchoate rebellion, but also to impose its own authority on the rebels. The people of the self-proclaimed and unacknowledged (even by Moscow) Donetsk and Lugansk "People's Republics" had largely not set out to become independent of Kyiv, but soon found that they had little choice as to their fate, unless they were willing to flee into the rest of Ukraine. The rebellion that the "Russian Spring" represented was not a mass movement, but nor for that matter was it opposed by the bulk of the local population. Just as in 1917, most kept their heads down as an array of opportunists, gangsters, mercenaries, and Russian proxies fought to impose their own visions of what the Donbas needed.

The Bolshevik Revolution and the "Russian Spring" in the Donbas – incomparable as they seem to be at first glance – nevertheless bore certain parallels summarized quite well nearly a century earlier by Karl Marx: "The class struggle took place only within a privileged minority, between the free rich and the free poor, while the great productive mass of the population, the slaves, formed the purely passive pedestal for these combatants."[44] Marx was talking about ancient Rome, to explain the 1851 coup in France by Napoleon Bonaparte's nephew, Napoleon III. However, his words came to be prophetic for those who mourned the broken hopes of Russia's socialist revolution. Marx warned that any attempt to bring socialism to a nation not ready for it with a strong, coherent, and politically mature proletariat would be a disaster, creating a regime with all the unleashed energies of revolution, yet all the instincts of the old order. Neither Russia in 1917 nor the Donbas in 2014 was ready for its historical moment, in both cases brought about more by state collapse that created opportunities for radical minorities to, in effect, seize power by coup rather than consensus.

In Russia, the erstwhile rebel would build on the authoritarian foundations laid by Lenin and impose a return to autocratic traditions, even if wrapped in a red flag. Moscow had not forgotten this lesson, though, and was not willing to let others follow the same path. In the Donbas, the rebels who might have dreamt of becoming tsars would find themselves one by one co-opted, excluded, imprisoned, or simply assassinated. Igor Girkin, the Russian nationalist who, by his own account, "pulled the trigger on the war" when he led a motley force of volunteers into the Ukrainian town of Sloviansk, and then later became the rebel "defense minister," was forced out of office in August 2014. He would become an outspoken critic of the Kremlin, until his arrest in 2022. Then there were militia commanders such as Alexander "Batman" Bednov, Alexei Mozgovoi, and Arseny "Motorola" Pavlov, gunned down in January 2015, May 2015, and October 2016, respectively. By the time Alexander Zakharchenko, the leader of the "Donetsk People's Republic," was murdered by an unusually sophisticated bomb in August 2018, Moscow was in essentially undisputed control of these regions it still hardly wanted.[45] By 2022, the Kremlin had subordinated the interests of the pro-Russian separatist movement to its wider proxy war with the West. Whatever the "Russian Spring" was or could have been was stifled by the very patrons to whom they had looked for leadership and support. As one of the Russian nationalist activists who joined the separatist movement said to me in 2019, "We were fucked over by people who never even understood what we were trying to do."[46]

7

The Dissidents

"I must say what I think –
and the results do not concern me"

Of the leading lights of the Snow Revolution, two are dead. Boris Nemtsov, a former parliamentarian and a longtime Putin critic, was assassinated in February 2015 by thugs alleged to be acting in the interests of Chechen strongman Ramzan Kadyrov, a murder that, while it embarrassed him, Putin ultimately chose to brush under the rug. Alexei Navalny, after surviving a poisoning in 2020, was jailed when he returned to Russia in 2021. He died in prison in 2024, under circumstances the state has yet properly to explain. A number more would go to jail, including one of the most vocal liberal activists, Ilya Yashin. Vladimir Kara-Murza, a journalist and dissident, had also survived two poisonings, in 2015 and 2017, yet continued relentlessly to criticize Putin's Kremlin, organize opposition committees, and leverage his dual Russian–British citizenship to draw international attention to the Kremlin's violation of human rights and lobby for sanctions. On March 15, 2022, after Moscow launched its full-scale invasion of Ukraine, Kara-Murza addressed the Arizona House of Representatives and accused Putin's government of committing war crimes. He spoke out against the Kremlin's "war of aggression," warned against the appeasement of dictators, and then, on a hopeful note, pointed out that "there are millions of people in my country who fundamentally reject, who fundamentally disagree with everything the Putin regime represents."[1] Then, he boarded a plane back to Moscow. The following month, while driving, he saw men in black uniforms and masks following his car in his rear-view mirror. He was arrested under a new law criminalizing spreading "fakes" about the Russian armed forces. Two months later, the authorities charged him with treason for his Arizona speech. He was sentenced to twenty-five years in prison in April 2023. "The day will come when the darkness over our country will dissipate," he said in his final hearing. "Even today, even in the darkness surrounding us, even sitting in this cage, I love my country and believe in our people."[2] Yashin and Kara-Murza would be released from prison in 2024, exchanged for a Kremlin assassin and several other spies, effectively exiled to the West.

Yashin, as will be discussed in the final chapter, had become one of the new generation of Russian opposition politicians who, like the more famous Navalny, would seek to build a wider alliance for change, reaching out to a variety of constituencies, from disgruntled soldiers to leftist radicals. Kara-Murza, on the other hand, was very much a dissident of the old school, driven by a passionate moral outrage that accepted no compromises.

It was telling that, before his arrest, Kara-Murza had produced a documentary about the life of Father Georgy Edelstein, a Soviet priest who, from the day he was ordained in 1979, consistently and methodically decried the abuses of the Soviet regime and the treachery of Church bishops who tried to "run ahead of the authorities." Hounded by the government for his criticism, he was dismissed from the priesthood in 1987, but the following year, when *perestroika* was already in full swing, a meeting with US President Ronald Reagan helped get him reinstated. Thirty-five years later, when the government was swinging back towards repression, Edelstein was among the few Russian priests who denounced the war in Ukraine. "We cannot shyly close our eyes and call black white, evil good, and say that Abel was probably wrong and provoked his older brother," he told his congregation from his church.[3]

When I attended the screening of Kara-Murza's film in Washington in February 2023, a particular statement Father Georgy made stood out to me: "If we stay silent, we participate in the evil that is happening in our world. I must say what I think – and the results do not concern me."[4]

Something about those last words, and the priest's unmovable, uncompromising conviction, struck me as paradoxical. If we take "results" to mean the direct consequences for Father Georgy himself – the authorities' potential decision to persecute him over his convictions – then his courage and herculean strength are remarkable. Yet in an environment where the government frequently resorts to collective responsibility to keep people in line, what if the consequences of your words are borne by others? Edelstein's wife, Anita, for instance, lost her job as a result of her husband's choices. Her colleagues, she recalled, were expected to fire her, but did not want to be the "bad guys," so persuaded her to resign instead. The family's combined income went from 700 rubles a month to 92. What does it mean when the consequences of your stance affect people for whom you are responsible, maybe people who, unlike Anita or, indeed, Evgenia, Kara-Murza's wife, lack your moral strength?

The unwavering certitude of the Communist Party, entrenched by the Stalinist repressions of the 1930s, turned opinions first into facts and then into scripture, and questioning them became a heresy which could be punishable by death. For dissenting opinions to survive, their holders often were required to adopt the same unwavering certitude in return. To shield those principles from compromise, they sometimes had to place them upon a pedestal well above their love or obligations to family or to friends.

In the totalitarian Soviet Union, dissidents might by day work in research institutes as engineers and physicists, and by evening gather in their kitchens to exchange illegal copies of banned books, so-called *samizdat*, and voice their views. In a outwardly rigid conformist country where emigration was difficult, those who failed to conform receded into the "internal emigration" of private spaces and tight-knit dissident networks. Because KGB informers were common, close trust was paramount, so dissidents formed close communities that often developed a reflexive distrust of outsiders as a result. If the ancient peasant commune fostered mistrust, insulation, and atomization due to the harsh requirements of the soil, in the Soviet Union a similar atomization was replicated by the brutality of Party rule.

After all, the escape of "internal emigration," retreating from the world of crushing Marxist-Leninist hypocrisy and propaganda, didn't have to be political. To flee that stifling outward conformity, one could recede into music, into literature. Either way, though, it tended to create tight cliques where you belonged and where your tastes and your views were a way to distinguish *svoi*, your own, from *chuzhoi*, the other. This may have created stronger bonds with those of their own circle, but it also alienated them from the outside world, from other communities, and from many of their own countrymen. Like the persecuted Old Believers, one adopted an almost religious zeal to protect principles and practices from an oppressive establishment.

A thaw from above

The definition of the Soviet dissident is almost as controversial as the history of the Bolshevik Revolution – each framed the concept based on his or her own values, type of resistance, or activity. Sometimes cliques developed, fiercely gatekeeping their status from others who they believed dissented in the "wrong" way, or did not dissent enough, but this came much later. In the beginning, as always, was the word: the sudden freedom to give a name for that which had been, for decades, eradicated and unspoken. After all, it is difficult to talk about any kind of "dissident movement" during the blood-soaked Stalin years. There were many brave individuals, of course. Numerous artists and writers fell foul of the murderous system by accident, but others knowingly made a stand. Osip Mandelstam's satirical poem about "the Kremlin highlander," concluding that "every killing for him is delight," earned him internal exile to Voronezh and then a labor camp, where he died. There were even some who tried to fight violence with violence, like Savely Dmitriev, a Red Army corporal who shot at what he thought was Stalin's car (it actually turned out to be Politburo member Anastas Mikoyan's) in 1942, to avenge the loss of life as a result of the Generalissimo's disastrous mishandling of the German invasion. Either way, dissent was often fatal, as it could lead to up to twenty-five years in a Gulag labor camp under the infamous Article 58 of the Penal Code, on "anti-Soviet agitation" (which could mean whatever the prosecutors wanted it to), or even a bullet in the back of the head.

Under Stalin's successors, it could still mean prison, but also a range of other penalties, from internal exile to being delivered to a *"psikhushka"* psychiatric hospital and pumped full of psychotropic drugs. Nonetheless, after Stalin's death in 1953, it began to be more possible to question, if not challenge, the regime, and a movement would begin to emerge. Sergei Kovalyov, the biologist and human rights activist who stood at the heart of the nascent movement, and who would go on to spend seven years in the infamous Perm-36 labor colony for "anti-Soviet propaganda" in the 1970s, described its origins nebulously, but zeroed in on its uniting principle of "moral incompatibility" with the regime. Towards the second half of the 1960s, he recalls:

> I found myself in a new environment that was just taking shape, developing its own norms of behavior, methods of struggle, formulating principles and goals, and that, generally speaking, did not have a specific name. The term "dissidents" did not yet exist, and the awkward word "human rights activists" was also not very popular. Viktor Krasin, an economist, a former prisoner of the Stalin era, a friend of Pavel Litvinov and Pyotr Yakir, used the expression "democratic movement." Although, to be honest, what kind of movement was it? No positive program, no clear social base, no ideology, no structure. Thus, a conglomerate of friendly groups, united, in essence, by only one thing: an active rejection of official lies and a willingness to publicly and openly resist legalized lawlessness and lack of rights. I think that it was a great success for the movement in defense of human rights in the USSR – to start just like that, without programs, theories, and structures, based solely on moral incompatibility with the existing regime.[5]

In many ways, that nascent "democratic movement" was, like the liberal ideals that inspired the Decembrist uprising, a product of reforms instigated by the Soviet government itself. Stalin's death left in its wake a society exhausted and traumatized by the millions of lives sacrificed to war and repression in the name of power. A whole generation had internalized cognitive dissonance as a way of life: conditioned to live in fear of falling victim to what was essentially a quota system for rounding up "enemies of the people," many at the same time revered Stalin, the man behind this inhuman state, as a secular demigod, a replacement for the religion that the Bolshevik party had taken great pains to eradicate. I will never forget an elderly woman breaking down in tears in the archives of the

Memorial human rights organization in Moscow in 2010 when she was handed an order for the execution of her father, signed by Stalin himself. Even with the proof in her hands, it was still excruciatingly difficult for her to hold the leader of her country responsible for such injustice, to be deprived of any excuses for his excesses, and see someone in whom she had placed so much hope and faith turn out to be a human being of ruthlessly arbitrary power, unmitigated by law or principles.

But for the Soviet regime, the death of the unparalleled leader without – as often happens in Russian history – an heir or an institutionally sound method of succession created a profound challenge to the Party's ability to stay in power. The industrialization imposed upon the country by Stalin and the need to compete with a Western superpower forced the Soviet Union to chase ambitions that an ineffective economy and an exhausted, apathetic population could not attain. Nikita Khrushchev proclaimed a "new course" that involved intro-ducing more flexible bureaucratic and economic standards, and "strengthening Soviet legality" to encourage more trust and cooperation from a population that had, for a genera-tion, been conditioned for anything but.[6] To do this, however, required a degree of dangerous iconoclasm.

On February 25, 1956, at the Twentieth Party Congress, Khruschev publicly denounced Stalin in his speech, "On the Cult of Personality and Its Consequences," to a shocked audi-ence of Politburo members and Party delegates. He exposed specific crimes by his predecessor not only against the coun-try's laws, but more importantly also against the very tenets of Marxism-Leninism, not least physically eliminating most of the "Old Bolsheviks" behind the 1917 revolution, shooting a hundred or so Party delegates who had voted against him during the Seventeenth Party Congress in 1934, and arrest-ing more than half of the total delegates. By doing so, he had violated the very foundations of the kind of democracy the revolution had sought to build.[7]

Although these crimes would not be revealed to the wider public until several years later, in 1961, Khrushchev's "Secret Speech," as it came to be known, gave a powerful signal to members of the government and the elites. It was, of course, a cynical attempt to scapegoat Stalin for all the abuses in which Khrushchev and his peers were themselves implicated, but it wasn't just that. Even Stalin's henchmen were tired of the blood and the fear. It was a reflection of an already ongoing thaw in intellectual life when the Khrushchev leadership didn't just permit but encouraged writers to express themselves more freely, in the hopes of starting a gradual, contained process of de-Stalinization.[8] (Although, ironically, Khrushchev did revive the campaign against religion that had largely lapsed in the latter years of Stalin's tyranny.) The authorities may not have appreciated quite what they were doing when, like Mikhail Gorbachev thirty years later, they unleashed a process – albeit not nearly as dramatically as with the fall of the Romanov dynasty in 1917 – in which the elites would suddenly find themselves expressing a whole generation's worth of pent-up rage, grief, and hope.

At around the same time, a brilliant but shy young man who, through his hard work and intellect, had climbed to the apex of the Soviet scientific hierarchy was facing a moral conundrum. As one of the men who had helped the Soviet Union create the hydrogen bomb, Andrei Sakharov had managed to reconcile his work on weapons of mass destruction with his conscience, reasoning that mutually assured destruction – the inability of one superpower to launch a nuclear attack on the other without triggering a retaliatory strike – would encourage negotiation between the world's superpowers. He was rewarded with the best that the Soviet Union had to offer: 2,000 rubles a month (at a time when 300 rubles a month was considered a comfortable salary for an academic), special housing, a chauffeur, a bodyguard, and access to the kind of restricted imported goods that no ordinary citizen could find, let alone afford. In

1958, though, he learned that the Soviet Union was planning to resume atmospheric nuclear tests, a policy that Sakharov believed would cause escalation with the United States, not to mention increase the danger of fallout. He decided to use his privileged position as a member of the prestigious Academy of Sciences and his connections to some of the highest officials in the nuclear program to do something about it. He asked his friend Igor Kurchatov, the head of the Soviet nuclear program, to talk to Khrushchev himself. The intervention didn't work, but it was a turning point for Sakharov: he wasn't just a scientist anymore; he felt he had a duty to speak out against any actions of his government that he found morally unacceptable.[9]

Even for someone as privileged as Sakharov, a move like that came with enormous risks, the least of which was the loss of his position and, consequently, any ability to influence policy. But in the liberalizing climate of those times, the scientist's venture into public policy was not only permitted, but also seemingly encouraged. He went on to write open letters on education at a time when Khrushchev was enacting educational reform, and found himself transforming from scientist to public intellectual. That, however, required a moral reckoning with the environment in which he worked and lived. "I gradually began to understand the criminal nature not only of nuclear tests but of the enterprise as a whole," he told a *New York Times* correspondent in 1973. "I could not stop something I knew was wrong and unnecessary. It was terrible. I had an awful sense of powerlessness. After that, I was a different man. I broke with my surroundings. It was a basic break."[10]

In 1962, around the time that Sakharov was reinventing himself as a public intellectual, Khrushchev personally compelled the members of the Politburo to break another taboo and allow the publication of a short novel detailing life in the Gulag. The author, a charismatic former convict, Alexander Solzhenitsyn, owed its success both to his persistence – uncharacteristic of a Soviet writer in those days – and the patronage of the poet Alexander Tvardovsky, who was central to convincing Khrushchev to allow the publication.

A Day in the Life of Ivan Denisovich – a frank exposé of Stalinist repressions – was published in the literary magazine *Novy Mir* that November, in no small part thanks to the fact that the Party itself was enlisting writers to grapple with the contradictions of its history. Tvardovsky, as though justifying the publication of such a daring text in his prestigious monthly by citing the Party's permission, called it unusual in his foreword. Solzhenitsyn's material, he wrote, "carries within itself an echo of those painful phenomena in our development associated with the period of the cult of personality debunked and rejected by the Party, which, even though they are not so distant, feel to us as though they are in the distant past."[11]

Rather than pure liberalization, the publication was more a reflection of the value in having a powerful patron and also the degree to which Solzhenitsyn's book met the Party's needs at the time. Not so lucky, after all, was the poet, writer, and Gulag survivor Varlam Shalamov. Despite his work in the editorial offices of *Novy Mir*, he would not get to see his stories detailing the horrors of the camps published during his lifetime. From the Party's perspective, they were too dark, and exposed an experience that was too irredeemable. "If Solzhenitsyn tried to convey the idea of the inflexibility of a real person using camp material," wrote one Party critic, "then Shalamov . . . speaks about the inevitability of . . . the moral and physical death of a person in camp conditions . . . focusing on how hunger, cold, beatings, humiliation, and fear turn people into animals."[12] It was perhaps one of the reasons why he later broke with the main dissident movement, and in 1972 penned an article protesting the pirated circulation of his works abroad. Many saw his statement as a renunciation of the works he had written, a capitulation of sorts, as he was forced to choose between denouncing anti-Soviet publications abroad and never seeing his poetry published at home.[13] Instead, however, it exposed the controversial, exploitative nature of *tamizdat* – the term given to literature published *tam*, or *over there, abroad*. It was a valuable platform for writers censored at home, yet many of these foreign publications used their voices without permission as part of their countries' own political battles with the Soviet Union, with the writers themselves becoming collateral damage.

The backlash

But having unleashed a liberalizing movement, the authorities once again found themselves seeking to contain it. By 1964, the fear had spread to the top echelons of power that Khrushchev was going too far (bringing the world close to nuclear war over Cuba had not helped). His de-Stalinization campaign, moreover, was undermining relations with key Communist allies like China. That October, the head of the Supreme Soviet presidium, Leonid Brezhnev, quietly orchestrated Khrushchev's removal from power, accusing him of creating his own personality cult. Khrushchev did not resist, and the sudden transfer of power was smooth. "I'm old and tired," he wrote to his ally Mikoyan. "Let them cope by themselves. I've done the main thing. Our relationships with each other, our leadership style, have changed radically. Could anyone have dreamed of telling Stalin that he didn't suit us anymore and suggesting he retire? That's my contribution. I won't put up a fight."[14]

As they tried to contain the nascent opposition movement, Brezhnev's government turned to repression. In 1965, the Soviet authorities launched a show trial against two writers, Andrei Sinyavsky and Yuli Daniel, charging them with spreading anti-Soviet propaganda abroad in their *tamizdat* publications. The trial was meant to stem the tide, but instead served as a rallying call for the nascent dissident movement. On December 5, about 200 people, led by mathematician Alexander Yesenin-Volpin, physicist Valery Nikolsky, and artist Yuri Titov and his wife Yelena Stroyeva, came out to Moscow's Pushkin Square for a rally in solidarity with Sinyavsky and Daniel. About twenty were immediately detained, but then released, with no ensuing arrests. The leniency, however, invited more dissent. Dozens, then hundreds, began to speak out against the trial, journalists and academicians, playwrights and producers, all hoping to use their status to encourage the authorities towards mercy. The more they resisted, the more the government cracked down, the more the dissidents were transformed from critics, to activists, to oppositionists, albeit not in the classic political sense, since they had no chance to run for office as they would in the 1990s and even today. In a significant way, it was the behavior of the regime that shaped the movement, inadvertently nurturing it, even as it suppressed it.[15]

Increasingly, Sakharov himself would sign their petitions and attend the growing number of trials. By 1968, with the self-styled "democratic movement" concerned that Brezhnev's counter-crackdown wasn't just unraveling some of Khrushchev's reforms, but also leading to a rehabilitation of Stalin, he penned a memorandum advocating peaceful coexistence between the USSR and the West. It was a turning point: if the Soviet press had largely ignored him before, now it unleashed a wave of criticism. The public attacks were a precursor to more direct persecution.[16] Sakharov was discharged from his work on the nuclear weapons program, essentially losing his clearance and his job. By 1970, together with other physicists, he penned a respectfully worded open letter to Brezhnev, warning against scientific and economic stagnation, and called for democratization. By that point, Sakharov had abandoned any inclination to continue working with the authorities and declined invitations to join the Communist Party of the Soviet Union. "I'm convinced that by remaining outside the ranks of the CPSU I can be of more use to my country," he was said to have replied.[17] It would take another decade of an increasingly intense tug-of-war between Sakharov and the Soviet authorities before it culminated in his arrest and exile for denouncing the Soviet invasion of Afghanistan in 1979.

When the leftist dissident Roy Medvedev – of whom more below – met Sakharov in 1967 and shared his manuscript with him, they developed a friendship. They were, however, on somewhat different ends of the political spectrum, and to Medvedev, Sakharov appeared as someone who "lived for too long in some extremely isolated world, where they knew little about the events in the country, about the lives of people from other walks of life, and even about the history of the country in which and for which they worked."[18]

To some extent, however, the same could be said of Medvedev himself, and indeed about most of the dissident movement. The majority were extremely privileged members of the *intelligentsia* class. In one of its liberalizing moments, they were, in some respects, the narrow vanguard of the Soviet authorities' reform drive. The revisionist Soviet historian Sheila Fitzpatrick rather dismissively described them as "marginalized intellectuals whose modest challenges to the regime found encouragement and protection from the [Western foreign] correspondents."[19] While not untrue, it raises a much bigger problem: many Soviet dissidents *were* out of touch with broader currents of dissent in the country. They had come to think of their cause as an essentially moral one, with no room for compromise or cooperation. They were not to be satisfied with half-measures, nor were they in the main looking for allies of convenience, whether within the state and Party apparatus or amongst the workers. As Eliot Borenstein wrote, "It is now a truism that, on the whole, Brezhnev-era dissidents were fundamentally Soviet in their anti-Soviet opposition (reliant on the same binary oppositions that operated in the Soviet system, and often just as categorical as the people they opposed)."[20] As a result, they risked becoming a mirror image of the very regime they opposed, every bit as dogmatic, but simply in the name of a different cause, ultimately emigrating or accepting prison as the price for their righteousness.

In particular, the dissident movement often fragmented into cliques questioning each other's moral purity or, even more notably, failed to engage with the blue-collar opposition to the regime, which was generally driven by rather more immediately practical concerns, as well as being suppressed far more brutally than the intellectuals of Moscow and Leningrad could ever imagine. There were, of course, exceptions. The Jewish *refuseniks* campaigning for their right to emigrate, such as Yuli Edelstein and Natan Sharansky, spearheaded a movement explicitly supporting Jews across the country and of every social stratum. There were also champions of national self-determination, like the Ukrainian poet Vasyl Stus and the Estonian chemist Jüri Kukk, who would die in 1985 and 1981, respectively, both while on hunger strikes. Workers' advocates such as Alexei Nikitin, discussed below, focused on practical issues in the workplace. Then there were those like Anatoly Marchenko, an oil driller from Siberia driven to unyielding dissent by his incarceration for breaking up a fight, who would go on to expose the authorities' continuing reliance on the Gulag system. Yet too often what happened in the "provinces" rarely intersected with the dissident movement in the cities, whether centers of power like Moscow and Leningrad or academic hubs like Novosibirsk.

The silenced dissidents

On June 1, 1962, with Khrushchev's liberalization in full swing, locals in the southern town of Novocherkassk were expressing their dismay over a 25 percent hike in the price of meat and butter when they heard more bad news: their salaries at the Budyonny Electric Locomotive Factory were about to be cut by about a third. Within hours, a dozen-strong protest rally had swelled into a thousand-strong march blocking a local highway. Negotiations quickly broke down, and the army was called in to suppress the protest. They refused to fire on the demonstrators, but security troops had no such qualms, killing twenty-six and wounding eighty-seven more. The incident was effectively concealed from the public until 1990.[21]

While the massacre that ensued made it unique for the times, it was no isolated example of resistance. Even under Stalin, after all, there had been individual and collective protests.[22] Under his successors, every day, hundreds, thousands, of Soviet citizens fought against minor and major injustices, standing up when their rights as workers and citizens were being violated and when weak institutional control and local arbitrariness left them unprotected. The Soviet authorities usually resorted to silencing the victims, unable or unwilling to deal with the injustices that they were exposing. In his book *Age of Delirium*, the *Financial Times* correspondent David Satter calls these people "truth seekers," and describes thousands of them camping out at the train terminals of Moscow as they struggled to bring their petitions to the relevant offices of the powers that be, confused, isolated, and ultimately left powerless and maligned. Just as in pre-revolutionary times, there was a touching faith that somehow this was all a mistake, and that if only the tsar – or general secretary – could be apprised of what was happening far from his gaze, all could be resolved.

There was no protection for these dissenters; no petitions or rallies by the urban class in their support. Abandoned by the hollowed-out trade unions that were nothing more than additional organs of state control, they were, for the most part, ignored by the dissident intelligentsia. In one case described by Satter, Alexei Nikitin, a coal miner from the Donbas, fought tirelessly for years against safety violations at one of the mines where he worked, only to die after several years of confinement in a psychiatric hospital. "What happened to Nikitin," a friend of his recalled, who himself would go on to be arrested, was what happens to a lot of people in his position. He started out by sensing that there was an injustice and embarked on a series of actions, the consequences of which convinced him that his instincts had been accurate. But instead of it being just an injustice in the mine where he worked or in one city, he gradually learned that it was the injustice of a whole system. . . . The only way [to save himself] would have been for him to have gone crawling back to the authorities and to have begged their forgiveness, but he had suffered too much for that.[23]

Nikitin was persecuted so harshly precisely because he reached out to foreign correspondents like Satter. Thousands of others across the country were faced with the same choice as Nikitin: continue to fight, or face death in prison or be reduced to a vegetable in a psychiatric facility, pumped full of drugs. Thousands fought and capitulated, thousands kept fighting to the end, organizing rallies, strikes, and petitions. Certainly, by the 1970s, it was harder and harder to find anyone who believed in the official creed. In the words of the anonymous author of a 1979 *samizdat* pamphlet called "There will be no Second Coming":

[T]he victim who was silent and obedient does not want to live as a victim anymore. She does not want to work at a dirty collective farm, and she is no more satisfied by the minimum wage at a factory; she listens to [Western] radio voices but does not buy the *Pravda* newspaper; she reads Brezhnev only when she has to, but she is happy to read and even to reprint a Samizdat manuscript. Communism is dead in the mass mind.[24]

Yet what could the blue-collar rebels do about it, in an atmosphere of surveillance, propaganda, and repression? There were countless strikes, unofficial stoppages, and so-called "Italian strikes" (go-slows). Even the widespread practice of stealing from the workplace, whether stealing goods or simply stealing time, clocking in and then leaving to queue for food or moonlight, was also often justified as a kind of resistance to a regime which affected to uphold the interests of the workers while exploiting them more ruthlessly and comprehensively than any capitalist robber baron. What they could not do, though, was generally organize more widely than the group of friends, the factory, or maybe, occasionally, the town. The KGB, the latest iteration of the Soviet political police, was especially vigilant in preventing any attempts to build wider connections and alliances. Things would change in the 1980s, when Gorbachev rose to power, but attempts to create genuine unions such as SMOT, the Free Interprofessional Association of Workers, established in 1978, tended to be both small-scale and short-lived, before the authorities quickly cracked down – and without high-profile advocates, they tended to be as little known in the West as at home. Even the underground *Chronicle of Current Events*, which in the period 1968–82 did sterling work covering the trials and repressions the state would rather not have seen publicized, tended to focus on explicitly political rather than labor issues, and the suppression of the intelligentsia.

That the unhappy workers existed largely in a parallel reality from that of the pro-Western urban dissident intelligentsia was not really the fault of either: the Soviet Union worked ruthlessly to further the endemic atomization that had plagued Russian society for centuries. The dissidents may have stood largely for values that would also have benefited the workers, but they had little chance to unite with or advocate for them. Indeed, even some of those protesting against local injustice often themselves regarded the dissidents, if they thought about them at all, as privileged, patronizing sell-outs to the West. The legacy of that atomization would continue to haunt the protest movement even after the brutal Soviet repressions were merely a traumatic memory.

Emigration vs. "staying useful"

Yet there were those who did try to find a balance between an uncompromising rejection of the system or craven compliance, in the hope of being able to maintain some traction, however limited, with the state. In 1971, Roy Medvedev, a Communist Party member and an academic, was faced with a choice. For the last decade or so, he had been writing a book that was essentially a reckoning with the crimes committed by Stalin and an attempt to find a way forward, reconciling his Party with its original ideology. In 1970, he had signed an open letter penned by Sakharov, calling for democratic reforms, but his status as a Party member had shielded him from the repercussions faced by more outspoken and less protected signatories. Taken together, though, his activities were beginning to make him a problem for the authorities.

The Politburo didn't quite know what to do with someone like Medvedev. The ideological zealot Mikhail Suslov wanted him arrested, but the more legalistic KGB chief Yuri Andropov wanted him co-opted to write an official – approved – work instead, as he felt that as the book was "based on tendentiously picked, but authentic data, accompanied with an astute commentary and catchy, demagogical conclusions," it would likely find quite a wide underground following.[25] As a compromise, Medvedev was expelled from the Communist Party and lost his job. Prosecutors raided his apartment and confiscated his archive, issuing him a summons to report for questioning.

"I decided not to go there," he recalled decades later, when he was in his eighties. Instead, he fled from Moscow to wait out the storm, but not abroad. "For some time, I was in an illegal situation in the [Soviet] Baltic states, and when I returned home, no one even called me in for questioning. The books came out, the press was good, they forgot about me and didn't interfere with me until Brezhnev's death, and although there was another search in 1975, it had no consequences."

Medvedev knew exactly what was at stake. His Communist father had been arrested in the 1930s on trumped-up charges of propagating Trotskyism and died in a prison camp in 1941. Medvedev refused to join the Party until his father was officially rehabilitated in 1956. His twin brother, the biologist Zhores Medvedev, had been forcefully confined to a psychiatric facility over his criticism of pseudoscientist Trofim Lysenko. After the leading dissidents of the day, including Sakharov, came to his defense, he was released, but while on academic leave in the United Kingdom, Zhores was stripped of his citizenship and, therefore, prevented from returning. This was a common tactic for dealing with dissidents who were too high profile or outspoken for arrest, such as Yuri Orlov, one of the founders of the Moscow Helsinki Group human rights organization, or the satirical author Vladimir Voinovich. It got the job done, and although the dissident was still able to speak out, it was essentially only to a Western audience.

At the time, though, the noose was closing around Roy as well. He could have emigrated himself and joined his brother. He could have doubled down on his criticism, fighting vigorously back against not just the legacy of Stalinism, but also his own unfair treatment, which would almost certainly have led to his arrest. He could have ceased his activities altogether, in effect capitulating to the demands of the Party, in exchange for his own safety. Roy Medvedev did none of those things, though. He decided to stay and carefully continue doing what he could. "I had a certain direction – socialism with a human face," he explained when asked in 2013 why he didn't emigrate, "and there were a lot of dissidents working in close contact with me, perhaps some less famous, but who had interesting thoughts, and who were always eager for discussion."[26]

In my own experience, there is something like a wormhole, an interdimensional gateway, separating those who have left and those who stay behind. For those on the outside, it is sometimes hard to grasp why a dissident would, given the choice, choose to continue living in that kind of an environment. Indeed, in later decades, Medvedev would be criticized both for deciding to stay in the Soviet Union and, more importantly, for managing to stay out of jail. Ultimately – as with Navalny many years later – he felt it was more important to be inside the country rather than free outside it.

"Of course, everyone knows that the best places to write books on Soviet history are Stanford and Princeton, much more than Moscow and Leningrad," a friend of Medvedev, the Italian diplomat Roberto Toscano, would recall. "The difference between the Sovietologist who works in the Hoover Institution library and Roy Medvedev in his little room stuffed with books, with a list of materials that, if he is lucky, he will find in the possession of a Soviet friend or foreign correspondent, is as big as the difference between the Wright brothers and engineers working at NASA."[27] And yet, he went on, there was something incredibly important in Medvedev's craft, something that you couldn't get from the tomes written abroad with the best resources Western universities had to offer. There was also the very fabric of daily life – the same one that became almost alien, exotic, and mysterious, prone to distortion and mystification, once you emigrated – the experience of which was so crucial in understanding the political processes of your country. While Medvedev was having to, in his own words, "exercise the necessary caution in expressing my thoughts," he avoided the stigma of being an exile – and thus, in the eyes of the Party and many Soviet citizens, a traitor – and could continue to espouse that "socialism with a human face."[28] He recalled, much later, the experience of his friend the dissident historian Alexander Nekrich, who was hounded out of the Soviet Union and emigrated to Boston in 1976. "He was living in poverty. He didn't know who to work with. He wrote a book, launched a weekly magazine, but he needed financial support and he could only get it from the CIA." Hence, "here I felt that I was useful, that I had a job, but abroad I had nothing to do."[29]

Sakharov undeniably remained the benchmark of principled liberal dissent within the USSR. Solzhenitsyn was deported to Germany in 1974, and would go on to become as bitter a critic of Western liberal capitalism as he had ever been of the Soviet system. Roy Medvedev's writings, and especially his critique of the deforming legacy of Stalin on Marxism-Leninism, helped inform the reformists who cohered around Mikhail Gorbachev and his quixotic bid to save it from itself. He rejoined the Communist Party in 1989, and was elected to the Congress of People's Deputies, the closest thing to a genuinely representative body since the Bolsheviks forcibly dissolved the Constituent Assembly in 1918. In the terms they themselves used, he was arguably not truly a dissident but perhaps, to use Hedrick Smith's phrase, a "carefully calibrated nonconformist."[30] By choosing to compromise, though, by not directly challenging the state in the hope of retaining some small measure of influence, he may have helped in his own way to nudge the Party towards reform. In this, he seems to have been a harbinger of the democratic oppositionists – men and women more interested in political results than moral purity – who emerged after that reform program had shattered the USSR into fifteen new or renewed states.

8

The Democrats

"You are Other, but not Russia"

It was a splendid conference: the glossiest hotel Moscow had to offer, a luxurious banquet, glitter and lights, rich blue curtains, and a chance for the stars of the Russian opposition to join forces and shine together.

In the summer of 2006, the long-splintered opposition seemed to have managed to do the unthinkable. The pro-market reform former prime minister Mikhail Kasyanov shook hands with National Bolshevik Party leader and veteran renegade Eduard Limonov. The laissez-faire former economic advisor Andrei Illarionov broke bread with the radical Communist Viktor Anpilov. The Other Russia conference, organized as an attempt to form a coalition of the non-systemic opposition that President Vladimir Putin was increasingly trying to marginalize, was immediately pronounced as a success. Numerous dignitaries from abroad, including British Ambassador Anthony Brenton and President of the US National Endowment for Democracy Carl Gershman, took part, along with a phalanx from the foreign press corps, all decrying Putin's looming dictatorial tendencies. The Chairman of the Moscow Helsinki Group, Lyudmila Alexeyeva, one of its organizers, praised the "bright and festive mood" of the conference, and Garry Kasparov, the chess champion-turned-liberal activist, claimed that it exceeded their wildest expectations.[1] For the first time, it felt, different voices were at last proclaiming a single message. This message was a broad and simple one: "We are gathering together because we are united by that which is most important – disagreement with the current course of the Kremlin and growing concern for the present and future of Russia."[2]

There was something about that festive, glossy veneer that didn't sit right with me. As a young reporter on the news desk of Moscow's oldest English-language weekly, *The Moscow News*, I was still too timid to approach big names and spent my time instead talking to lesser-known local activists, cops, independent trade unionists, nationalists, leftists, and just regular people. They very often opposed and criticized Putin, but the issues they discussed and cared about didn't seem to fit with the narratives I was hearing as I meandered from panel to panel. I struggled to understand what, if anything, all these people had in common and, much more importantly, what they were going to do, aside from send a consolidated message that they didn't like Vladimir Putin. Everybody seemed to know each other. Each of the participants and their own friendly clique of reporters spoke their own shorthand, operating within unspoken assumptions which were supposed to be common knowledge. In that way, their world seemed to be completely alien to that outside of that hotel. While Alexeyeva and other liberal politicians criticized Putin over the widespread violations of human rights perpetrated by law enforcement (which undoubtedly happened), opinion polls indicated that an overwhelming majority of citizens didn't associate these abuses with Putin at all, and still supported him (and this was long before draconian repressions cowed people into refusing to talk to pollsters, as they did after 2022). While most hoped

Putin would stick to democratic and market reforms, they had very low expectations of what the government as a whole could achieve: only a quarter believed it could attain any kind of progress at all.[3] Their main concerns were poverty, crime, and corruption,[4] but compared to the 1990s, all of these indicators were improving. Real incomes had been steadily growing since 2000 at a rate of at least 10 percent a year.[5] Homicide rates had plummeted from a peak in the 1990s.[6] As for perceptions of corruption, while still negative, they had largely improved throughout Putin's tenure.[7] Alexeyeva presented a report on police brutality, which was a persistent and endemic problem, but it had been far worse in the 1990s, largely due to police impoverishment and corruption.[8] This was not something Putin had created, in other words, but something which he had inherited from the previous government of Boris Yeltsin. According to the summary by dissident and human rights activist (and longtime Yeltsin supporter) Lev Ponomaryov, though, Putin had instigated "mass repressions" and "recreated the Gulag."[9]

To be sure, dissent was still a very dangerous profession. That October, investigative journalist Anna Politkovskaya was shot to death outside her apartment in Moscow. While her immediate assailants and organizers – including three Chechen men and a police officer – were eventually convicted, the murder was not solved, and it was widely alleged that this was because it came from as high as Chechen President Ramzan Kadyrov. In a bold interview two years earlier, Politkovskaya had tried to hold Kadyrov accountable for his mounting human rights abuses as then-head of the restive republic's security bloc. In a subsequent article, she recalled how he was "mad" and "screaming" at times throughout their interview, and repeatedly threatened to have her shot.[10] The following month after her death, the FSB defector and outspoken Putin critic Alexander Litvinenko died from polonium poisoning allegedly administered by two Russian agents in London. Beyond that, a

great number of lesser-known activists or local reporters challenging powerful officials would find themselves beaten and
otherwise attacked, with law enforcement sometimes finding
the direct assailants, but doing little to bring the actual organizers to justice. Yet in most of these extrajudicial attacks and
killings, the victims had clashed with powerful local or regional
officials or businessmen, often over their personal corruption.
They were attacked not for criticizing the Kremlin per se, but,
as another victim of one these brutal attacks, Oleg Kashin, put
it, for personally offending someone mean enough, powerful
enough, or criminal enough to go after you.[11] That law enforcement often found itself powerless against such untouchables
was certainly a failing and the responsibility of Putin's Kremlin,
but it was a leap to claim that the Kremlin orchestrated most
of these reprisals.

Most importantly, these brutal attacks – while often intimi-
dating activists into silence – were a far cry from the kind
of organized, "legal" Soviet repression that many of the pro-
Western liberal dissidents were so used to fighting. Instead
of Putin's attempts to backtrack on democracy, these were
often symptoms of a law enforcement system riddled with
corruption. The human rights abuses, in other words, were
not so much sanctioned by a political party intent on repression. They were, instead, by-products of the corruption and
lawlessness that had become entrenched during the 1990s. Of
course, Putin should have been held responsible for failing to
live up to his campaign promises of imposing a "dictatorship
of the law" and ending the lawlessness, but he himself was not
its fundamental source. Yet the way these political activists
spoke, the corruption and lawlessness that concerned a majority of the population were all caused by the KGB officer who
had assumed the presidency, rather than being legacies of bad
governance that would take generations to change.

The rapid political and market reforms they themselves had
espoused during the 1990s had not, contrary to expectations,

reduced corruption, lawlessness, and rights abuses, but often made them worse. What were the specific abuses on which leading human rights activists tended to focus? The arrest of individual political activists (this was long before the repressive crackdown and draconian laws of the later Putin era); their barring on trumped-up pretexts from local elections; the illegal transfer of an oil company from a non-state oligarch (who had himself obtained the company illegally) to another state oligarch; the pressure exerted on an oppositionist journalist. These were all very far removed from the experiences of the average citizen. As for the claim that they were primarily because of Putin's attempts to "roll back" democratic reforms, that rollback had actually begun long before Putin was anywhere near the presidency. For dissidents like Ponomaryov and Alexeyeva, fearing a KGB officer and everything he represented was understandable: they were fighting the monster they knew rather than the societal ailments that came to the fore once that monster was gone. Much like Putin, who saw violent revolution and revolt in every peaceful, unthreatening protest and overreacted rather than seeing that he had any number of safe options to reform his system, so too some of the old-school political activists often failed to see that this was no longer the Soviet Union, that they were up against different societal ills that required new ways of holding the government accountable. It wasn't just about the man in the Kremlin. Many would start taking back nascent democratic institutions that had been abandoned and corrupted throughout the 1990s and further eroded under Putin, but it would take years to develop the civic skills that would require. For now, back in those times, long before Putin actually began reversing democratic reforms, a common phrase I'd hear from all sorts of members of the liberal intelligentsia, regardless of whether they had faced prior repression, was, "I just don't like his face."

It was not surprising, then, that the feeling was mutual. The authorities, even though they allowed the conference to take place at one of Moscow's most sought-after venues, detained some twenty participants to prevent them from attending,[12] and some of them were framed by planting drugs on them. Meanwhile, pro-Kremlin youth groups demonstrated outside; a counter-protester held up a sign saying, "You are Other, but not Russia." To many of them, youngsters from blue-collar families who had benefited from state-funded political initiatives, these self-styled opposition leaders were focusing on problems that affected only a very rich, very privileged segment of the population – in other words, themselves – but were doing it in the name of actual democracy.

Provocateurs roamed the lobby, looking for trouble. (It did not help, to say the least, that part of the security was provided by the National Bolsheviks' militant wing of skinhead anti-fascists.) Inevitably – for I had seen such scuffles at the liberal protests before – one of them managed to get a rise out of one of the speakers, in this case Garry Kasparov. State security dressed in civilian clothes pounced on four National Bolsheviks, including one woman, and began to drag them to police vans outside. Kasparov shouted out: "Aren't there any foreign correspondents here? Look at what they're doing!"

To be fair, Kasparov blurted this out to try to avoid them getting detained. The remark, in other words, was in part addressed to Russian law enforcement, and counted on their desire to keep up a veneer of due process and democracy. During his first two presidential terms, Putin feared that his Western counterparts would regard him as an oriental despot, and still strove to keep up appearances. But at the time, I also couldn't help feeling a little embarrassed at Kasparov's words. Why was it the *foreign* reporters and not Russian ones to whom he was so intent on appealing? Had he written off the entire Russian press as collaborators of the state, even though this was a time of unprecedented media pluralism, the likes of which the country would not see again for many years? Or was it just that he was never really interested in talking to Russians, the ordinary

Russians from outside the capital, the provincial *sovoks* – a derisory term for people who seemed not to have progressed beyond Soviet values and tastes – who couldn't manage to provide the reporters in Yeltsin's entourage with something as basic as freshly squeezed mandarin juice? (This may sound like a bizarre statement, but there is a persistent story of a Kremlin pool reporter complaining about not being able to find a decent café with mandarin juice when out of the capital.) After all, they had demonstrated a pesky tendency to not vote for these liberal politicians when given the chance to do so.

What it amounted to was this: despite liberals' attempts to shake hands with leftists like Anpilov, the forum was dominated by their own pro-market, pro-Western agenda. They claimed to speak in the name of the entire Russian opposition while in essence representing only a fraction of it. At least on paper, their platform differed little from the Kremlin's: democratic and market reforms (though in practice this was merely a promise rather than a reality). If there was a Russian opposition with substantial reach and a network throughout the country, it was the Communist Party, but it faced pressure from both sides. On the one hand, the Kremlin, while allowing the Communists second place in parliament, ensured that they remained only a token force, their leaders' position largely scripted by the Presidential Administration.[13] On the other, the liberal opposition, those who in the 1990s had supported Yeltsin's course, claimed to speak in the name of the entire Russian opposition while largely failing to bring genuine Communist oppositionists into their ranks. The opposition's preoccupation with Vladimir Putin – to the point where even the liberal politician Irina Khakamada criticized participants for their lack of any sort of program for the future – was peculiar. In hindsight, however, there is another explanation for their oversized dislike of Putin, however deserved. These democratic forces had played a unique and pivotal role in Russia's history, and in Putin's story as well.

I was still a young reporter, but I was old enough to remember what many of these liberals were doing just six years earlier, when Yeltsin and his circle had effectively stage-managed Putin's ascent to the presidency: having made him prime minister, Yeltsin unexpectedly resigned, so that he became acting president and could hold a snap election with the advantage of incumbency, as well as the mass media support of Yeltsin's allies. Hoping to stave off a Communist revanche (and getting some badly needed support for their own parliamentary campaign from the Kremlin in return),[14] the Union of Right Forces party – which included the leaders of the liberal opposition – had themselves backed Putin as the defender of the new market economy, turning a blind eye to Yeltsin's manipulation of nascent democratic institutions in the process.

The dissident and the rebel

Three generations after a group of rebels had taken control of the Russian government and inaugurated a new dynasty of tsars, a dissident and a rebel were locked in a vicious power struggle, the fruits of which would become, however briefly, the only democracy that Russia had ever known. Both were powerful officials – leaders, even – of the Soviet government, a gargantuan bureaucracy overseeing an empire fraying at the seams. For the last five years, the dissident, emerging as the supreme leader by virtue of the fact that he was the youngest, most energetic official of the aging Politburo that ruled the empire, had been pushing through a series of ambitious reforms to democratize the state apparatus he had inherited. Drawing on many of the programs and tenets devised by the Soviet dissidents during the thaw of the 1960s, he believed in the spirit of their movement. This "last believer" tried to stay true to the democracy and collegiality that he still felt was at the heart of Marxist-Leninist doctrine, and rejected the repressive unwritten laws of the Communist Party in which doing or saying anything without the explicit permission of the authorities was forbidden.[15] To make the government work in accordance with its written laws and stated values, he encouraged free speech, lifted much of the press censorship, and embarked on a campaign of economic and political restructuring. Carried to its conclusion, this would have decentralized decision-making to give all of the constituents of the Soviet Union, particularly its fifteen national republics, a genuine voice in how they were governed. To revive the economy, he lifted some of the Party's controls and allowed citizens to legally run private enterprises for the first time since the 1920s. To curb the dictatorial powers of the Politburo and give the governed a voice, he created the Congress of People's Deputies, something of a return to the very early days of 1917–18, when the country was briefly, until the emerging Politburo of Lenin's Bolshevik party ultimately stripped them of their representative and legislative powers, ruled by locally elected *soviets*, or councils. The Congress replaced the acting Supreme Soviet of the Soviet Union, which was a *soviet* in name only since it was appointed, not elected. Now the Congress, which consisted of about 1,000 directly elected deputies, elected the Supreme Soviet.

Initially, the rebel was no rebel at all, but a protégé of the dissident, likewise believing in democratic reform. A career Party member, he rose through the ranks until the dissident appointed him Party chief of Moscow. Having assumed power, though, he grew frustrated with the constraints of Soviet inertia, dismissed local functionaries to replace them with younger ones of his choosing, and began to fall out with the dissident. Both thought of each other as somewhat domineering, which was perhaps inevitable given the caliber of egos required to fulfill their respective positions. Finally, the rebel handed in his resignation in protest, and the dissident let him go, blackening his name as he left. With much more efficient democratic

institutions now in place, the rebel used them to *rebel*. Thanks
to his vision and charisma, he rose through a series of democratic elections, first to the Congress of People's Deputies of
the Russian Republic, then to chairman of its Supreme Soviet.
He was not the leader of the USSR – that would still be the
dissident. But through the first democratic institutions the
country had ever known instated by the dissident, he emerged
as the first democratically elected leader of Russia.

But here's the thing about Russian leaders. Throughout
history, they have known no higher authority than God (or
an ideology that sought to replace it). Over the course of the
next several years, the rebel would declare Russian sovereignty
within the USSR, call a presidential election and win it, and
then use his new powers to abolish the Soviet Union altogether
(albeit this was no great feat by that time, given that it was col-
lapsing under the weight of its own contradictions), followed
by the very institutions that he had used to rise to power, and
which he had vowed to uphold in the vision of Russia that had
encouraged millions to elect him in the first place.

The dissident, as the reader has surely figured out by now,
was Mikhail Gorbachev; the rebel was Boris Yeltsin, the policy
of free speech was *glasnost*, and the reforms were *perestroika*.
Biases about these words and people have since calcified into
untested assumptions and so it is vital to try to get back to the
basics. History may tell us that Russian leaders have tolerated
no constraints other than those imposed by God, and there
are certainly enough Russians who, while looking today at yet
another failure of democracy, succumb to this depressing path
dependency. Putin himself, perhaps, is the most prominent
among them. But history is not gospel. It explains the past,
but shapes the future only when members of society choose
to let it. That democratic moment in 1991 failed not because
history ordained it so. Instead, by the end of 1991, when Yeltsin
emerged as a victor, most educated Russians, and especially
those in the West, were assuming that democracy had won,

and the battle was over. In hindsight, it is now clear that the struggle for Russian democracy was only just beginning.

The rebel as leader

On August 19, 1991, Boris Yeltsin, who just two months earlier had become the first directly elected president of the Russian Soviet Federative Socialist Republic (RSFSR), found himself barricaded in the White House, the seat of the Russian parliament, as a crowd of Muscovites swelled outside in his support. That morning, a group of hardliners, led by KGB Chairman Vladimir Kryuchkov and Soviet Vice President Gennady Yanayev, had placed President Gorbachev under house arrest, announced a state of emergency, and sent tanks into the city to stop what they saw as the calamity that had been unleashed by the reformers' liberalization campaign. The economy had collapsed, with people struggling to find, let alone buy, basic food staples, and five republics were seeking to secede from the Soviet Union. Gorbachev, to stem the tide, had negotiated a new Union Treaty that would in effect give each republic as much sovereignty as it needed, while still preserving a union. But the Union Treaty also stripped the Communist Party, including many prominent members like Kryuchkov and Yanayev, of a great deal of their authority. It was due to be signed on August 20, and the coup plotters had to act fast.

Whether out of genuine support for the reforms and a rejection of the repressions that the coup plotters stood for, or simply spotting his chance to seize the reins from his floundering rival, Gorbachev, Yeltsin also realized that he had to act fast. Seeing the tanks approaching from the window of his office, he got up, signaled to the deputies next to him, and said, "Let's go!" Down below, demonstrators had already managed to get the commander of the tank squadron sent by the hardliners to join them. One of them had simply climbed up onto a tank, and asked the commander, Major Sergei Yevdokimov, "Are you going to shoot at us? Or maybe you'd rather come over to our side and start defending the parliament?" After a moment of deliberation, Yevdokimov ordered his tanks to turn around, pointing their guns outwards – defending the building from the very people who had given him orders in the first place.[16] It was one of Yevdokimov's tanks that Yeltsin clambered onto to deliver his iconic address to the people. "Regardless of the reasons given for his removal," he said, in a terse reference to Gorbachev, referring to him only as president of the country and not mentioning his name until the very end of his speech, "we are dealing with a rightist, reactionary, anti-constitutional coup. Democratic process in the country is acquiring an increasingly broad sweep and an irreversible character."[17]

It was at that very moment that the rebel found himself transformed into a leader. The will of a people he clambered onto that tank to lead – people who were willing to die for what they believed – prevailed over that of the hardliners, who were not ultimately willing to spill blood in the name of an ill-thought-through attempt to revive a system already beyond resuscitation. The coup collapsed. "In 1991, Yeltsin was a hero," an exiled businessman and former officer of the General Staff would recall decades later. "But that would not always be the case."[18]

With Gorbachev politically incapacitated, Yeltsin used the power he had amassed in the RSFSR in effect to rule over the entire Soviet Union by decree, essentially dismantling many of the cumbersome vestiges of the old regime. That December, he abolished the Communist Party. He ignored the March 1991 referendum on the Union Treaty, in which 76 percent voted in favor of retaining the Soviet Union's federal system. Instead, he discarded the treaty, and declared, together with the leaders of Ukraine and Belarus, that the Soviet Union no longer existed. His decrees and declarations may have been representative of the will of many of the republics that had declared independence from the Soviet Union, such as the Baltic states and Ukraine, but in that they circumvented the democratic due process of the new Russian republic, they were, arguably, not representative of the will of his own nation, and the members of that nation who found themselves residing in these newly foreign, and sometimes hostile, states. It was something for which his nascent opposition would never forgive him.

On New Year's Eve, 1991, the USSR ceased to exist, and a whole new country emerged, the Russian Federation. But unlike the fourteen other republics gaining sovereignty from the Soviet Union and identifying themselves via their ethnicity and their independence from Moscow, Russia – on the one hand a nation, on the other still an ethnically diverse federation – couldn't really claim either identity. Nearly 150 million exhausted, demoralized people needed a unifying vision. Boris Yeltsin offered them Western-style capitalism, and turned all his efforts towards dismantling the Communist Party. He focused upon rapid market reform – essentially the direct opposite of all that the Communist Party stood for – as the bedrock of the new democracy. "The *glasnost* of the day simply put a minus sign instead of a plus sign," a Russian journalist remarked to me of that period.[19] In practice, it would prove to be neither a bedrock, nor democratic.

The time of the "seven bankers"

In 1990, the dissidents Sergei Kovalyov and Lev Ponomaryov drafted a Declaration for a newly created political body, the Democratic Russia Election Bloc. They called for the abolition of the one-party rule of the Communist Party, but also for a smoother transition to the market economy that included retail price freezes.[20] The faction they would go on to form in the Congress of People's Deputies would be instrumental in helping Yeltsin win his presidential election the following year. Their coalition then passed legislation central to the reform, and proved key supporters of Yeltsin and his government, which would include the controversial market reformer Yegor Gaidar.

But after two years of shock therapy – the rapid privatization espoused by Gaidar – the economy continued its free-fall and millions of people saw their savings wiped out. Democratic Russia started to lose its support. Parliament ousted Gaidar, the acting prime minister, at the end of 1992. A standoff began between the president and his parliament that would culminate in Yeltsin shelling the very White House he had been defending two years earlier, as will be discussed in the following chapter. Ponomaryov's Democratic Russia began hemorrhaging members and seats in parliament, but even the rebooted Democratic Choice alliance only managed to get nine seats in the new parliament after 1995, down from sixty-two. Some of its members, like Viktor Sheinis, would go on to form the liberal Yabloko party with its founder, Grigory Yavlinsky, and many others would go on to be absorbed in 1999 by the Union of Right Forces (SPS), a pro-market reform bloc led by Gaidar, charismatic Deputy Prime Minister Boris Nemtsov, and another influential Kremlin official, Sergei Kiriyenko. In the 1999 State Duma elections, SPS and Yabloko managed to win 8.5 percent and 6 percent of the vote, respectively, but they would never be a match for the Communist Party, which took a quarter of the total seats.

To their credit, many in the Democratic movement vocally opposed many of Yeltsin's policies, especially his brutal military operation to rein in Chechnya. In 1996, Sergei Kovalyov resigned from the presidential human rights commission which he headed in protest against the violence in Chechnya as well as Yeltsin's backtracking on democratization.[21] Others, like parliamentarian Galina Starovoitova, not only called

Yeltsin "Bloody Boris" over his war in Chechnya, but also fought for accountability in the murky world of foreign aid in St. Petersburg. She was murdered in 1998 in connection with her work.

Meanwhile, the market reforms continued to bleed the country, to the point where Yeltsin's government struggled simply to secure cash for its operations. By the end of 1995, a curious new formation emerged that was neither democratic nor inherently statist: the *semibankirschina*. It is hard to translate what that really means: the "time of the seven bankers" or perhaps the "seven banker outfit," with a certain negative connotation. Named after the *semiboyarschina* of the Time of Troubles, when Russia was essentially ruled by seven boyars, the new name referred to the seven bankers who had managed to elevate themselves so high that Yeltsin owed his Kremlin seat as much to them as he did to his voters, and perhaps rather more.

In the summer of 1995, just a year before the next presidential elections – partly because Yeltsin would need their support in the face of a strong Communist challenge, and partly because his government was laboring under a 50 trillion ruble debt – the seven bankers in question, Vladimir Potanin, Vladimir Gusinsky, Mikhail Khodorkovsky, Pyotr Aven, Mikhail Fridman, Alexander Smolensky, and Boris Berezovsky, wound up with the choicest spoils of Russia's oil and gas industry for next to nothing. It was these men, according to journalist Andrei Fadin, who went on to "form the will of the president."[22] The "loans for shares" program saw the government offering shares of oil refineries as collateral for loans to the state worth hundreds of millions of dollars. Everyone knew the state would never pay these loans back, but it was a way of circumventing a State Duma ban on privatizing strategic oil assets. In all, between November and December of 1995, twelve enterprises were auctioned off to these seven bankers, who promptly sold the shares back to themselves through offshore and shell companies in a rigged privatization that few even pretended was fair.[23]

One, Boris Berezovsky, would assume a particularly important political role, organizing the so-called "Davos Pact" between Russian business leaders attending the World Economic Forum to bankroll Yeltsin's re-election campaign in 1996 and throwing his media empire behind him. This gave him a powerful voice within what became known as "the Family," the clique of relatives, cronies, and advisors around the ailing president, and looks likely to have meant that Berezovsky was able to broker Putin's appointment as prime minister in August 1999, and then help orchestrate his ascendency to the presidential seat.[24] When Yeltsin handpicked Vladimir Putin as his successor, he had two sets of allies: the group of bankers who financed his election and the liberal reformers in the Union of Right Forces party.[25] It seemed like a win-win: with his energy and KGB background (many KGB officers had reinvented themselves in the 1990s as shadow brokers and security providers for the business community), the hope was that Putin could safeguard the market reforms and manipulate democratic institutions to ensure there would be no Communist revanche.

Ready for democracy

Mikhail Khodorkovsky, for one, seemed to know exactly how this new world worked. Referring to Vladimir Putin as his "boss," he would joke that "I don't own anything, I rent it."[26] He would explain that he would even step down as head of his own bank if the then-prime minister asked him – because the "state is the dominant force in the economy."[27]

Yet, in 2003, he felt it was time to go against this wisdom. Feeling he had atoned for the "incestuous" acquisition of his oil assets in 1995 by making his company more legally transparent and efficient than pretty much any other in Russia, he undertook to build a transnational oil empire. At the same time, he seemed to have political ambitions, not to stand for office or even, as figures like Berezovsky clearly fancied themselves, to be the power behind the throne, but rather to play an important role in the evolution of the country, and especially by challenging the corruption and autocratic power baked into the system. Pyotr Aven, Putin's close friend from his time in St. Petersburg and later the head of Alfa Bank, told an American journalist that Khodorkovsky was "openly going around Moscow saying they would like to buy one-third of the Duma to be able to block an institutional majority."[28] Khodorkovsky would also publicly speak out on corruption, and not in the accepted way, by criticizing the "bad boyars" as a way of praising the "good tsar," but as a top-to-bottom problem.

Mikhail Kasyanov, who served as Putin's prime minister at that time and then fell utterly out of favor for his staunch support for Khodorkovsky – and who would never see his opposition parties allowed anywhere near the election process – suggested that the problem was simpler: that Khodorkovsky was refusing to defer to Putin. "It wasn't a question of [him funding] liberal or illiberal parties," he told me in an interview in 2010.

> It could have been the other way around. The main problem [for Putin] – and this surprised me – was that besides the legal support that businesses could give political parties, a business had to obtain secret approval from the president for this activity. It didn't matter what parties were approved or not. What was important was that this permission be obtained.[29]

Like the Yeltsin government before him, Putin must have considered his hold on power too weak to withstand this kind of insubordination. "I have eaten more dirt than I need to from that man," Putin reportedly told BP chief John Browne in a private remark shortly before Khodorkovsky's arrest.[30] In October 2003, Khodorkovsky was arrested and tried for tax fraud, tax evasion, and embezzlement. His ponderous, Kafkaesque trial highlighted the extent to which the state was willing to use the judiciary to its own ends. Much of his oil company Yukos ended up nationalized by the state-owned Rosneft oil company, controlled by Putin ally Igor Sechin, and Khodorkovsky would spend the next decade in prison, until he was suddenly amnestied by Putin in 2012, on condition, of course, that the errant boyar spend the rest of his life abroad. Unlike Ivan the Terrible, Putin would feel no need to directly polemicize with these exiled dissenters.

* * *

Putin's facilitation of the hostile takeover of independent TV station NTV in 2001 by another state-owned company, Gazprom, first alerted the liberal opposition to the mistake they had made when they welcomed him into the Kremlin. But it was Khodorkovsky's trial that ultimately cemented it, and the oligarch became one of the unlikely icons of the liberal resistance. In this, they had little wide support: for much of the population, Khodorkovsky was the robber-baron who had profited from their poverty. In a 2005 poll, the majority of respondents felt either neutral or negative about him, and were split evenly on whether he should be released, even while most understood that the Kremlin had put pressure on the judiciary.[31] But here was the problem: an oligarch who enriched himself in the 1990s thanks to extralegal machinations was now being stripped of his assets thanks to extralegal machinations. The Yukos case certainly corroded Russia's independent court system, but that corrosion had been established years before.

None of this excuses Putin's entrenchment of corruption and his manipulation of the law to achieve his aims and ensure his security. Nor should the democratic opposition be blamed.

Their failures to establish a potent solidarity with other sectors of Russian society was not down entirely to their splintered, divisive inner debates. Arguably, though, there is another dimension to their dislike of Putin that proved as problematic: a deep-seated, class-driven antagonism between the urban intelligentsia and the "uneducated" provincial masses that, to them, Putin came to represent, for all that he was a native of Leningrad/St. Petersburg. His deliberate use of street slang to assert his tough-guy credentials, his bare-shirted bravado, his apparent lack of real interest in culture and art, all of this meant that he was considered the epitome of *poshlost'*, a particularly Russian sense of vapid, trashy tastelessness.

To a degree, this is also what endeared him to so many ordinary Russians exasperated with Muscovite snobbery. In fairness, though, his apparent success in returning prosperity and order to their lives – whether Putin really can take the credit or simply benefited from economic and social changes is another matter – and the spectacle of a leader who, unlike the increasingly inebriated and incapable Yeltsin, looked the part, actually counted for rather more. The point was, however, that from the first, the man who would be tsar was able to reach past the social elites and play the masses against them.

The rebel who had become a president, Boris Yeltsin, had taken full advantage of the growing crisis of the Soviet order to destroy it. In the process, he had briefly managed to ally elite oppositionists with an unhappy populace. The marches and protests supporting him against the 1991 coup plotters had brought together miners and mathematicians, choreographers and street cleaners. However, this would prove a moment, not a movement. The irony was that the dissident movement gave way to a democratic opposition that would prove to have a pivotal and crucial role to play in 1991, dismantling many of the structures of the old order, from the Party state to the moribund planned economy. Without their drive, without their faith and sometimes misguided zeal, those ruthless transformations may not have been able to take place. But just as much as someone needed to sweep out the old, someone, too, needed to build something new. For Democratic Russia and the other liberal movements of the time, as with the Other Russia forum, "disseminating ideas became more important than putting them into practice," in the words of political scientist Vladimir Gelman.[32]

Believing that almost any change was good, they sat back while rapacious entrepreneurs redefined the Soviet economy to their advantage, scavenging its remnants and creating monopolies, without allowing the emergence of the kinds of legal and regulatory frameworks which allow free capitalism to exist. In the name of preventing a Communist revanche, they cheered on the creation of a distorted and managed pseudo-democracy, heedless of how far this would lay the foundations for Putin's electoral dictatorship. That the Communists were riding high in the polls was seen as a sign of the political immaturity of the masses, who could clearly not truly be trusted, rather than a desperate protest vote against hunger and fear. Putin shared their skepticism, and, in private, reportedly told a journalist close to the Kremlin around 2010 that "the Russian people are not yet ready for democracy."[33] The road to authoritarianism turned out to be paved with good intentions. These rebels no more seemed to understand or appreciate the people in whose name they claimed to be acting than had Lenin, or the *narodniki*.

That did not mean that a new generation could not do better, though. Writing from prison in August 2023, Alexei Navalny first called for a reckoning with Yeltsin-era reformers that had been virtually taboo up until then. As he put it, "I hate Yeltsin and the rest of the corrupt family who put Putin in power. I hate the swindlers, whom we used to call reformers for some reason."[34] His foundation then produced a film series called *Traitors* detailing how Putinism was a continuation of Yeltsinism, and how the pro-market reformers who later became his foes actually played a role in bringing him to power. The virulent backlash against Navalny's Anti-Corruption Foundation (ACF) and the film's narrator, Maria Pevchikh, was telling of the painful chord the series struck among liberals, many of whom liked to hold others to account for supporting Putin or not opposing him enough, but were unprepared to hold their own principles, their own sacred cow, Yeltsin, accountable for making Putin possible. Mikhail Khodorkovsky even threatened to prevent Pevchikh from doing anything to judge him – in effect, suggestive of silencing her, even as he compared her to Putin's prosecutors.[35] But as the scholar Lev Kadik detailed, back in Russia the films had a great deal of resonance, sparking a reckoning with past mistakes and forcing a new generation of political activists to ask themselves if the liberals had actually been that liberal – or, indeed, to what extent they had been truly democratic.[36]

To be fair, a protest movement rooted in the dissident era could, arguably, not be expected to have a clear vision of the future beyond sweeping away the regime which had repressed it. But many of the oppressive conditions that engendered distrust, isolation, and alienation in the Soviet Union no longer applied in the 1990s and even during Putin's rule. Some of the liberal reformers – most notably Boris Nemtsov – would go on to take a leading role in the Snow Revolution of 2011–12. But there, they were part of a new, younger emerging movement, one that would begin to learn some of the lessons of the 1990s and from that try to overcome the divisions of the past and reach out to the rest of the country at large. Even in the deep freeze of Russia's current political winter, that process continues to this day – although it is not only liberals and democrats who are seeking to build wider constituencies, as nationalists and xenophobes can be dissidents, too.

9

The Russian Spring

The "banality" of Putin

I met Eduard Limonov in the spring of 2009, the year he tried, unsuccessfully, to register as the "single" and "natural" candidate from the opposition. He emerged from the subway underpass, a tall, thin figure with the face of Leon Trotsky, flanked by two young skinheads in army boots and leather jackets – bodyguards who never left his side. "I've been attacked before," he said baldly, waving in their direction to explain their presence, without me having to ask.

We walked for a while through a rather affluent neighborhood in south-central Moscow, near where I lived at the time, to an office he rented in a Stalinist high-rise, some of the most sought-after real estate in the city. In that room – something between a safe-house and a studio – we talked for about an hour about his life as an eternal rebel, the travails of unifying the opposition, and Vladimir Putin.

"The trouble is," he said towards the end of our interview, "is that he's just a very banal politician. From his suits to his politics, Putin is just . . . banal."[1]

That was a powerful indictment coming from a poet who

got his start sewing clothes for bohemian bards and artists in the 1960s. In his career, he managed to piss off everyone, from KGB Chairman Yuri Andropov, who called him an "anti-Soviet" in 1973, to the FBI and the DST (then, the French security service), as he trampled proudly over the artifices of human conformity in his black leather boots. He was born Eduard Savenko, but soon adopted Limonov, a name more fitting because it not only reflected his lemon-shaped head, but also paid homage to the slang word for a hand grenade, the *limonka*. Moving to New York City in the 1970s, he perfected an unabashedly vulgar prose style, dabbled in homosexuality (at least as described in his autobiographical novel *It's Me, Eddie*), cavorted with the Socialist Workers Party, and chained himself to the building of *The New York Times* over their refusal to publish his anti-capitalist screeds. Finally, disillusioned with America's shallow sanctimony and censorship, in 1980 he left the country and headed to France, where he had more luck on the socialist scene, members of whom lobbied the government to grant him citizenship.[2] When the Soviet government collapsed and Russia became the place to be for anyone who wanted to make trouble, he restored his citizenship and returned to the country in 1991. After war broke out following the breakup of Yugoslavia, he fought on the side of Serbia in its war against Bosnia. In 1993, amid a growing opposition to Boris Yeltsin, he founded the National Bolshevik Party (NBP, or *natsboly*, as they became colloquially known), espousing an amalgam of progressive socialism, nationalist revanchism, and just the right dash of fascism. "The essence of National Bolshevism is withering hatred of the anti-human SYSTEM of the trinity: liberalism/democracy/capitalism," their program proclaimed in 1994. "A man of rebellion, the National Bolshevik sees his mission in destroying the SYSTEM to the ground. . . . We denounce the Belavezha Accords" – whereby the presidents of Russia, Ukraine, and Belarus agreed amongst themselves in December 1991 to break up the USSR

– "and as a result, Russia's borders will be revised. Let's unite all Russians in one state. The territories of the 'republics' that have broken away from us, where the Russian population is more than 50 percent, will be annexed to Russia through local referendums and their support by Russia (Crimea, Northern Kazakhstan, Narva region, etc.)."[3] Limonov's followers adopted the style of the Nazi skinheads not out of admiration, but in irony, to pursue and beat the shit out of them in Moscow alleyways and underpasses.

Enfant terrible and provocateur that he was, at a time when loving Russia was not considered *comme il faut*, Limonov considered himself a genuine patriot. He believed that Yeltsin – ostensibly the father of the first Russian nation – had committed a criminal travesty by breaking up the Soviet Union, and Limonov's party was one of the earliest and most radical to stand up against what they believed to be anti-democratic and anti-Russian reforms. When Russian police arrested him and several other *natsboly* in a tiny town in Russia's Altai region in 2001, just north of the border with Kazakhstan, the first thing he said to the cameras was, "I'm a Russian patriot."[4] He was convicted and jailed on charges of buying weapons and planning an insurrection in Northern Kazakhstan. While he denied those charges, Limonov's activism in support of ethnic Russians in Northern Kazakhstan was notorious (whether they wanted it or not). "Kazakhs have no right to these cities along the border," he would continue saying years later, when that incident would suddenly gain a whole new relevance. "They were not built by them, and they do not own them, since they got them by accident. Justice was violated when 327 million Russians remained outside of Russia, and I said back in the early 1990s that sooner or later it would explode."[5] Even as Limonov spent two years in jail, his *natsboly* continued their activism among ethnic Russians in Northern Kazakhstan, hoping to foment a revolt, perhaps even a confrontation between Russia and Kazakhstan.[6]

Limonov was therefore an unlikely figure to emerge as one of the leaders of the mostly liberal March of Dissenters, a series of demonstrations numbering up to about a thousand people held regularly in the aughts. These rallies were – not wholly unfairly – regarded as reflecting the interests of no more than a tight clique of affluent, educated cosmopolitans with time and money on their hands. In fairness, they stood in defense of a noble cause, human rights, yet some critics couldn't help but joke that in order to defend them, they had to get them violated first. Limonov had joined forces with the liberal opposition because he believed that only a common front could stand up to Vladimir Putin. To that end, his NBP even toned down its original program, putting the focus instead on civil society and grass-roots activism: the bedrock of the democracy they had earlier denounced.[7]

They needed a single presidential candidate, and Limonov believed himself ideally suited for the role. The trouble was that so did Mikhail Kasyanov, the liberal former prime minister, widely known as "Misha 5 Percent," a reference to the kickbacks people allegedly paid during his time in office, and so did Garry Kasparov, and so did Boris Nemtsov, a former parliamentarian and one of the leaders of Right Cause, a movement at a time when to be "right-wing" in Russia meant to be in favor of the free market, democratic reform, and social liberalism. Limonov had a point, in that the chief challenge facing the fractured opposition wasn't Putin's increasing clampdowns, but their inability to find common ground with others who believed in different platforms, potentially forming something with more reach than their cosmopolitan clique with their own network of cafés to frequent. That was why the Other Russia forum in 2006 represented, initially, such a profound milestone: for the first time, market liberals, socialists, and nationalists managed to sit down around the same table and have a conversation.

But it was short-lived, and by 2009 Limonov was beginning to fall out with his peers. In 2012, he and his National

Bolsheviks took part in the Bolotnaya Protests, but the lines between liberal, left, and nationalist forces were by that point once again becoming clear – in a symbolic representation of this new disunity, even though all took part in the demonstrations, they marched in their own respective columns.

But then, something happened. All of a sudden, this renegade rebel, one of the fieriest nonconformists of the Putin era, started appearing on state-owned television channels and writing columns in the pro-Kremlin press. As demonstrators gathered on Kyiv's central square in the winter of 2013–14, protesting the same government corruption and lies that Limonov himself persistently stood up against in Russia, he decried their rallies and praised the valor of the Berkut riot police deployed by President Viktor Yanukovich to hose them down in subzero temperatures. He rejoiced when Putin moved to annex Crimea. And when thousands of nationalists, veterans, rogue security officers, and men looking for a purpose scrounged up some military gear, waded through the swamps around Ukraine's southwestern border, and joined the pro-Russian separatist movement against Kyiv's new pro-Western government, he was among the first to form his own battalion of eager *natsboly*, who went to fight for a Russian Donbas. By 2015, he was calling on the Kremlin to shut down the publications of the "enemy" and exile pro-Western oppositionists for their "anti-Russian treachery."[8]

Limonov had always been a nationalist, and on some level, especially given his activism in Northern Kazakhstan, none of this should have been surprising. But there was something else here, perhaps more important than his "patriotism": Limonov had a nose for revolution, and what started to happen in Russia in 2014, after the suppression of the Snow Revolution two years earlier by a government that had lost its sense of quite what to believe in, was just such a revolutionary moment. Putin would initially lean on it and try to use it to shore up his own legitimacy, but he was equally afraid of it because these people had something he clearly lacked: a vision. He would, through 2014 and 2015, by turns try to distance himself from and then embrace the new nationalist revolution. As he dithered, that revolution ended up co-opting him. Putin broke from the constraints of banality, and joined the very thing he had so long resisted, and could never beat. This revolution became known as the Russian Spring.

Revanchists for democracy

The nexus and origin of what has been happening in Russia starting in 2014 and through to the present lie two decades earlier, in 1993. If there is one thing that unites nationalists of all colors in Russia, from Limonov to those who took up arms and went to Ukraine in 2014, it's that the ones who were old enough stood up, one way or another, to Boris Yeltsin then in his bloody standoff with his own parliament. They lost.

Konstantin Malofeyev, a young parliamentary aide eager to take part in Russia's new democracy, was glued to the radio. It was October 1993, and he was holed up in the White House, the seat of Russia's parliament, at the time an elected institution theoretically as powerful as the presidency. The president's constitutional standoff with the Congress of People's Deputies and the Supreme Soviet that it elected from among its membership had been brewing for months. His own vice-president, Alexander Rutskoi, opposed his widely unpopular economic reforms, as did a majority of parliamentarians, calling it "economic genocide."[9] The sudden privatization and liberalization of prices sent the ruble into free-fall, and if people had trouble finding food during *perestroika*, when there was still a modicum of a social safety net, the majority now found themselves in even greater hardship. A new class of obscenely rich businessmen zoomed through the streets of Moscow in their Mercedes, buying off the police and running their own protection rackets that defended only those rich enough, while government officials and liberal intellectuals extolled the virtues of capitalism and democracy from the safety of their relatively protected central Moscow apartments. It was no wonder that young *natsboly* were so confused about what "democracy" meant that they signed up to a party that vowed to destroy it. The opposition in parliament also challenged the terms of the Belavezha Accords, the document that formally ended the Soviet Union. But what it ultimately came down to was a power struggle between the president and the legislature. Temporary constitutional amendments granting the president special powers to rule by decree had expired at the end of 1992. Yeltsin was demanding that the parliament adopt a new constitution that would make such powers permanent. Parliament was refusing.

In April, Yeltsin had tried to break the constitutional logjam through a four-part referendum on his leadership and his policies, but also on holding early presidential and parliamentary elections. He got his personal vote of confidence and support for his policies – with 59.9 and 54.3 percent, respectively – but not the mandate for early elections, so he was stuck in his constitutional deadlock. True to form, he bulled ahead anyway and in September announced early parliamentary elections and, in clear breach of the constitution, the dissolution of the legislature. The Congress of People's Deputies escalated in turn, declaring that as a result Yeltsin was no longer head of state and declaring Rutskoi president.

At this point, the constitution was more on the side of the parliamentarians. However, after barricading themselves into the White House, their defenders and loyalists amongst the police escalated. On October 3, urged on by Rutskoi, they stormed out to take the offices of the Moscow mayor and even tried to seize the Ostankino television center. Rutskoi began appealing to soldiers to join his cause. The prospect of *bunt*, of armed rebellion and mayhem in the heart of the capital, not only delegitimized the parliamentarian side, it also gave Yeltsin the excuse and opportunity to act with a ruthless decisiveness that, ironically enough, the 1991 coup plotters had been unable to muster.

Malofeyev suddenly heard on the news that somebody in the basement was handing out weapons to anyone who wanted to defend the White House. "And we were all joyful, ran down to the basement, thinking we'd get weapons, only to find a sleepy policeman who [chased us away]."[10] In any case, it would hardly have made a difference. Tanks from the Kantemirov Division began shelling the White House as special forces stormed the building, and Moscow witnessed the first civil violence on its streets since 1917. Yeltsin called what had happened the defeat of a "fascist–communist armed rebellion," but many would later characterize it as his October Coup.[11] In six days, 147 people were killed and over 400 injured. The self-professed democrat got his way, the Congress of People's Deputies was dissolved and replaced with a new, weaker parliament, the constitution was rewritten retrospectively to make what Yeltsin did legal, and arguably Russia's budding democracy began to wither before it had had a chance to take root. Malofeyev would later recall that this was when he lost his faith in humanity, or at least in politics. "Everything that Yeltsin was doing was illegal. . . . When I saw all those bodies in the White House, . . . I realized that this was such a cynical and terrible story that I definitely didn't want to have anything to do with it ever again. After finishing studies in constitutional law, I left politics and went into business."[12] Twenty years later, when Putin began to move to annex Crimea, Malofeyev joined forces with his old comrades from 1993 and began secretly to finance the volunteers who joined pro-Russian separatists first in Crimea and then in the Donbas. Long before the Kremlin was ready to commit regular troops, Malofeyev had become the chief financier of the Russian Spring.

To this day, there is an extensive memorial to the suppressed uprising of 1993 just across from the White House, with stands displaying photos of the fallen and newspaper clippings from the most revanchist elements of the Russian press. Excerpts from leftist-nationalist ideologue Alexander Prokhanov's newspaper *Zavtra* hold prominence, and conspiracy theories casting doubt on the actual death toll abound.

In the years after the events of 1993, and in the early years of the Putin era, the shelling of the White House seemed like a necessary evil: the liberation of the media and political parties from the last legacies of the Soviet era. The Congress of People's Deputies had, after all, been elected in 1990 and originally a majority of its members had been members of the Communist Party, although most quickly shed that affiliation, even before the USSR was dissolved. It led to a ferment in which, as well as liberal and humanitarian ideologies, all sorts of ugly repressed currents of thought would emerge, from outright racism and antisemitism to the performatively nationalist Liberal Democratic Party of Russia (LDPR). Created initially as a fake party with presumed ties to the KGB, its populist leader, Vladimir Zhirinovsky, soon gained a considerable following thanks to his violent solutions for society's ills. Long before Putin suggested "wasting terrorists" in outhouses on national TV, Zhirinovsky was proposing nuclear strikes against the "bandits" in Chechnya.[13] In the election to the newly reformed lower chamber of parliament, the State Duma, in December 1993, his party gained 23 percent, or fourteen seats. For the still largely pro-Western intelligentsia, it was both a warning and a relief. Violent revanchists in parliament were hard to accept, but at the least it was a weakened parliament.

The nationalist revolution

There is a political chasm between the likes of Eduard Limonov and Konstantin Malofeyev, between the new-generation *natsbol* Zakhar Prilepin, who likewise turned into a Donbas battalion leader after a long stint as an oppositionist novelist, and the statist ideologue of the Russian Spring Yegor Kholmogorov. Limonov and Prilepin are or were (the former died in 2020) revolutionaries: nationalists who look to destroy the present, so that they can remake a future in their own image. Malofeyev and Kholmogorov are conservatives, looking to restore the (heavily mythologized) pre-revolutionary past. The post-Soviet nationalist movements of Russia are even more varied, disparate, and disunited than the liberal opposition. Throughout the Yeltsin and Putin administrations, until 2014, they were plagued by the same squabbles, vanities, and ambitions – even more violent in their case – that prevented them from ever forming a unified front. Statist nationalists argued with anti-immigration activists; both flirted with skinhead groups when it suited them, and denounced them when necessary, and, through the NBP and other quasi-leftist organizations, even maintained links with the Communist revanchists. They may have been just as out of touch with the Russian population at large as the liberal opposition, but they offered a message that resonated with them far more. In a nation paralyzed by a profound inferiority complex, they were, at the very least, not *blaming* Russians for their own ills, not discarding the Russian identity wholesale over the evils of its past in favor of a Western model. At a time when the educated elite and the government were trying so hard to be like someone else, implying that being Russian was somehow *wrong*, inferior, and when the worst forms of Russophobia paraded under the guise of a reckoning with the Stalinist past, the nationalists were telling over a hundred million Russians that it was OK, good even, to be who they were.

The trouble, of course, was how one *defined* Russian: by ethnicity, citizenship, or something else? For the ethno-nationalists it was by ethnicity (they were helped here by the fact that Soviet passports included the "nationality," i.e. Ukrainian, Armenian, or Jew, well into the 1990s), for the statists it was citizenship, but in the end neither really filled the void.

* * *

Konstantin Krylov, one of the most influential Russian nationalists to emerge during the Putin era, looked like a *kolobok*, an animated bread roll or pancake from Slavic fairytales that, in pagan times, represented the sun. Short, round, with his reddish beard, Krylov, of all things a Zoroastrian by faith, fitted that profile – a solid, robust presence who took such a vibrant joy in good food and drink that I found myself buying him all the vodka shots and toasted black bread he could eat. At a time when I was trying to get Western institutions to understand the grass-roots nature of Russia's intervention in Crimea and the Donbas, these boozy conversations seemed to be what expense accounts were created for.

"Imagine a communal apartment with five rooms," he liked to tell me, long ago, over Armenian mulberry moonshine. "When it's privatized, a room goes to the Kazakhs, another to the Ukrainians, the Chechens, the Georgians, the Latvians. The Russians get the corridor."

It was a questionable but also telling analogy. The nationalists felt they had lost out when the USSR was dissolved. The ethnic republics of the USSR, from Armenia to Uzbekistan, went on to form their own nations, but Russia remained a federation with twenty-one internal ethnic republics. The largest ethnicity without its own republic was Russian.

"Yeltsin couldn't even bring himself to call us Russians, or *Russky*," he complained. "What kind of word is *Rossiyanin?* It's Newspeak."

He was referring to the linguistic convolutions required by the government of a multi-ethnic, multi-confessional new state that was still trying to get round the fact that it was the Russian Federation, but not purely *ethnically* Russian. The word *Russky* was understood to mean ethnically and culturally Russian, while *Rossiysky* was being used more broadly, for the Russian state (after all, the original RSFSR had technically been *Rossiyskaya*, not *Russkaya*), and a *Rossiyanin* was the term that emerged for a citizen of the Russian state, who need not actually be ethnically *Russky*.[14] For nationalists like Krylov, it was an affront not to recognize that as more than three-quarters of the population of the Russian Federation were *Russky*, they ought to define its identity.

Yet he was a democrat, in his own terms. As someone who believed that only democratic institutions and free and fair elections could guarantee the kind of national state, in the name of the people, that he envisioned, Krylov joined the demonstrations of 2011–12, leading columns of nationalists down to Bolotnaya Square. Since 2006, he had been an organizer of the annual Russian March, a nationalist answer to the liberal March of Dissenters. He was already in trouble with the authorities over his work with the Movement Against Illegal Immigration (DPNI), which had taken part in thousands-strong protest rallies in central Moscow, and in 2011 was arrested and charged with inciting racial hatred for chanting "Stop Feeding the Caucasus" at a protest rally, a reaction to the extensive federal subsidies provided to the impoverished and unruly North Caucasus regions.

In our conversations, I noticed a barely suppressed xenophobia that Krylov was self-aware enough to both acknowledge honestly and yet rationalize. He praised the State of Israel and both admired and envied the Jews for their consolidated communities, looking to them as an example of what Russians could be if they could overcome their self-hatred, but also sounded embittered when he spoke about the issue. I had met him and Yegor Kholmogorov when both were editors of *Konservator*, a conservative newspaper that also had the liberal poet and activist Dmitry Bykov as editor. Krylov fell out with Kholmogorov over the latter's increasing support of Putin, whereas for Krylov, the Kremlin represented an anti-national, corrupt, oppressive, and autocratic regime.

"In fact, nationalism and democracy are practically the same thing," he said in a 2010 interview.

> Now it is important to rid Russian organizations of the last remaining prejudices towards civil society, democracy, and the free market. Authoritarian sympathies are more like a disease for the movement, like chickenpox or measles, you need to get over it. But those who recovered from the disease received immunity for life. In fact, I believe that the best democrats come from former fascists.[15]

While his xenophobia and imperialism deeply disturbed me, I couldn't help but admire his honesty and revulsion of performative self-flagellation on both a personal and a political level. The human being, he believed, was born free.

"My mother used to tell me, what did you borrow so that you owe so much?"

While Krylov focused most of his efforts on domestic issues, the problem of millions of Russians who became foreigners in their own homes overnight with the breakup of the Soviet Union directly affected how he and his cohorts saw national identity. When popular protests in Ukraine toppled President Yanukovych in 2014, and when the new, pro-Western government in Kyiv began to proclaim an increasingly nationalist policy in which the Russian language and identity had little place, counter-protests erupted in the Russian-speaking east of Ukraine, and Krylov believed it a point of honor to come to their aid. The Ukrainian separatists and the Russian nationalists who took up their cause sought to create a new state of

Novorossiya in the Donbas, reviving an older name for Russia's frontiers. Yet what they really seemed to be after was a New Russia, both a nation and an empire, both a republic and a despotate, one that rejected Western democratic notions even as it sought to recreate them. Perhaps it was the very Russia that many of them had envisioned in 1993, and then lost.

Novorossiya betrayed

Krylov joined forces with Igor Girkin, who was better known by his callsign Strelkov ("Shooter"), the former FSB officer who, with Malofeyev's financial support, led fifty-two volunteer militants over the Russian–Ukrainian border in April 2014 and headed up groups of pro-Russian separatists who saw in him the Russian intervention that they had so eagerly awaited since the annexation of Crimea in February. While he didn't fight himself, Krylov did help organize humanitarian aid to the civilians of the Donbas. Later, in 2016, he would try to form a political movement with Strelkov,[16] but by then the Kremlin had removed him from the Donbas and abandoned the grass-roots groups on which it had initially relied.[17] Indeed, it was killing off inconvenient separatist warlords who refused to take orders from Moscow, while co-opting the separatist statelets so that it could push them back into Ukraine, albeit on Moscow's terms, as little more than disruptive Trojan horses.

"I was asked to go there and talk to the fighters, mostly the ones who came from Russia," Krylov recalled. "There were a lot of them. Their motives were different. I was in a car riding with two, one was a completely gone Communist, and another was a Slavic pagan, and they bantered with each other. It was a national elevation, I had thought it was impossible, I had thought Russians were inert: but no, there were thousands who went."[18]

The Russian Spring, as this uprising came to be known, was described by its proponents in the language of the "color" revolutions in Ukraine and other former Soviet states and also of the Arab Spring, where people rose up to take charge of their destiny. From Limonov's *natsboly*, to Alexander Zaldostanov's Night Wolves biker gang, to Eurasian-imperialist monarchists raised on clippings from *Zavtra*, thousands took up the new cause. They hopped on trains and airplanes, first to Crimea and then to the Donbas, as a way of releasing some of the long-pent-up tensions about Russian national identity that the Kremlin had, until then, taken such great pains to suppress. The movement's initial alignment with the Kremlin was a marriage of convenience: as Putin moved to annex Crimea, he was unsure what to do with the eastern Ukrainian mainland, which lacked the same political resonance, strategic importance, or easy defensibility. Allowing and encouraging unofficial Russian volunteer fighters to help the rebels (most of whom were not even separatists at this stage) was an appealing strategy at first, until it mired the Kremlin in a war that it wasn't sure it even wanted to fight. After uprisings in Donetsk and Lugansk led to the proclamation of "people's republics," Putin told the separatists to hold off on referendums on independence from Ukraine.[19] Ultimately, though, he was unwilling at the time to go all in and recognize or annex these pseudo-states, nor was he willing to abandon what might be a useful weapon against a new Ukrainian government that didn't realize, as he saw it, that its rightful place was within Moscow's sphere of influence, and not America's. By that summer, Moscow had started imposing its control over the motley assortment of Ukrainian and Russian militants who had taken control of southeastern Donbas, and in August it sent limited contingents of regular troops to prevent them falling to government forces and help them cement their positions. But it wouldn't acknowledge this intervention, nor would it recognize the statelets or their referendums until 2022, shortly before it annexed them, too.

The Russian Spring and the Novorossiya that it tried to create, in other words, were a genuine movement that the Kremlin at first encouraged, then tried to co-opt, then betrayed and subsumed. However much we tend to equate opposition to Putin with the liberals, these, too, were rebels. When the nationalist volunteers went into the Donbas in the early weeks of the war, they had to dodge Russian border guards. Strelkov himself was said to have switched off his phone so that he could not be tracked, but also to prevent Malofeyev or some similar figure from trying to recall him.[20] Some of them genuinely believed they were simply anticipating Putin; others hoped he would support them, but were honestly unsure. They were right to be skeptical, because when Putin finally did stop dithering, he would not support this revolution but try to tame it, with political pressure, economic blackmail, corruption, and outright murder. If Strelkov himself, according to Krylov, used to have a portrait of Putin hanging behind his desk, by 2016 it was gone. For Krylov, Novorossiya ended the moment the Kremlin co-opted it. "They fucked us over," he said. "In the Donbas, they have come to the conclusion that Russia is a two-faced and treacherous partner, and I've heard this from them since 2015, one that you can't really rely on. But in the absence of other allies, they have no one else to turn to, and have to work with it."[21] In the words of one volunteer fighter, "For Russia we were like luggage without handles – it's hard to carry, but a pity to throw it away."[22]

Few among the supporters of Novorossiya had any doubts that the only thing holding Putin back from selling them to Kyiv – had the Ukrainian government been willing to pay his price – was not any commitment to their cause, but fear of alienating the nationalists at home. Those nationalists were, after all, increasingly numerous, and while in many ways they had been granted the scope to expand by the Kremlin's own acts, from the brutal suppression of Chechen secessionism to increasingly belligerent foreign policy rhetoric, they quickly outpaced Putin and were becoming impatient. The Russian Spring provided them at last with a unifying focus. "It was like a pyramid," Krylov said. "For every man with a machine gun who goes there, there are ten people who helped, supported him, gave him money; for each of those there are a hundred who approved, and for each a thousand who wrote an approving post. It was a massive uprising."[23] Movements from the neo-fascist Russian Imperial Legion, through ethnonationalist ones such as Cossack associations, to the *natsboly* all funneled volunteers to go and fight. Even after Moscow had decided to provide guns, money, and, where necessary, deployments of regular troops to keep the undeclared war going, though, there were few illusions as to how cynical and limited this commitment was. Many would go on to echo – albeit in more profane terms – the words of Ukrainian citizen but pro-Moscow militia commander Alexander Khodakovsky when in 2018 he wrote on social media about his disappointment at Putin's unwillingness either to recognize the self-declared states of Novorossiya or to annex them: "We believed in the reasonableness of Moscow, forgetting that there are people there, too, who are prone to making mistakes."[24]

I often wonder what Krylov would have thought about the full-scale invasion of 2022, but he passed away in the spring of 2020. I doubt, however, that he would have said anything positive about it: for Krylov, a big war was only in the interests of the Ukrainian nationalists.[25] As for the Kremlin, he felt it tended either to follow the lead of its Western "partners" or reflexively and unthinkingly oppose them, or else be swayed by whomever it fleetingly leaned on to shore up its legitimacy. In other words, it had no real ideology, no core moral or political values, just opportunism and an instinctive response – positive or negative – to what others might be doing, whether in Washington, DC, Kyiv, or Bolotnaya.

Either way, by 2022, the war had become a Kremlin project. It will take decades to understand fully what finally spurred

Putin on that February night to do something that seemed to make so little sense, even to the proponents of a Russian Donbas. Yet one explanation for the invasion and everything that happened after seems to be an attempt to contain and manage a potential national revolution. In hindsight, after the government had oppressed, expelled, and even assassinated its way through them, it became clear that it may well never have been the liberals whom Putin really had to fear, but the nationalists. With his annexation of Crimea that so quickly and powerfully raised their hopes, and then his vacillations over the Donbas – "Novorossiya" – that so quickly dashed them, he finally gave them that focus, that cause around which so many could unite in their disappointment with him. Furthermore, they were found not so much in the cafés and tech hubs of Moscow, but in the security services and the military. Men with guns: if he had tacitly unleashed and thought to use them on Ukraine in 2014, then unless he was careful, it was only a matter of time before they turned on him. Within a year of the start of the invasion, parliamentarian and former Presidential Administration staffer Oleg Matveychev was warning that "2023 will be very dangerous," because of the threat of the so-called "turbo-patriots": with the liberals having "all run away," then it was the nationalists who posed "the only danger to our state."[26]

That year did indeed prove dangerous, because turn on him they did. When mercenary leader Yevgeny Prigozhin led a march on Moscow with thousands of well-armed Wagner private military fighters, it was a taste of what could happen if nationalist forces were diverted from fighting Ukraine and turned on the Kremlin instead. Indeed, when the mutiny began, what was striking was just how unwilling the security apparatus seemed to do anything to stop it. They may not have joined this latter-day Pugachev, but instead they largely stood back as if they didn't care which opportunist devoured which. As it was, a scratch force of paratroopers, police, and security troops was eventually thrown together to try to prevent the mutineers from crossing the Oka River south of Moscow – although Prigozhin struck his deal before this was tested – but it certainly demonstrated the degree to which the monarch could no longer count on his troops. Indeed, it was some of the most nationalistic of his generals, such as Sergei Surovikin, known as "General Armageddon" for his brutal methods in Syria, who were later charged or dismissed under suspicion of having sympathized with the mutiny. The increasingly belligerent tone of the rhetoric coming from the government (especially the president's erstwhile liberal substitute Dmitry Medvedev, now reinvented as an outspoken nationalist imperialist) is less a reflection of Putin's own changing views than a desperate attempt to win back the so-called "turbo-patriots." If Putin could not fight the creeping nationalist insurgency, then he had to lead it.

While the Krylovs, Girkins, and Prigozhins may not have found an answer, they were at least asking the right question: what is Russia? However imperfectly, working societies develop some kind of overarching sense of belonging to something bigger than themselves. When that sense of identity or unity is absent, broken, or dysfunctional, some regimes and revolutionaries seek to create it by force, from above or below, respectively. Often, this is by a fascistic effort to mobilize society through creating a common enemy, to identify their nation through what it is not, rather than through what it is, finding an "other" within or without. Many of even the most tolerant modern democracies once had to go through this bloody process, whether in the persecution of Catholics in the sixteenth-century English Reformation, or the way the American Revolutionary War bound republicans, opportunists, impoverished farmers, and business magnates through a common tale of resistance to foreign imperial rule. "Novorossiya" was, in many ways, just such a project, started from below by chauvinists and opportunists in the Donbas and their Russian helpmeets, and then imposed from above as Putin co-opted it. Floundering in the face of the need for some national identity beyond cynicism and corruption, Putin tried to replicate this on a national scale at home, making the war – or the "special military operation," to use the approved euphemism – the central, mobilizing principle of his regime. As the joke in 2022 went, the "People's Republics" of Donetsk and Lugansk couldn't get themselves annexed by Russia for eight years, so they ended up annexing Russia instead.

As in 2014, Putin's attempt to align himself with the "turbo-patriots" in 2022 would fail. As before, he enjoyed a brief reconciliation, only to anger and alienate many nationalists when it became clear just how incompetent and unproductive his Ukrainian adventure would turn out to be. In April 2023, Strelkov was among the nationalists founding the "Club of Angry Patriots," but this has largely withered since his arrest in July of that year. Nonetheless, in the age of the internet – and especially for dissidents who can still meet and talk in the police station ready room, the battalion wardroom, and while sitting in a car during a political police surveillance stakeout – it is much easier to close down openly registered movements than to suppress the ideologies for which they stand. Liberal and nationalist dissidents alike may not currently be able to march and campaign, and their leaders may be in prison, in exile, or in the grave, but they have neither been won over, nor been defeated.

10

The Russian Winter

Making politics real again

It was 2006, long before a law banned smoking in public places, and Bilingua, a stylish hipster café in central Moscow frequented by the city's creative intelligentsia, was filled with tobacco haze. A young blogger from the youth wing of the liberal Yabloko party was moderating a political debate between a member of the opposition and a pro-Kremlin publicist. The debate series had become wildly popular, pitting political activists of all camps against each other in a no-holds-barred discussion. No topic seemed off limits: liberal parliamentarian Vladimir Ryzhkov faced off against the leader of the nationalist Movement Against Illegal Immigration Alexander Belov about the growing popularity of nationalist marches and their worrying neo-Nazi components;[1] libertarian Yulia Latynina argued about the democratic movement with the pro-Kremlin publicist-for-hire Maxim Kononenko. It was *the* place to be at the time, and not without drama or incident. In 2007, for instance, the neo-Nazi Maxim "Tesak" Martsinkevich showed up to a debate between Latynina and Kononenko and started shouting "Sieg heil!" – after which the moderator of the debates, who was a lawyer by training, filed criminal charges for inciting racial hatred under the controversial Article 282 of the Criminal Code,[2] and got him sent to prison.[3]

In those days, nothing seemed more vibrant than Russia's budding, beleaguered democracy. From the smoky caverns of Bilingua to the streets off Mayakovsky Square, where liberals held demonstrations in homage to the dissidents who had gathered there in Soviet times, to the blogosphere where the journalist Oleg Kashin and Maxim Kononenko argued about who was the most notorious "Kremlin cocksucker," there was something *real* about these debates. In hindsight, it is clear where their power came from: high politics in Putin's Russia was a façade, a pretence in which its actors went through the motions in a sort of de-fanged dress rehearsal of democracy. With a parliament emasculated by Boris Yeltsin in 1993 and with free elections further discredited with the vote rigging that delivered Yeltsin a victory in the 1996 presidential race against Communist leader Gennady Zyuganov, what was left for Vladimir Putin was simply to consolidate power, even as he observed the pretences and rituals of democratic procedure. Which was exactly what made those grass-roots political movements of the aughts so vibrant: on some deeper level, everyone, from their participants to members of the Kremlin charged with overseeing them, was secure in the knowledge that none of these debaters would take part in real politics, because politics in Russia at the time wasn't exactly real. You could, therefore, say anything.

In a particularly poignant exchange after one of these debates in December 2006, the moderator pointed his camera at Kononenko and asked, "Do you, as a running dog of the bloody Kremlin regime, support our debates?" He was using the epitaph almost ironically, a friendly chide between people of opposite camps, an exchange so innocent it could not be imagined a decade later. Not one afraid to alienate even his own friends, though, he was also exposing and even overcoming a taboo, prevalent in those circles, against associating with Kremlin supporters. "These debates are *great*," the half-drunk Kononenko proclaimed. "My [Kremlin] curators think they're great."[4]

The moderator was an energetic 30-year-old lawyer, entrepreneur, and budding political activist named Alexei Navalny. What set him apart was that he talked to everyone, even and especially those who did not necessarily share his views. This was at a time when much of the liberal opposition policed its own members to prevent association with those who were not *rukopozhatnyie*, or "handshakable" – those whose principles of opposition to the authorities did not align purely enough with their own. In that context, it wasn't just Navalny's nationalist sympathies, but his fearless association with anyone and everyone, while sticking to his own beliefs, that rubbed some within the dissident scene the wrong way. The following year, in 2007, the liberal Yabloko party expelled him over his participation in the nationalist Russian March, but this did nothing to stem his budding popularity.

Eighteen years later, neither Navalny nor Kononenko would be among the living. Kononenko, a Kremlin loyalist who was horrified by Russia's invasion of Ukraine in 2022 but continued making money as a propagandist for the Kremlin's RT television channel, drowned his depression in alcohol until it killed him in May 2024.[5] Navalny, in jail since 2021, having survived a near-fatal poisoning, died in his prison cell, the cause – state media suggested a blood clot[6] – so widely disputed, even officially,[7] that it left little doubt that, whether through the lingering effects of the poisoning or the poor conditions in prison or potentially something more sinister, it was the government that killed him. But the possibility of civic discussion and debate that they started, however ironically and superficially at first, opened the country's new civil society to the potential of integrating differing views and policies, of not *fearing*, at the very least, the *other*.

"We're the adults now"

It was a long way from that smoky café to an Arctic prison cell, but what Navalny had managed to accomplish in a decade was what arguably no Russian politician outside of office had managed before: he had started to build a grass-roots solidarity around a common cause that wasn't just *against* the Kremlin, but *for* a vision of a Russian future. He rebelled against the very notion that Russians weren't ready for democracy, that making politics *real* would herald too many dangers to be worth it. In that, he even borrowed a key tenet of the nationalists: that Russians – whether as an ethnos or a nationality – were already good enough. His, therefore, was a simple, optimistic vision: corruption is eating away at our country, and it's time to take back our laws from a government that abuses them, and use them to live like the normal European country that we are. Sure, we might have our cultural uniqueness, our painful and complex history, and our political disagreements with our Western neighbors, and even with each other. But the essential point was simple: we are *already* a democratic country founded on the rule of law, just like any other European country. It's simply that our leaders haven't gotten the memo yet, and we haven't made sure that they have. Vladimir Putin's Kremlin had spent more than a decade trying to impose the dictatorship of the law in letter, while gradually becoming a lawless dictatorship in spirit. Navalny emerged claiming that Russians already had laws. They just needed to start using them.

He did so first through a series of legal exposés of government corruption and then, more crucially, through his Anti-Corruption Foundation (ACF), which he created in 2011 to conduct investigations of government officials and use legal means to combat corruption. Intended to push officials to carry through on promised reform, the initiative managed to resonate and find a constituency that ran through the working poor in the regions and the affluent middle class in the cities, liberal intellectuals and patriotic nationalists, hopeful youth and angry pensioners. It also reputedly had sympathetic patrons among liberal businessmen close to the Kremlin: one of its initial benefactors was Vladimir Ashurkov, a top manager at Alfa Group, the country's largest privately owned investment conglomerate. While Ashurkov was public in his support and, indeed, was persuaded to leave Alfa Group by its chief, the oligarch Mikhail Fridman, over his closeness to Navalny,[8] it was widely believed that there were other, not so public, benefactors. As early as the mid-aughts, Navalny was buying minority stakes in state companies not for the sake of profit, but to better monitor and expose corrupt schemes using public funds, in his role as an activist shareholder.[9] This undoubtably earned him connections in high places – and made him enemies and supporters alike. It also helped him do something that other activists had failed to achieve: building alliances with powerful economic interests, from VTB Bank to the Transneft pipeline company. They may not necessarily have had an interest in wider political reform, but they, too, were tired of being stolen from, and they saw in Navalny someone who was standing up for their concrete, tangible interests. As he publicized their concerns, they helped him document and expose cases of graft.

When the Kremlin, at the request of Moscow Mayor Sergei Sobyanin, allowed Navalny to run in the September 2013 mayoral elections, he won 27 percent of the vote. Of course, Sobyanin, who had publicly urged municipal deputies to sign petitions for Navalny, had his own angle. He sought to use the popular blogger to shore up the legitimacy of the poll when he won, as he did with 51 percent of the vote. Nonetheless, it was striking that a key figure within the government was eager enough to engage with Navalny, even in elections he knew he would win, thanks to "administrative resource" and the authority of his position, at the same time as the Kremlin was trying to put him in a prison camp. At the time, after all, Navalny was on trial for alleged embezzlement from the Kirovles timber company, and in July 2013 was sentenced to five years in prison in what was widely seen as politically motivated prosecution. After thousands of protesters gathered steps away from the Kremlin on the day of the sentencing, though, prosecutors, in an unprecedented move, suddenly appealed the sentence.[10] Later that fall, it was suspended altogether. Even Vladimir Putin, speaking to a youth camp that August, called the Kirovles verdict "strange"[11] – a powerful signal that indicated a sudden shift in the Kremlin's approach to Navalny. The Kremlin's new leniency raised questions among Navalny's skeptics. Yabloko leader Grigory Yavlinsky would later accuse him of being not only a nationalist, but a "Kremlin agent" as well, precisely over the government's initial handling of the Kirovles case.[12]

Labeling anyone who manages to forge connections with different camps – especially with those in power – a "Kremlin agent" is a popular tactic within opposition groups, but it has largely served only to divide and insulate them from each other. In some ways, it has also served the most repressive government purposes, of keeping civil society atomized and therefore weak. As one FSB officer in the Kirov region described to Mark Galeotti in 2012, "My job is, well, you could say that it's to make sure that if there is new Solidarity, you know, the Polish union, well, it doesn't start in my region."[13]

Navalny was no "Kremlin agent." Rather, he was doing something that seemed unprecedented: building solidarity not just within the opposition, but out in the country, and even among some in the government elites. In 2017, he angered supporters and critics alike when he took up the dare of nationalist fighter and Donbas veteran Igor Girkin to hold a public debate. For nearly an hour and a half, the two argued about corruption and patriotism, and even as Navalny's supporters decried him for associating with a war criminal, Navalny the lawyer held fast to his legalist principles: "If he is a war criminal, it is up to the courts, not Alexei Navalny."[14] Far from marginalizing him, the criticism seemed only to expand his appeal. By 2017, when Navalny announced his presidential campaign, he had head-quarters in sixty of Russia's eighty-nine regions and republics. The following year, while the authorities, predictably, refused to register his candidacy, he mustered 124 regional delegates in Moscow for a summit to found a new party, the Future Russia.[15] At one point in 2017, Navalny's associate Vladimir Volkov told me that the opposition's strategy was waiting out the Kremlin: if it was too dangerous to protest now, the key thing was to work on building up networks and supporters across the country who could and would act once it became safe to do so.

And so, despite a criminal conviction and an open criminal investigation, despite ten arrests between 2011 and 2019 alone,[16] despite the persecution and extra-legal attacks against him (including twice being splashed with the antiseptic green dye known as *zelyonka*, which left him with impaired vision in his right eye) and also against his supporters across the country, Navalny had created a nationwide movement. Through projects ranging from the Smart Elections program, which sought to help voters select independent and oppositionist candidates who were most likely to get into office and encourage people to take part in local and regional elections, to supporting efforts to hold local officials accountable through the courts for the quality of municipal services, Navalny's team had developed a grass-roots network of lawyers, activists, and social workers. In effect, it worked as a sort of shadow civil society in a country where, for centuries, the government had held a veto over public organization and activity.

To be sure, Navalny was no saint, nor did he aspire to the moral purity of many Soviet-era dissidents. He could be ruth-less; he and especially his ACF staff were not immune to the pernicious habit of accusing those who disagreed with them of being Kremlin collaborators.[17] In 2013, Navalny fell out with his ally and one-time campaigner Maxim Katz, one of the young, urban oppositionists who managed to win and hold a municipal council seat in Moscow during the Snow Revolution. Three years later, Navalny publicly called him a grifter, while his campaign manager, Leonid Volkov, alleged that while he was on their campaign staff in 2013, Katz threatened to report any unlawful activity among the staff to the authorities. Katz denied this and claimed that Navalny saw him as a rival because the political projects he headed were gaining a comparable online readership.[18] Either way, their feud continued and flared up again in 2024, when Katz, now also in exile over his anti-war views, asked the ACF leadership about widespread allegations that their treasurer, Alexander Zheleznyak, had embezzled money. Instead of replying to Katz's inquiry, ACF leaders accused him of working for Russian intelligence.[19]

And yet, whether because of the success of Navalny's approach or the optimistic zeitgeist of the Snow Revolution, other groups – supporters, competitors, and critics of Navalny alike – were inspired to form pathways of negotiation and feedback between activists and local officials even at a time when few could actually run for office. In 2014, now working from abroad, Khodorkovsky had revived his Open Russia organization to help civil society groups and independent politicians form networks and hone their campaign skills. Drawing on Navalny's success with his Smart Elections project, he launched the Open Elections platform, helping opposition candidates most likely to win against the United Russia party. Earlier in 2012, Maxim Katz, together with blogger Ilya Varlamov, had founded the City Projects Foundation, a grassroots organization that worked with locals to improve urban environments not just in Moscow, but eventually a number of regional cities where they established branches. Later on, drawing on both Smart Elections and Open Elections, Katz launched his own, dubbed Political Uber, aimed at simplifying the registration process for people who hoped to register for local elections.

As for Navalny, his political pragmatism went beyond keeping his rivals at bay and involved outreach with the more established opposition. He made inroads with those members of the Communist Party who, unlike their aging and compromised leaders, actually thought the job of the opposition was to oppose. Arguably, Moscow city Communist leader Valery Rashkin's incautious decision to thank Navalny for "smart voting" and then offer to leak him information for another of his corruption exposés was the point at which his card was marked.[20] Within a few months, he was arrested on charges of illegal hunting and lost his position.[21] Yet it had been an open secret for some time that Rashkin was cooperating with Navalny and nothing had been done until he went public about it. It was the sight of a moderately senior figure within the systemic opposition openly forging such an alliance that was unacceptable for the Kremlin, precisely because, there and then, Navalny was demonstrably bridging that centuries-old alienation between the government and the governed, and between different political camps. Having honed his practice in the political theater of Putin's Russia, Navalny was making politics *real.*

By 2020, the Kremlin had finally decided that even making a martyr out of him was a small risk to take compared to letting him continue building his base at large. After surviving a poisoning with the nerve agent Novichok, Navalny himself prank-called Konstantin Kudryavtsev, one of the FSB officers involved, and got him to give a detailed description of how exactly a military-grade nerve agent was rubbed on the crotch area of his underwear and how he cleaned his trousers afterwards. The whole exchange was recorded and published, with an incredulous Navalny trying not to laugh as Kudryavtsev asked if they were speaking on a secure line.[22] Putin called the exposé a falsification, but added, tellingly, "If there was such a desire [to successfully poison Navalny], it would have been done."[23]

Already afraid of Navalny but not too sure what exactly to do with him, the Kremlin felt that this last humiliating exposé crossed a line. The calculus, if there was one, seemed to have been that he would either die in the poisoning or flee the country – indeed, an initially reluctant Kremlin facilitated his evacuation to Germany for treatment, in response to international pressure.[24] Abroad, after all, was exactly where it wanted him, just another embittered émigré railing at Putin from exile. But Navalny called the Kremlin's bluff and did neither: once he was well, he decided to return. By doing so, it set him apart from so many other members of the opposition, especially some of his more liberal former cohorts, who had long ago left the country. It established him not just as someone willing to put his faith in the rule of law (knowing full well that he would be fighting an uphill battle that he could well lose), but as a patriot who loved his country, and who chose to believe in it. It also spelled his doom.

It was understandable, then, that Navalny's sudden death in February 2024 dealt such a demoralizing blow not only to his supporters, but also to those in Russia and abroad who had dared to believe that the country had a future. Kilometer-long lines formed as crowds waited at the church where his coffin was to arrive for the funeral, with confused police standing by, not exactly sure what to do. Supporting Navalny publicly had become a crime punishable by jail ever since ACF was classified as an "extremist organization" in 2021, but the authorities also seemed to be aware that this was not a crowd daunted by them. At his protest rallies, Navalny would chant, "Who is the power?" and the crowd would roar back "We are the power!" Of all the jailed dissidents, he had the greatest potential to someday emerge, in a post-Putin Russia, as a popular, democratically elected leader. Those hopes now seemed dashed.

And yet there was another, much subtler glint of hope in the days after his death. As people emerged from their mourning, their drinking, and their depressions, a common refrain among his supporters became, "If he's taught us anything, it's that we're the adults now."[25] Instead of waiting for a savior from above, one like Navalny, they would have to build their salvation themselves.

The dissidents abroad

After the invasion of Ukraine in February 2022 and the sudden passage of draconian laws curtailing free speech, Russia saw an exodus of as many as a million people, not just over their political convictions, but over fears of the generally repressive climate that had descended on the country. Among them were many members of Navalny's team and ACF. They joined many who had left years earlier. Garry Kasparov had fled persecution in 2013. Mikhail Khodorkovsky left for Switzerland as an unwritten condition of his pardon in 2013, and has been living in London since 2015. Mikhail Kasyanov, the former prime minister and leader of the liberal Parnas Party, left the country for Latvia after the 2022 invasion. Together with Khodorkovsky, he tried to unify the Russian opposition in exile with a series of anti-Putin summits, but despite their attempts at coalition-building, these groups remain as splintered as they were in Russia.

The parliamentarian Ilya Ponomaryov, who marched with a megaphone through the streets of Astrakhan as part of the White Ribbon movement that warm April day in 2012 when so much was still possible, would later flee to Ukraine, dividing his time between Kyiv and Washington, DC. Two years later, after the Kremlin launched its full-scale invasion of Ukraine, he turned to armed dissent. Joining forces with the National Republican Army (NRA), a Russian militant group, he called for armed attacks against the Putin regime, including against civilians on Russian territory, as the only effective form of resistance. Ponomaryov described the NRA as consisting mostly of "educated people with fire in their eyes" who were "probably no different from those people who supported the Bolsheviks at the beginning of the twentieth century." His own role, he continued, was to publicize the activities of the NRA and offer "help with security . . . and material-technical" support.[26] Trying to unite exiled politicians, he helped launch the Congress of People's Deputies, a self-styled "interim parliament and potential successor parliament" consisting of deputies at some point elected to Russia's federal or, more often, local parliaments who opposed the annexation of Crimea.[27] Yet it had limited support due to stringent requirements that its members vocally oppose the war in Ukraine at a time when doing so, even in exile, could be dangerous. More to the point, a number of Russians questioned its legitimacy as a representative parliament without electoral procedure,[28] but, in particular, its endorsement of violent resistance and terror turned a number of Ponomaryov's supporters against him and diminished support for his cause.

Meanwhile, Khodorkovsky cofounded the Russian Anti-War Committee, but also found little success. The exiled members of ACF wanted nothing to do with him. "We constantly tell the guys from the Anti-Corruption Foundation . . . that it would be great if we all met not only in front of television cameras, but sat down at the table," he said in January 2024.[29]

Navalny's widow, Yulia, vowed to continue her husband's work abroad, and has made powerful appeals before the European Parliament, while also encouraging Russians at home to do what they can to stand up in support of Navalny's values.[30] But while some have expressed hope that she could emerge as a charismatic leader in her own right, without having been elected to any posts, she, too, lacks a formal mandate to represent Russians abroad.

Ilya Yashin and Vladimir Kara-Murza – two liberal, pro-Western opposition activists – were released in 2024 after spending two years in Russian jails in a prisoner exchange that the Kremlin used to get rid of some of its most vocal critics without having to kill them. There is an understanding that no matter their stature at home, there are limits to what émigré dissidents can do from the outside. While in prison, Yashin regularly published sketches of his conversations with fellow convicts – some of them soldiers who fought in the war and supported Putin – as a way of helping bridge the gap between the liberal opposition and those it had most alienated.[31] Even in prison, Yashin felt he was making a difference, and he vocally protested his release, saying he did not consent to it. He understood, too, that the dialogue that mattered was not so much with anti-war Russians, who needed no convincing, but with those who were complacent or who outright supported the war. "We need to talk to them, and we need to pull these people out of the shackles of Putin's propaganda," Yashin said at a demonstration after his release in Berlin. "We need to explain that this monstrous war against Ukraine . . . is a war against Russia too, because this war is crippling . . . entire generations. It is taking away the future of our country."[32]

Yet Yashin's eagerness to engage with those he disagreed with was an exception to the rule, and it highlighted the difficulties émigré dissidents face trying to continue their work from outside the country. The chief struggles that plagued them at home – splintering, bickering, competing for leadership – have been compounded abroad. "They are like sharks battling for a small pie, for their own tiny slice in it," an exiled oppositionist said of them, though she singled out Yulia Navalnaya as a politician with a great deal of strength and poise. "The scope for civic action is so limited by the government that it becomes a war of the vanities."[33]

Indeed, so long as the chief objective of many of these groups is to produce an opposition that can claim some kind of leadership role over Russia, in effect a government in exile, these groups are bound to face splintering and marginalization. This is due not just to their own cliquishness, but to their lack of connection to Russians back home. The Free Russia Foundation, for example, which has done a great deal of valuable advocacy on behalf of the Russian opposition, has succeeded in legislative engagement, but that has been largely abroad. There is little understanding of how exactly this kind of engagement reflects back, or is indeed perceived by, people at home. "I don't think people understand this," said an exiled journalist trying to engage with Russians in Russia. "They don't see what all this looks like from the perspective of a Russian in Yekaterinburg, who is living in a completely different reality. He doesn't want to be lectured by people abroad living in safety and comfort." The main opposition in exile, he said, "hasn't really accomplished that much, and that creates certain perceptions."[34]

There are other groups working not towards political goals but towards helping the millions of Russians who have fled the country since 2022, who are reviled at home and often harassed and maligned in exile. Kovcheg (Ark) claims to be the largest, helping émigrés with legal support and adaptation to their new countries, as well as supporting anti-war Russians at home,[35] while Georgia-based Idite Lesom (Go by the Forest – an expression meaning "get lost") more explicitly has sought to help Russians flee the country to evade mobilization. Meanwhile, organizations like the Russian Democratic Society, in addition to supporting Russian émigrés, help raise funds for Ukraine, supporting towns hit hardest by Russian attacks to rebuild generators and clinics.[36] These groups arguably have more potential to overcome the social fractures that have been exacerbated by Russian government repressions, though what they can do from afar remains limited. While many of these may one day return to Russia and play a pivotal road in rebuilding a new country, the key to and the glimpse of the country's future lies elsewhere – back home, in Russia, in the confines of a political winter.

A new civil society

Navalny may have been among the most charismatic and successful of the protest leaders seeking to build a strong, nationwide network, but he wasn't the only one. The failure of the protests of 2011–12 had a curiously invigorating effect on many younger activists, who had their baptisms of fire at these demonstrations. Commentators mulling over how to channel the activist drive in a politically repressive environment where the opposition has little leverage revived a nineteenth-century movement called "the theory of small action." This focused on promoting local interests rather than fighting the leviathan of the government. Other activists and journalists criticized this approach as useless and even collaborationist, wasting time on petty matters rather than addressing their root cause.[37] Theory aside, though, the practice demonstrated unexpected results. Indeed, one might even suggest that Russians' increasing willingness to donate time and money to charity from around this time may reflect on some small level this new reorientation away from grand abstract causes and towards practical goals. According to the British Charities Aid Foundation, in 2010, Russia was close to the bottom of the global league tables, yet another depressing index of social atomization, but by 2013, it had begun to rise from this low base, and "nearly 40 million Russians (33% of the population) provided direct help to strangers in need."[38]

Activists involved in the protest movement soon separated into clusters focusing on a range of apparently non-political niche initiatives. A long-haul truckers' strike in late 2015 became something larger when they reached out to wider constituencies to protest new road pricing tolls imposed as part of the Platon system. Beginning in Dagestan, the truckers' protests spread to other regions, reaching Moscow with a "rolling roadblock" that alarmed federal authorities.[39] Within a few months, the strike had spread to forty-three Russian regions,[40] and was even able to attain limited success. The Communist Party spoke out in support of the protesters,[41] one of the rare times that any systemic – tame – opposition party has done so in the past decade, while the government reduced the fines levied on truckers who fell foul of Platon, and offered talks. Soon after the protests began, the Kremlin lowered the penalties from 450,000 rubles to 5,000 rubles.[42] The fact that Platon was half owned by a state corporation and half by Igor Rotenberg, son of one of Putin's closest friends, the oligarch Arkady Rotenberg, gave a particular political dimension to this issue. On the one hand, it helped mobilize non-truckers to the cause, but, on the other, it allowed the opposition forces to use it to demonstrate to a blue-collar constituency how the lack of checks and balances at the top of the system hit them directly in their pockets.

In 2019, when investigative journalist Ivan Golunov was arrested after police planted drugs on him, a public outcry involving protests and petitions not only got Golunov released, but also helped launch a criminal investigation against five police officers involved in the fabrication, leading to their imprisonment. Interior Minister Vladimir Kolokoltsev even sacked two police generals, including the head of the Moscow drug squad. What was particularly noteworthy about the case was how many different voices – from Navalny's ACF to a slew of even pro-Kremlin newspapers – united in solidarity to stand up for Golunov and against police abuse.[43] It was a small step, and it wasn't without its pitfalls. The case highlighted, for example, that Golunov got justice because he had a whole community of journalists and public figures behind him, which was not something on which the thousands of ordinary Russians finding themselves facing similar abuses could rely. But in its tiny way, it set a precedent, and created certain expectations, both for civic activists learning how to achieve their goals, and for state authorities learning how to negotiate with dissenters and take them seriously.

There were many other examples of successful results-driven political and civic activism – from Khodorkovsky's aforementioned Open Russia to Katz's City Project Foundation and Political Uber. But possibly the best – and one that continues to work in Russia's current repressive conditions – is that of OVD.info, a human rights and media project launched in 2011 to provide legal aid to protesters and those persecuted for their political beliefs. Partnering with the Memorial human rights group, OVD.info spread across the country and by 2023 included over 5,000 volunteers in addition to their staff: lawyers, experts, and consultants who offered a free twenty-four-hour hotline, lawyers' visits, and legal defense in courts.[44] After the invasion of Ukraine in 2022, OVD.info spread its efforts in particular to help those speaking out against the war. Its research arm, meanwhile, covers protests, monitors and analyzes repressions, and reports on politically motivated persecution, making it one of the few statistical resources in an increasingly closed political climate. It continued to do this despite the fact that, in 2021, Russian authorities designated the organization a "foreign agent" and blocked its website, hampering its financing and operation.[45]

Meanwhile, even at a time when competitive elections are stifled, with inconvenient candidates jailed and parties discouraged from taking part in local polls, and amid artificially engineered apathy, the watchdog Golos identified real political competition during mayoral and local municipal elections held in the summer of 2024 – a testament to continued progress despite tightening repressions.[46]

Why are all these cases important, and do they represent anything beyond a temporary revival of civil society, quickly quashed by the repressions that descended upon the country in 2022? Can one even speak of a civil society at a time when reporting honestly about the war is punishable by jail? They are important because, despite the temptation to write off the last decade as a period of civic retreat, these clusters of local and national grass-roots initiative demonstrate exactly the opposite. They may not technically represent rebellions, dissent, or revolt, but in their own way they offer something more important, and potentially more lasting: rather than tearing down repressive edifices, they are building something alongside them, with thousands of lawyers, activists, labor organizers, community volunteers, and municipal council candidates establishing networks and practices, accumulating and honing civil skills, and fighting to build electoral procedures that may be brought to bear in subsequent years. These are the nameless people working with discreet solidarity. They are not the ones lobbing Molotov cocktails and making the news, they are the ones quietly talking to the very people the rest of the world has chosen to isolate, hoping, little by little, to prevail upon them for the sake of the activists and citizens they are defending and empowering. In doing so, they are overcoming one of the chief hurdles that the rebels have faced for centuries in Russia: the alienation between various sectors of society, and especially the alienation between the government and the people.

On a daily basis, they interact with police, security officers, prosecutors, judges, and officials, advocating on behalf of the rights of citizens, holding them to account and teaching them, little by little, to act in accordance with their country's laws. Take OVD.info's 5,000 volunteers, and consider how often each one of those engages with a member of the state apparatus. In April 2024 alone, its volunteers visited at least a dozen police stations and attended over a hundred trials in sixteen towns across Russia, achieving the retrial or acquittal of twelve administrative cases – in a country with a 99.6 percent conviction rate.[47] As for criminal offenses, in that month they provided aid to ninety-eight people facing charges.[48] Over the course of a year, that translates to at least a thousand government officials who were confronted, on a person-to-person level and on a regular basis, about the legality of what they were doing. It is not impossible to imagine that some of those thousands may quietly shift their tactics, and while continuing to work within a repressive government machine, will try to avoid egregious abuses, or even work from within to reform the system. It's a dangerous, uphill battle, and it's a great deal harder and far less glorious than penning withering indictments of Russia's imperialist culture from the safety and luxury of Western campuses, but when the next Thaw arrives, these thousands of nameless Russians will have formed the building blocks of a new, unique Russian democracy.

The Russia of the future

The fight for democracy that began in Russia in the late 1980s turned out not to be about defeating an authoritarian government after all. The decaying Party state defeated itself. The challenge that proved insurmountable was the same challenge that democracies around the world are facing today: learning how to talk to people you dislike and with whom you disagree, and finding common ground. At some point during the next political Thaw, the liberal opponents to Putin's regime will have to sit down and have a conversation with the nationalists and the turbo-patriots. They will have to talk openly and frankly about the war in Ukraine – and that will mean listening to and accepting different and irreconcilable points of view. They will have to have a conversation about the future of Russia, the social and legal contract between the rulers and the ruled, and on what exactly that contract will be founded. And they will inevitably disagree. At that point, each side will be faced with a critical choice: look for rhetorical, informational, or possibly even actual weapons to defeat your opponent and impose your own will upon the rest of the country, or look instead for bridges and compromises. The history of Russia has shown that the rebel who sweeps away the edifices of the government in the name of defeating repression ends up putting the crown upon his own head. With an intimate knowledge of the kind of existential threat that he himself faces from the opposition, as well as a narrow base of support, he is keenly aware of the violence and volatility of total regime change, and also his own vulnerability. So, whether it is Lenin dispatching the Red Guards to close down the Constituent Assembly rather than negotiate with the rival revolutionary parties which had actually won the election, or Yeltsin shelling the White House, the rebel-turned-tsar will deploy all his resources towards silencing dissent rather than take a chance and listen to the new dissenters and see if he can work with them. Many of the dissenters, themselves radicalized by government repression, will fight with the same belligerence in a struggle to defeat what has so clearly become their foe. The cycle, therefore, repeats with tragic predictability.

The next choice, therefore, will be the same one that Russians have faced at regular intervals: revolution or evolution? Building on existing laws and institutions and reforming them will be a lot more difficult (and less exciting) than sweeping them away wholesale, and the question will be whether the leaders deciding Russia's fate will have the courage to resist both wholesale revolt, on the one hand, and passive inertia, on the other. At their disposal, they will have the channels and networks that have been created both by those in power and by civil society groups. They can help build the kind of bridges between civil society and the state that, in the end, can bolster each. It will be in the interests of the statists, the patriots, and the conservatives to convince their opponents that a strong government will make them, their opponents, stronger as well. And it will be in the interests of the liberals to convince their opponents that a strong civil society makes for a strong government.

It can also help close the other fissures which for so long have perversely weakened both the state and the rebels: the failure to connect different social estates and form wider solidarities.

For the state, this atomization leaves it vulnerable, forced to adopt maximalist solutions because it lacks a reliable foundation for its rule. On the one hand, the elite were perennially mistrusted or openly rebellious. Ivan IV sought to blackmail his boyars by retreating to his *oprichnina*, and relying on his *oprichniki* to cow them, until he realized that this new elite was no more loyal, and arguably rather more dangerous, than the old. The Cossacks, personally bound to the tsar, seemed to represent a way of building a separate power base until Pugachev and his ilk proved that obligations go both ways and they can also be the state's worst enemies. Catherine and her successors were forced to return to a reliance on the regular aristocracy and gentry, for all their concerns about their loyalty and capability. The Decembrists set the broodingly suspicious tone of Nicholas I's reign. The Bolsheviks in effect tried to reshape society, something brought to its murderous climax by Stalin, but the new elite of the *nomenklatura* (the name for the system which limited key positions to the politically approved) quickly acquired the same habits as their tsarist predecessors. They did not so much rebel – at least, not until 1991 – as inadvertently undermine the state through the backsliding and embezzlement that would be such a scourge in the 1970s.

On the other hand, the state seemed unable to genuinely rely on its subjects, for all that they may sing hymns to the tsar as God's representative on earth, or attend meetings of the factory's Communist Party cell, or duly vote for United Russia. Such expressions of superficial loyalty were often products of coercion, or a simple lack of alternatives. In the absence of good options, the truly desperate were otherwise often driven to bad ones: whether the chance to join Pugachev's rising, or to go and fight in the Donbas in a cause the Kremlin hadn't yet decided if it wanted to back.

When co-option fails, the government thus turns again to repression. After the 1905 Revolution, Tsar Nicholas II began bringing more and more regions under special "Reinforced

Guard" and "Extraordinary Guard" provisions – in effect, martial law – precisely because he felt he could trust neither the peasants nor the local officials meant to control them. At first Putin relied on propaganda, targeted repression, and a theatrical facsimile of democracy to control the population, while seeking to cultivate the emerging middle class. The Snow Revolution then shook him so much that he overreacted, turning to authoritarian rule and, eventually, martial law by other names, never daring properly to trust and reconcile with a discontented public.

Yet the rebels and dissidents also felt isolated, unable to assemble the kind of cross-estate alliances which might allow them to demand change with authority. What was left, many of them felt, but violence? When the peasants rejected the *narodniki* when they "went to the people," the radicals instead turned to terrorism, much like Ilya Ponomaryov now claims, to the horror of many of his former allies and supporters, that "armed resistance remains the only means to challenge Putinism."[49] While many of the Soviet-era dissidents did understand the need for wider alliances as a precondition for effective political change, their own perspectives and the activities of the KGB helped keep them apart, such that even when they spoke *for* the workers, they too rarely were able to speak *with* them. And yet Russians of every class marched in support of Boris Yeltsin in 1990–1 and resisted the 1991 August Coup. While many of their hopes were dashed in the 1990s, the new wave of activists and opposition leaders seem to a degree to have learned a number of lessons.

The main one is that democracy doesn't happen overnight, after whatever tyrant in power has been deposed. While Russian history, like any other, may be cyclical, these cycles are not repetitions. Without in any way excusing or minimizing his abuses, Putin is not Stalin and will never be. Millions of political prisoners perished in the Gulag system, but according to OVD.info, there have been 3,984 politically motivated persecutions since 2012, less than half of which were serving jail time as of 2024.[50] This is a lot, but historical perspective matters. It matters too that when workers organized a strike in Novocherkassk in 1962, the authorities killed twenty-six people, while independent organizers wasted away in psychiatric hospitals. By contrast, the biggest worker strikes in Putin's Russia were usually handled by a mix of co-option and concession – and, rarely, targeted but brief arrests for some of the organizers.[51] And while the Decembrists consisted of armed officers willing to kill to overthrow the tsar, the Snow Revolution was about peaceful, legal protest.

At any given point in the cycle, however repressive the current turn, there are new options and opportunities for society to evolve. Some of the most effective grass-roots institutions were being developed in the last two decades not by political activists eager to proselytize, but by human rights advocates, charities, and local campaigners trying to help people defend and use their lawful rights rather than promoting any political platform. Building a new Russia will depend on closing not just the gap between rulers and ruled, but also gaps amongst the ruled.

After all, violent revolt is typically a result of weak democratic institutions, whereby dissenting voices lack peaceful, legal means to be heard and to affect the way their society functions. Having missed the chance to talk it out meaningfully in parliament, the revanchists are now fighting it out on the battlefields of eastern Ukraine. Compromise is the inevitable byproduct of the checks and balances that make those peaceful, legal means possible in the first place. Russia will always have its rebels. The real Russian Spring that will inevitably follow its Winter will depend on whether the dance of the rebel and the tsar is bloody or civil. A solidarity between the two – if one can be formed – will ultimately create the foundations of a state strong and secure enough that it will have no need to start wars against its neighbors or to jail, maim, and kill its dissenters.

Notes

Chapter 1 The Optimists

1 Alena Popva, interview with the author, Washington, DC, November 2022.

2 Amie Ferris-Rotman, "Trolling the patriarchy with photos of battered women – one woman's quest to change Russia's domestic violence laws," *Elle*, February 22, 2018.

3 Anna Arutunyan, *The Putin Mystique: Inside Russia's Power Cult* (Bloxham: Skyscraper Publications, 2014), p. 285.

4 From the author's online correspondence with Oleg Kashin, June 2017.

5 Andrew Roth, "Journalist Oleg Kashin knows who tried to kill him," *The Washington Post*, September 18, 2018.

6 From the author's online correspondence with Oleg Kashin, June 2017.

7 Gini Index – Russian Federation. World Bank data. https://data .worldbank.org/indicator/SI.POV.GINI?locations=RU.

8 "Russia's 'YouTube policeman' Dymovsky accused of fraud," BBC, January 22, 2010. http://news.bbc.co.uk/1/hi/8475649.stm.

9 Yegor Sozayev-Guriev, "Путин невиданно открылся для оппозиции и экспертов [Putin opened up to the opposition and experts in an unprecedented way]," *Izvestiya*, September 20, 2013.

10 Nadezhda Azhgikhina, "Is Russia waking up?" *The Nation*, June 6, 2019.

11 This became Navalny's campaign slogan during his unsuccessful 2018 presidential bid. https://2018.navalny.com/post/492/.

12 "Russia PM Vladimir Putin accuses US over poll protests," BBC, December 8, 2011. https://www.bbc.co.uk/news/world-europe-16084743.

13 Ibid.

14 "'Яблоко' выдвигает Явлинского и отвергает Навального [Yabloko nominates Yavlinsky and rejects Navalny]," BBC, December 18, 2011. https://www.bbc.com/russian/russia/2011/12/111218_yabloko_yavlinsky_presidency.

15 "Navalny boards flight for Russia," Associated Press, January 17, 2021. https://www.rferl.org/a/navalny-boards-flight-for-russia/31049881.html.

16 "Russia: Navalny arrested at border control," Sky News, January 17, 2021. https://www.youtube.com/watch?v=1LVQC5xSbiI.

Chapter 2　The Traitor and the Tsar

1 "Putin refused to say Navalny's name. Here's what he called him instead," *The Moscow Times*, 28 April 2024.

2 "Первое послание Курбского Ивану Грозному [Kurbsky's first message to Ivan the Terrible]," Electronic Library of the Pushkin House of the Russian Academy of Sciences. http://lib.pushkinskijdom.ru/Default.aspx?tabid=9105.

3 Ian Grey, *Ivan the Terrible* (London: Hodder & Stoughton, 1964), p. 159.

4 "Переписка Ивана Грозного с Андреем Курбским [Correspondence between Ivan the Terrible and Andrei Kurbsky]," Infolio Electronic Library. http://www.infoliolib.info/rlit/drl/grozny.html.

5 Alexander Yanov, *The Origins of Autocracy: Ivan the Terrible in Russian History*, trans. Stephen Dunn (London: University of California Press, 1981), p. 11.

6 Andrei Pavlov and Maureen Perrie, *Ivan the Terrible: Profiles*

in Power (London: Pearson Education Limited, 2003), pp. 60–1.

7 Grey, *Ivan the Terrible*, p. 73.

8 Pavlov and Perrie, *Ivan the Terrible*, p. 92.

9 Grey, *Ivan the Terrible*, p. 152.

10 "Переписка Ивана Грозного с Андреем Курбским [Correspondence between Ivan the Terrible and Andrei Kurbsky]."

11 Alexander Zimin, *Реформы Ивана Грозного* [The Reforms of Ivan the Terrible] (Moscow: Izdatelstvo sotsialno-ekonomicheskoi literatury, 1960), p. 158.

12 Yanov, *The Origins of Autocracy*, p. 11.

13 Richard Pipes, *Russia under the Old Regime* (London: Penguin Books, 1995), p. 1.

14 *The Russian Primary Chronicle, Laurentian Text*, trans. and ed. Samuel Hazzard Cross and Olgerd P. Sherbowitz-Wetzor (Cambridge, MA: The Medieval Academy of America, 1953), p. 59.

15 Paul Michael, "The *Iaroslavichi* and the Novgorodian *veche* 1230–1272: a case study on princely relations with the *veche*," *Russian History*, vol. 31, no. 1/2, 2004, p. 45.

16 F. C. Conybeare, *Russian Dissenters* (London: Forgotten Books, 2019), p. 4.

17 Pipes, *Russia under the Old Regime*, pp. 9–10.

18 Christine Worobec, *Peasant Russia: Family and Community in the Post-Emancipation Period* (Princeton, NJ: Princeton University Press, 1991), p. 13.

19 Jerome Blum, *Lord and Peasant in Russia: From the Ninth to the Nineteenth Century* (Princeton, NJ: Princeton University Press, 1971), p. 32.

20 John Maynard, *The Russian Peasant and Other Studies* (London: Victor Gollancz Ltd., 1947).

21 Blum, *Lord and Peasant in Russia*, p. 106.

22 Sergei Ivanov, *Блаженные похабы: культурная история юродства* [The Blessed Profane: A Cultural History of Holy

Fools] (Moscow: Yazyki Slavyanskykh Kultur, 2005), pp. 50, 265–6. Available in English as *Holy Fools in Byzantium and Beyond*, trans. Stephen Franklin (Oxford: Oxford University Press, 2006).

23 Paul Avrich, *Russian Rebels: 1600–1800* (New York: W. W. Norton & Co., 1972), pp. 13–14.

24 Yanov, *The Origins of Autocracy*, p. 1.

Chapter 3 The Rebel and the Tsar

1 "Пригожин записал видео к 9 мая – про 'победу дедов' и какого-то 'счастливого дедушку', который может оказаться 'законченным мудаком' [Prigozhin filmed a video about the victory of the grandfathers and some 'happy gramps' who turns out to be a 'complete asshole']," Meduza, May 9, 2023. https://meduza.io/video/2023/05/09/prigozhin-zapisal-video-k-9-maya-pro-pobedu-dedov-i-kakogo-to-schastlivogo-dedushku-kotor yy-mozhet-okazatsya-zakonchennym-mudakom.

2 Pjotr Sauer and Andrew Roth, "'Someone will fall victim': insiders reveal elite anguish as Russia's war falters," *The Guardian*, 7 October 2022.

3 "Победа будет за нами – Путин [Victory will be ours – Putin]," United Russia official site, February 23, 2012. https://er.ru/acti vity/news/pobeda-budet-za-nami-putin_75844.

4 For more on this, see Anna Arutunyan and Mark Galeotti, *Downfall: Prigozhin, Putin and the New Fight for the Future of Russia* (London: Ebury, 2024).

5 Alexander Pushkin, *Капитанская дочка* [The Captain's Daughter], Alexei Komarov Internet Library, Chapter 13. https://ilibrary.ru/text/107/p.1/index.html.

6 Alexander Pushkin, *История пугачевского бунта* [The History of the Pugachev Rebellion] (Moscow: AST Press, 2023), p. 44.

7 Author's interviews with modern Russian Cossacks, Moscow, 2011.

8 Anna Arutunyan, *The Putin Mystique: Inside Russia's Power Cult* (Bloxham: Skyscraper Publications, 2014), pp. 245–7.

9 Pushkin, *История пугачевского бунта* [The History of the Pugachev Rebellion], p. 7.

10 Ibid., p. 9

11 Paul Avrich, *Russian Rebels: 1600–1800* (New York: W. W. Norton & Co., 1972), p. 182.

12 V. Mavrodi, *Крестьянская война под руководством Пугачева* [A Peasant War under the Leadership of Pugachev] (Moscow: Znaniye, 1973).

13 V. Maul, "Загадка болезни Е.И. Пугачева (об одном казусе из предыстории русского бунта XVIIIi столетия) [The mystery of E. Pugachev's disease (about a case from the preface to a Russian rebellion of the eighteenth century)]," *Вестник Томского государственного университета* [Chronicle of Tomsk State University], no. 382, 2014, pp. 113–18.

14 Avrich, *Russian Rebels: 1600–1800*, p. 192.

15 Pushkin, *История пугачевского бунта* [The History of the Pugachev Rebellion], p. 46.

16 Ibid., p. 52.

17 Alexander Pushkin, *История Пугачева: Пушкин, А.С. Полное собрание сочинений* [The History of Pugachev: A. S. Pushkin, Complete Works] (Leningrad: Nauka, 1978), 10 vols, Vol. 8, p. 132.

18 Avrich, *Russian Rebels: 1600–1800*, p. 190.

19 Alexei Ivanov, *Вилы: увидеть русский бунт* [Pitchforks: To Witness the Russian Rebellion] (Moscow: Alpina Non-Fiction, 2024), pp. 9–12.

20 "Пригожин развернул колонны 'Вагнера' и объявил об уходе в тыловые лагеря [Prigozhin turned around his Wagner columns and announced withdrawal to the rear camps]," RBC, June 24, 2023. https://www.rbc.ru/politics/24/06/2023/649727e69a7947620cff0826.

21 "Обращение к гражданам России [An address to the citizens of Russia]," presidential site, June 26, 2023. http://kremlin.ru/events/president/news/71528.

Chapter 4 The Revolt of the Elites

1 "Russia protest: white ribbon emerges as rallying symbol," BBC, December 9, 2011. https://www.bbc.co.uk/news/world-europe-16097709.

2 "В.Сурков: Лучшая часть нашего общества требует уважения к себе [V. Surkov: The best part of our society is demanding respect]," RBC, December 23, 2011. https://www.rbc.ru/politics /23/12/2011/5703f1189a7947ac81a6350c.

3 Andrei Kolesnikov, "С выступающим Новым годом [With a demonstrating New Year]," *Kommersant*, December 26, 2011.

4 Conversations with demonstrators and their political leaders, Moscow, winter 2011–12.

5 "Алексей Кудрин предложил себя в посредники между митингом и властью [Alexey Kudrin offered himself as a mediator between the rally and the authorities]," *Vedomosti*, December 26, 2011.

6 "Deputy Prime Minister – Chief of the Government Staff Vladislav Surkov's answers to audience questions at the London School of Economics and Political Science," official website of the Government of the Russian Federation, May 1, 2013. http:// archive.government.ru/eng/docs/24158/.

7 "Кудрин пока не планирует ходить на митинги оппозиции [Kudrin does not yet plan to attend opposition rallies]," RIA Novosti, May 29, 2012. https://ria.ru/20120(529/660063382. html.

8 Matvei Muravyov-Apostol (ed. S. Shtraikh), *Декабрист М. И. Муравьев-Апостол: Воспоминания и письма* [Decembrist M. I. Muravyov-Apostol: Memories and Letters] (Petrograd: Izdatelstvo Byloye, 1922). https://www.prlib.ru/item/1290601.

9 Oleg Chistyakov (ed.), *Российское законодательство X–XX вв* [Russian Legislation Tenth–Twentieth Centuries] (Moscow: Yuridicheskaya Literatura, 1988), Vol. 6.

10 Carolyn Harris, "150 years ago, Sochi was the site of a horrific ethnic cleansing," *Smithsonian Magazine*, February 7, 2014.

11 A. Kornilov, *Курс истории России XIX века* [Course on the

History of Russia in the Nineteenth Century] (Moscow: Eksmo, 2004), pp. 211–12.

12 Andrei Zubov, "Размышления над причинами революции в России [Reflections on the causes of the revolution in Russia]," *Novy Mir*, no. 7, 2006.

13 *Энциклопедический словарь Брокгауза и Ефрона* [Brockhaus and Efron Encyclopedic Dictionary], Vol. 24a, 1898. See also N. Turkestanov, *Граф Аракчеев и военные поселения 1809–1831* [Count Arakcheyev and the Military Settlements] (Moscow: Russkaya Starina, 1871).

14 W. Bruce Lincoln, *Nicholas I: Emperor and Autocrat of all the Russias* (DeKalb, IL: Northern Illinois University Press, 1989), pp. 36–7.

15 Muravyov-Apostol, *Декабрист М. И. Муравьев-Апостол: Воспоминания и письма* [Decembrist M. I. Muravyov-Apostol: Memories and Letters].

16 M. Nechkina, *Декабристы* [The Decembrists] (Moscow: Nauka, 1984), pp. 20–2.

17 Ibid., p. 22.

18 Alexander Herzen, *Былое и думы* [My Past and Thoughts] (Moscow: Izdatelstvo Pravda, 1975), Vol. 4, p. 38. Available in English as *My Past and Thoughts*, trans. Constance Garnett (London: Chatto & Windus, 1968), 4 vols.

19 Herzen, *Былое и думы* [My Past and Thoughts], p. 36.

20 Lincoln, *Nicholas I*, p. 19.

21 Liudmilla Trigos, *The Decembrist Myth in Russian Culture* (New York: Palgrave Macmillan, 2009), p. 41.

22 Maya Kucherskaya, *Константин Павлович* [Konstantin Pavlovich] (Moscow: Molodaya Gvardia, 2013).

23 Lincoln, *Nicholas I*, p. 40.

24 Kucherskaya, *Константин Павлович* [Konstantin Pavlovich].

25 As quoted in Lincoln, *Nicholas I*, p. 44.

26 M. Nechkina, *Движение Декабристов* [The Decembrist Movement] (Moscow: Russian Academy of Sciences, 1955), Vol. 1, p. 7.

27 Natan Eidelman, "'Доброе дело делать . . .': Страницы жизни Сергея Муравьева-Апостола ['To do a good deed . . .': pages from the life of Sergei Muravyov-Apostol]," *Zvezda*, no. 12, 1975, pp. 18–59.

28 Herzen, *Былое и думы* [My Past and Thoughts], Vol. 4, p. 58.

29 "Democracy has to be fought for," Meduza, May 16, 2024. https://meduza.io/en/feature/2024/05/16/democracy-has-to-be-fought-for.

30 "СМИ: Пресс-секретарь В.Путина пообещал разогнать 'гуляния' оппозиции [Media: Putin's press secretary promises to disperse opposition 'protests']," RBC, May 11, 2012. https://www.rbc.ru/politics/11/05/2012/5703f7479a7947ac81a67cc1.

31 Orlando Figes, "Putin needs to show more restraint than hero to avoid a new Crimean war," *The Guardian*, February 28, 2014. See also "Путин рассказал анекдот об императоре Николае I [Putin tells an anecdote about Nicholas I]," *Izvestia*, August 15, 2015.

32 Lincoln, *Nicholas I*, p. 84.

33 Mark Galeotti, *A Short History of Russia: From the Pagans to Putin* (London: Ebury Press, 2020), pp. 124–5.

Chapter 5 The Will of the People

1 Author's interview, Astrakhan, April 2012.

2 Alexei Navalny's Livejournal post from April 9, 2012. https://navalny.livejournal.com/698954.html.

3 Author's interview, Astrakhan, April 2012.

4 Author's interviews, Moscow region, March 2012.

5 Yuri Pelevin, "'Хождение в народ,' 1874–1875 гг ['Going to the people,' 1874–1875]," *Voprosy istorii*, no. 4, April 2013, p. 64.

6 Vladimir Fyodorov, "Освободительное движение 60-х–начала 80-х гг: Русское народничество [Liberation movement of the 60s–early 80s: Russian populism]," chapter 4 in *История России, 1861–1917* [History of Russia, 1861–1917], 2nd edition (Moscow: Yurait, 2011). http://krotov.info/libr_min/21_f/ed/orov_04.htm.

7 As quoted in Pelevin, "'Хождение в народ,' 1874–1875 гг ['Going to the people,' 1874–1875]," p. 78.

8 Ibid., p. 69.

9 Ibid., p. 68.

10 Ibid., p. 80.

11 Alexander Kornilov, *Александр II: Курс истории России XIX века* [Alexander II: Course on the History of Russia in the Nineteenth Century] (Montreal: Literary Heritage, 2008), p. 10.

12 As cited in Fyodorov, "Освободительное движение 60-х– начала 80-х гг [Liberation movement of the 60s–early 80s]."

13 The account of the revolt and the tsar's response comes from General Alexander Apraksin's report: S. Okun and Z. Kudryavtseva, *Крестьянское движение в России в 1857-мае 1861, сборник документов* [The Peasant Movement in Russia in 1857–May 1861, Collection of Documents] (Moscow: Izdatelstvo sotsialno-ekonomicheskoi literatury, 1963), pp. 350–5.

14 Fyodorov, "Освободительное движение 60-х– начала 80-х гг [Liberation movement of the 60s–early 80s]."

15 As cited in Kornilov, *Александр II* [Alexander II], pp. 225–6.

16 As cited in Avram Yarmolinsky, *Road to Revolution: A Century of Russian Radicalism* (Springfield, OH: Collier Books, 1968). https://www.ditext.com/yarmolinsky/yar0.html.

17 See video by Yevgeny Gladin, of *Moskovskiye Novosti*, December 6, 2011. https://www.youtube.com/watch?v=24XBX0Wkmpw.

18 "Ridiculed star of internet meme to join NTV," *The Moscow Times*, July 9, 2012.

19 "Tank town a welcome bastion of Putin support," *The Moscow Times*, February 28, 2012.

20 Anna Arutunyan, *The Putin Mystique: Inside Russia's Power Cult* (Bloxham: Skyscraper Publications, 2014), pp. 38, 74.

21 Author's interview, Astrakhan, April 2012.

Chapter 6 The Rebel as Tsar

1 Shaun Walker, "Ukrainian far-right group claims to be co-ordinating violence in Kiev," *The Guardian*, January 23, 2014.

2 Volodymyr Ishchenko, "Denial of the obvious: far right in Maidan protests and their danger today," Vox Ukraine, April 16, 2018. https://voxukraine.org/en/denial-of-the-obvious-far-right-in-maidan-protests-and-their-danger-today. See also Sean L. Hanley, "Ukraine: provoking the Euromaidan," UCL School of Slavonic and East European Studies, December 3, 2013. https://blogs.ucl.ac.uk/ssees/tag/svoboda-party/.

3 Telephone conversation, Moscow, May 2014.

4 Conversation, Kyiv, May 2015.

5 Conversation, Sevastopol, March 2014.

6 "'Укропы' и 'валенки' — риторика войны ['Dill' and 'felt boots' – the rhetoric of war]," Radio Azatutyun (RFE/RL), September 18, 2014. https://rus.azatutyun.am/a/ukropy-valenki-leksika-voiny/26591776.html.

7 Anna Arutunyan, "Pro-Russians finding less support for vote in east Ukraine," USA Today, May 8, 2014.

8 Richard Balmforth, "Street violence in Kiev dims prospects for peace effort in Ukraine's east," Reuters, September 3, 2015. https://www.reuters.com/article/world/street-violence-in-kiev-dims-prospects-for-peace-effort-in-ukraines-east-idUSKCN0R30YD/.

9 Michele Berdy, "Talking smack about Ukrainians and Russians," Moscow Times, July 24, 2014.

10 This and preceding quotes from interviews collected by the author in March and May 2014 in Simferopol, Odessa, Donetsk, and Mariupol, Ukraine; names have been withheld or changed for the protection of the sources and the author. For more on the origins of the conflict in Ukraine, see Anna Arutunyan, Hybrid Warriors: Proxies, Freelancers and Moscow's Struggle for Ukraine (London: Hurst, 2022).

11 Author's interviews, Donetsk, Ukraine, May 2014. See also Rebels without a Cause: Russia's Proxies in Eastern Ukraine, Crisis Group report No. 254, July 16, 2019. https://www.crisisgroup.org/europe-central-asia/eastern-europe/ukraine/254-rebels-without-cause-russias-proxies-eastern-ukraine.

12 Vladimir Lenin, *The Revolution of 1905* (London: Martin Lawrence Ltd, 1931), p. 10.

13 Ibid., p. 11.

14 S. Alliluyeva, *Только один год* [Only One Year] (New York: Harper & Row Publishers, 1969), p. 360.

15 I. Stalin, *Собрание сочинений* [Collected Works] (Moscow: Gosudarstvennoye izdatelstvo politicheskoi literatury, 1951), Vol. 13. https://www.marxists.org/russkij/stalin/t13/t13_19.htm.

16 Steven Rosefielde, "Stalinism in post-Communist perspective: new evidence on killings, forced labour and economic growth in the 1930s," *Europe-Asia Studies*, vol. 48, no. 6, September 1996, p. 975.

17 Ibid., p. 980.

18 V. Lenin, *Собрание сочинений* [Collected Works] (Moscow: Gosudarstvennoye izdatelstvo politicheskoi literatury, 1967), pp. 190–1.

19 Stephen Cohen, *Bukharin and the Bolshevik Revolution: A Political Biography, 1888–1938* (New York: Alfred A. Knopf, 1974).

20 Richard Pipes, *Communism: A History* (New York: Modern Library, 2001).

21 See Stefan Hedlund, *Russian Path Dependence* (London: Routledge, 2012).

22 Richard Pipes, *The Russian Revolution* (New York: Vintage, 1991), p. 343.

23 A. Naumov, *Из уцелевших воспоминаний: 1868–1917* [From Surviving Memories: 1868–1917] (New York: Izdatelstvo A. K. Naumovoi i O. A. Kusevitskoi, 1954), Vol. 1, pp. 42–4.

24 Maxim Novichkov, "Брат повешенного» становится революционером [The hanged man's brother becomes a revolutionary]," *Diletant*, August 25, 2017.

25 "'Из университета Ленин исключил себя сам.' Историк – о мифах вокруг вождя ['Lenin expelled himself from the university.' A historian talks about the myths around the leader]," *Argumenty i Fakty*, November 8, 2017.

26 According to police protocols from April 3, 1888. "Отношение департамента полиции в донское областное жандармское управление, от 3 апреля 1888 года, No. 942/274 [Relation of the police department to the Don regional gendarmerie department, dated April 3, 1888, No. 942/274]," archival documents. As cited in Anatoloy Ivansky, *Молодой Ленин* [Molodoi Lenin] (Moscow: Gosudarstvennoye izdatelstvo politicheskoi literatury, 1964). https://leninism.su/books/4309-molodoj-lenin-1964-g.html?start=5.

27 N. Veretennikov, *Володя Ульянов: Воспоминания о детских годах В. И. Ленина в Кукушкине* [Volodya Ulyanov: Memories of V. I. Lenin's Childhood Years in Kukushkino] (Moscow: Detgiz, 1957).

28 Novichkov, "Брат повешенного» становится революционером [The hanged man's brother becomes a revolutionary]."

29 A. Kostin, *История КПСС* [A History of the CPSU], (Moscow: Izdatelstvo politicheskoi literatury, 1964), Vol. 1. https://www.booksite.ru/fulltext/1/001/008/122/700.htm.

30 E. H. Carr, "Russian Revolution and the peasant" (Raleigh Lecture on History, January 30, 1963), *Proceedings of the British Academy* 49, 1963, pp. 69–93.

31 V. I. Lenin, "What is to be done?" https://www.marxists.org/archive/lenin/works/1901/witbd/ch03.htm.

32 Roy Medvedev, *Let History Judge: The Origins and Consequences of Stalinism* (Nottingham: Spokesman Books, 1976), p. 336.

33 N. A. Troitsky, *Россия в 19-м веке* [Russia in the Nineteenth Century], lecture course. https://tinyurl.com/mrena4pa.

34 Orlando Figes, *Origins of the Russian Revolution.* http://www.orlandofiges.info/section1_OriginsoftheRussianRevolution/TheConditionsoftheWorkingClass.php.

35 As cited in ibid.

36 Orlando Figes, *Revolution or Reform.* http://www.orlandofiges.info/section3_RevolutionorReform/WasTsarismReformable.php.

37 As cited in W. Bruce Lincoln, *Red Victory: A History of the Russian Civil War* (London: Cardinal, 1991), p. 36.

38 Konstantin Paustovsky, *Повесть о жизни: Начало неведомого века* [A Story about Life: The Beginning of an Unknown Century] (Moscow: Sovetskii pisatel', 1956).

39 Vladimir Mayakovsky, "Советская азбука ('Антисемит Антанте мил. . . .') [Soviet Alphabet ('The anti-semite is dear to the entente')]," in *Полное собрание сочинений в 13 томах* [Collected Works in 13 Volumes] (Moscow: USSR Academy of Sciences, Gorky Institute of World Literature, 1955–61), Vol. 2. https://feb-web.ru/feb/mayakovsky/texts/ms0/ms2/ms2-092-.htm?cmd=p.

40 As cited in Lincoln, *Red Victory*, p. 40.

41 Ibid., p. 43.

42 Ibid., p. 43.

43 John Reed, *Ten Days that Shook the World*, Chapter IV, "The fall of the Provisional Government." https://www.marxists.org/archive/reed/1919/10days/10days/ch4.htm.

44 Marx, Karl, *The Eighteenth Brumaire of Louis Bonaparte*, Preface to the Second Edition, 1869. https://www.marxists.org/archive/marx/works/1852/18th-brumaire/preface.htm.

45 See *Rebels without a Cause*.

46 Conversation, Moscow, March 2019.

Chapter 7 The Dissidents

1 Vladimir Kara-Murza, Speech on the House Floor, Arizona, March 16, 2022. https://www.youtube.com/watch?v=aIP6q_RJ8PM.

2 Vladimir Kara-Murza, "My only regret is failing to convince people of the danger Putin posed," *The Moscow Times*, April 11, 2023.

3 "Father Georgi Edelstein: we will not repeat the crimes of those who welcomed Hitler in 1939," *The European Times*, February 28, 2022.

4 *My Duty to Not Stay Silent. A Film about Father Georgy Edelstein,*

written and directed by Vladimir Kara-Murza, July 30, 2022. https://www.youtube.com/watch?v=7LBJU6TLGoQ.

5 Sergei Kovalyov, from his manuscript *Dissident*, published in German in 1996. https://web.archive.org/web/20090223102447/ http://www.hrights.ru/text/b20/Chapter1_2.htm.

6 Abraham Rothberg, *The Heirs of Stalin: Dissidence and the Soviet Regime, 1953–1970* (Ithaca, NY: Cornell University Press, 1972), p. 5.

7 "Nikita Khrushchev's Speech to the 20th Congress of the CPSU." https://www.marxists.org/archive/khrushchev/1956/02/24.htm.

8 Rothberg, *The Heirs of Stalin*, p. 13.

9 Andrei Sakharov, *Sakharov Speaks*, ed. Harrison Salisbury (London: HarperCollins, 1975), pp. 10–11.

10 Hedrick Smith, "Ideological bombshells from an atomic scientist," *The New York Times*, November 4, 1973.

11 *Слово пробивает себе Дорогу: Сборник статей и документов об А.И.Солженицыне 1962–1974* [The Word Breaks Its Way: Collection of Articles and Documents about A. I. Solzhenitsyn] (Moscow: Russky Put, 1998), p. 15.

12 Valery Yesipov, "Нелюбовный треугольник: Шаламов–Твардовский–Солженицын [Unloved triangle: Shalamov–Tvardovsky–Solzhenitsyn]," Shalamov.ru. https://shalamov.ru/research/101/#n1.

13 Yakov Klots, "Варлам Шаламов между тамиздатом и Союзом советских писателей (1966–1978) [Varlam Shalamov between *tamizdat* and the Union of Soviet Writers (1966–1978)]," Colta.ru, January 10, 2017. https://www.colta.ru/articles/literature/13546-varlam-shalamov-mezhdu-tamizdatom-i-soyuzom-sovetskih-pisateley-1966-1978.

14 Sergei Khrushchev, *Пенсионер союзного значения // Никита Сергеевич Хрущев: материалы к биографии* [Pensioner of Union Significance // Nikita Sergeevich Khrushchev: Materials for a Biography] (Moscow: Novosti, 1989), p. 282.

15 Howard Biddulph, "Protest strategies of the Soviet intellectual

opposition," in Rudolf Tökés (ed.), *Dissent in the USSR: Politics, Ideology, and People* (Baltimore: Johns Hopkins University Press, 1975), p. 114.

16 Hedrick Smith, "Soviet physicist assailed for 1968 memo," *The New York Times*, February 15, 1973.

17 Biography of Andrei Sakharov, Chapter 4, Sakharov.space. https://www.sakharov.space/bio/glava-4-povorot.

18 Roy Medvedev, "Из воспоминаний об академике Сахарове [From memories about Academician Sakharov]," *Vestnik*, no. 9, 2002, pp. 822–36.

19 Sheila Fitzpatrick, "Popular opinion under Communist regimes," in S.A. Smith (ed.), *The Oxford Handbook of the History of Communism* (Oxford: Oxford University Press, 2014), p. 379.

20 Eliot Borenstein, "A sovok is a person, place, or thing (Russia's alien nations)," NYU Jordan Center blog, March 29, 2019. https://jordanrussiacenter.org/blog/a-sovok-is-a-person-place-or-thing-russias-alien-nations.

21 Vladimir Shlapentokh and Anna Arutunyan, *Freedom, Repression and Private Property* (Cambridge: Cambridge University Press, 2013), p. 148.

22 Jeffrey Rossman, *Worker Resistance under Stalin: Class and Revolution on the Shop Floor* (Cambridge, MA: Harvard University Press, 2005).

23 David Satter, *Age of Delirium: The Decline and Fall of the Soviet Union* (New Haven, CT: Yale University Press, 2001), p. 144.

24 Quoted in "Soviet dissidents and religion: between human rights and national roots," ICLRS, December 22, 2022. https://talkabout.iclrs.org/2022/12/07/soviet-dissidents-and-religion/.

25 Barbara Martin, "Soviet dissident historians as a societal phenomenon of the post-Stalin era (1956–1985)," *International Journal of Russian Studies*, no. 3, 2014, p. 68.

26 Dmitry Gordon, "Известный писатель и диссидент, автор исторических портретов самых ярких политических деятелей советской эпохи Рой МЕДВЕДЕВ . . . [The famous

writer and dissident, author of historical portraits of the most prominent political figures of the Soviet era, Roy MEDVEDEV . . .]," *Bulvar Gordona*, January 8.

27 N. Krotov and M. Kholmskaya, "Медведев Рой Александрович [Medvedev Roy Alexandrovich]," *Observer*, no. 23(27). https:// web.archive.org/web/20151117022442/http://www.observer. materik.ru/observer/N23_93/23_05.HTM.

28 Ibid.

29 Gordon, "Известный писатель и диссидент [The famous writer and dissident]."

30 In Hedrick Smith, *The Russians* (New York: Ballantine, 1977), quoted in Philip Short, "Andropov's turn," *London Review of Books*, May 19, 1983.

Chapter 8 The Democrats

1 Ivan Grushin, "Странные сближенья: В Москве прошла конференция российской оппозиции 'Другая Россия' [Strange convergences: a conference of the Russian opposition 'The Other Russia' was held in Moscow]," Lenta.ru, July 13, 2006. https://lenta.ru/articles/2006/07/13/otherrussia/.

2 "Участники конференции 'Другая Россия' определили дальнейший курс Кремля [Participants in the 'Other Russia' conference identified the Kremlin's future course]," *Novaya Gazeta*, July 13, 2006.

3 Opinion poll, May 2006. "Социально-Политическая Ситуация В России В Мае 2006 Года (Часть 1) [Social and political situation in Russia in May 2006, Part 1]," Levada.ru. https://www. levada.ru/2006/06/04/sotsialno-politicheskaya-situatsiya-v-rossii-v-mae-2006-goda-chast-1/.

4 Opinion poll, July 2006. "Социально-политическая ситуация в России в июле 2006 года [Social and political situation in Russia in July 2006]," Levada.ru. https://www.levada.ru/2006/07/31/sotsialno-politicheskaya-situatsiya-v-rossii-v-iyule-2006-goda/.

5 "Реальные доходы россиян упали впервые с 2000 года [Real

incomes of Russians fell for the first time since 2000]," RBC, January 28, 2015. https://www.rbc.ru/economics/28/01/2015/54 c8ed8e9a79476360df32f3.

6　Intentional homicides (per 100,000 people) – Russian Federation, World Bank Group. https://data.worldbank.org/indicator/ VC.IHR.PSRC.P5?locations=RU.

7　See Transparency International's Corruption Perceptions Index from 1996 through 2023. https://tradingeconomics.com/russia/ corruption-index.

8　R. German, "Влияние оперативной обстановки на условия и результаты работы сотрудников органов внутренних дел на Дону в 90-е годы XX века: историко-правовой анализ [The influence of the operational situation on the conditions and results of work of internal affairs officers on the Don in the 90s of the twentieth century: historical and legal analysis]" (Rostov-on-Don: Publishing house of the Rostov Law Institute of the Interior Ministry of Russia, 2013), pp. 117–21.

9　Grushin, "Странные сближенья [Strange convergences]."

10　Anna Politkovskaya, "Центровой из Центороя. Интервью с Рамзаном Кадыровым [The central [man] from Tsentrovoi. Interview with Ramzan Kadyrov]," *Novaya Gazeta*, June 21, 2021.

11　Andrew Roth, "Journalist Oleg Kashin knows who tried to kill him," *The Washington Post*, September 18, 2018. Also author's conversations with Kashin, Moscow, 2009, London, 2022.

12　"20 делегатов конференции 'Другая Россия' задержаны милицией или избиты [Twenty delegates to the 'Other Russia' conference were detained or beaten by police]," Radio Svoboda, July 10, 2006. https://www.svoboda.org/a/163906.html.

13　Boris Kagarlitsky, "Russia: is there life for KPRF after Yeltsin?" Green Left, January 17, 2001. https://www.greenleft.org.au/ content/russia-there-life-kprf-after-yeltsin.

14　Andrei Pertsev, "Они боялись диктатора. И сами привели его к власти [They were afraid of the dictators. And brought him to power themselves]," Meduza, November 7, 2023. https://meduza

.io/feature/2023/11/07/oni-boyalis-diktatora-i-sami-priveli-ego
-k-vlasti.

15 The Memorial human rights group's attempt to define the multi-faceted dissident movement is probably the most objective. Memorial's archives, like those of many independent groups and media in Russia, have been removed from the Russian segment of the internet, but this entry can be accessed here: https://web.archive.org/web/20110316074723/http://www.memo.ru/history/DISS/.

16 Daniel Sandford, "Moscow coup 1991: with Boris Yeltsin on the tank," BBC, August 20, 2011. https://www.bbc.co.uk/news/world-europe-14589691.

17 Boris Yeltsin speech, August 19, 1991. Translated by the US Department of State. https://web.viu.ca/davies/H102/Yelstin.speech.1991.htm.

18 Conversation, London, 2024.

19 Conversation, Moscow, 2005.

20 Declaration, "Новые политические партии и организации России [New political parties and organizations of Russia]," *Analitichesky vestnik informatsionnogo agentstva Postfactum*, no. 4/5, April 1991.

21 Sergei Kovalyov, "Открытое письмо Президенту Российской Федерации Б.Н.Ельцину [Open letter to the President of the Russian Federation B. N. Yeltsin]." https://web.archive.org/web/20090429180755/http://www.hrights.ru/text/kniga/Chapter3.htm.

22 "Словарь русского публичного языка конца XX века [Dictionary of the Russian language at the end of the twentieth century]," *Kommersant-Vlast*, no. 24, June 23, 2003.

23 I. Karatsuba, I. Kurukin, and N. Sokolov, *Выбирая свою историю* [Choosing Your History] (Moscow: Kolibri, 2005), pp. 618–19. See also David E. Hoffman, *The Oligarchs: Wealth and Power in the New Russia* (New York: Public Affairs, 2003), pp. 297–315.

24 Although for a dissenting voice that suggests Berezovsky had another figure in mind for the presidency, see Robert Otto, "The

1999 Moscow bombings reconsidered," *Russian Politics*, vol. 8, no. 3, 2023, pp. 375–91.

25 Viktor Khamrayev and Ilya Bulavinov, "Конец правых сил [The end of the Right Forces]," *Kommersant-Vlast*, January 26, 2004.

26 Steve Liesman and Andrew Higgins, "Seven-year hitch," *The Wall Street Journal*, September 23, 1998.

27 Chrystia Freeland, *Sale of the Century: Russia's Wild Ride from Communism to Capitalism* (New York: Crown, 2000), p. 157.

28 Peter Baker and Susan Glasser, *Kremlin Rising: Vladimir Putin's Russia and the End of Revolution*, updated edition (Sterling, VA: Potomac Books, 2007), p. 281.

29 Anna Arutunyan, *The Putin Mystique: Inside Russia's Power Cult* (Bloxham: Skyscraper Publications, 2014), p. 174.

30 John Browne, *Beyond Business* (London: Weidenfeld & Nicolson, 2010). From an excerpt published in *The Times*, February 5, 2010.

31 Russian Public Opinion 2012–13, Levada Analytical Center, Moscow, 2013. https://www.levada.ru/sites/default/files/2012_eng.pdf.

32 Vladimir Gelman, "'Liberals' vs. 'democrats': ideational trajectories of Russia's post-Communist transformation," *East View Press*, vol. 51, no. 2, 2020, pp. 3–24.

33 Conversation with a Russian journalist, Moscow, 2010.

34 Alexei Navalny, "My fear and loathing," blog post August 11, 2023. https://navalny.com/p/6652/.

35 Mikhail Khodorkovsky, "Фильм 'Предатели'. Мое мнение без купюр [The 'Traitors' film. My two cents]," Khodorkovsky's vlog. https://youtu.be/yvCEULANjBg?si=u2blG5SKGKXZawIi&t=317.

36 Lev Kadik, *Wild Paroxysms of the Turbulent 90s – How the Traitors Documentary Exposed the Russian Liberal Milieu*, Friedrich Ebert Stiftung Russia Program report, July 2024. https://library.fes.de/pdf-files/international/21384-20240814.pdf.

Chapter 9 The Russian Spring

1 Author's interview, Moscow, April 2009.

2 Zakhar Prilepin, "Его имя – Эдуард Лимонов [His name is Eduard Limonov]," from Limonov's official campaign site: http://www.limonov2012.ru/biography.html.

3 Program of the National Bolshevik Party, 1994. https://web.ar chive.org/web/20071208041130/http://www.nbp-info.com /1573.html.

4 Dimitry Plotnikov, "На своей земле. Почему север Казахстана называют казачьими землями и как там живут миллионы русских [On your own land. Why is the north of Kazakhstan called Cossack lands and how do millions of Russians live there?]," Lenta.ru, January 16, 2022. https://lenta.ru/articles/20 22/01/16/north_kz/.

5 Ilya Azar, "Усть-Каменогорская народная республика. Ждут ли русские в Казахстане 'вежливых людей' [Ust-Kamenogorsk People's Republic. Are Russians waiting for 'polite people' in Kazakhstan]," Meduza, October 20, 2014. https://meduza.io/ news/2014/10/20/ust-kamenogorskaya-narodnaya-respublika.

6 Plotnikov, "На своей земле [On your own land]."

7 Program of the National Bolshevik Party, 2004. https://web.ar chive.org/web/20071017132229/http://nbp-info.ru/cat107/index. html.

8 Eduard Limonov, "Оппозиция откладывается [The opposition is postponed]," *Izvestia*, November 18, 2014.

9 Celestine Bohlen, "Yeltsin deputy calls reforms 'economic geno-cide,'" *The New York Times*, February 9, 1992.

10 Malofeyev's interview, Tsargrad TV, September 9, 2017. https:// tsargrad.tv/shows/krasnyj-ugol-s-elenoj-sharojkinoj-v-gostjah -konstantin-malofeev_84563.

11 "Портрет в датах [Portrait in dates]," *Nezavisimaya Gazeta*, January 6, 2000.

12 Malofeyev's interview, Tsargrad TV, September 9, 2017.

13 Remarks on Russian national television, December 13, 1999, as cited by Laura Belin, "Campaign advertising rarely mentions

Chechnya," RFERL, December 17, 1999. https://web.archive.org/web/20080214043842/http://www.rferl.org/specials/russian election/archives/07-171299.asp.

14 Helge Blakkisrud, "*Russkii* as the new *Rossiiskii*? Nation-building in Russia after 1991," *Nationalities Papers*, vol. 51, no. 1, 2023, pp. 64–79.

15 "Константин Крылов: 'лучшие демократы получаются из бывших фашистов . . .' [Konstantin Krylov: 'the best democrats come from former fascists . . .']," Natsional-Demokratichesky Allyans, May 10, 2010. https://web.archive.org/web/201201251 82938/http://www.nazdem.info/texts/110.

16 Anna Arutunyan, "The delayed threat of Strelkov's opposition movement," European Council on Foreign Relations, June 20, 2016. https://ecfr.eu/article/commentary_the_delayed_threat_of_strelkovs_opposition_movement_7045/.

17 Anna Arutunyan, "How the Kremlin stumbled on nationalism," European Council on Foreign Relations, August 5, 2015. https://ecfr.eu/article/commentary_how_the_kremlin_stumbled_on_nationalism3094/.

18 Interview with the author, March 2018.

19 "Putin urges Ukraine separatists to postpone referendum," Reuters, May 7, 2014. https://www.reuters.com/article/world/putin-urges-ukraine-separatists-to-postpone-referendum-idUS BREA460K4/.

20 Ilya Barabanov, "России все-таки пришлось вводить войска. Российские писатели о войне в Донбассе [Russia still had to send in troops. Russian writers about the war in the Donbas]," BBC, April April, 2019. https://web.archive.org/web/20221216 205426/https://www.bbc.com/russian/features-47938985. See also Anna Arutunyan, *Hybrid Warriors: Proxies, Freelancers, and Moscow's Struggle for Ukraine* (London: Hurst, 2022), p. 112.

21 For a wider assessment of this rapid disillusion, see Pål Kolstø, "Crimea vs. Donbas: how Putin won Russian nationalist support – and lost it again," *Slavic Review*, vol. 75, no. 3, 2016, pp. 707–25.

22 "10 years later, Russian volunteer fighters recall fueling the war in Donbas," *The Moscow Times*, April 23, 2024.

23 Interview with the author, March 2018.

24 Quoted in *Rebels without a Cause: Russia's Proxies in Eastern Ukraine*, Crisis Group report No. 254, July 16, 2019. https://www.crisisgroup.org/europe-central-asia/eastern-europe/ukraine/254-rebels-without-cause-russias-proxies-eastern-ukraine.

25 Konstantin Krylov, "Перемога. Три варианта [Victory. Three options]," APN, December 31, 2018. https://serg07011972.live journal.com/2365038.html.

26 Quoted in Mark Galeotti, "Putin's real threat comes from Russia's 'turbo-patriots,'" *Spectator*, February 7, 2023.

Chapter 10 The Russian Winter

1 "Дебаты в клубе Билингва [Debate in the Bilingua Club]," Scilla.ru, November 23, 2006. https://scilla.ru/content/view/2045/.

2 "Тесак и Навальный. Какая связь между самоубийством националиста и оппозиционером [Tesak and Navalny. What is the connection between the suicide of a nationalist and an oppositionist]," Life.ru, September 16, 2016. https://life.ru/p/1345673.

3 "Неонацист Тесак получил девять лет колонии [Neo-Nazi Tesak received nine years in prison]," BBC, June 27, 2017. https://www.bbc.com/russian/news-40414321.

4 "Паркер о дебатах. Воробьёва рядом [Parker on the debate. Vorobyova is nearby]," Alexei Navalny's Youtube, December 20, 2006. https://www.youtube.com/watch?v=Ock6MnDrOGA.

5 Masha Morozova, "Официальный шут – это я [The official jester is me]," Kholod, June 26, 2024. https://holod.media/2024 /06/26/maksim-kononenko/.

6 "'An unlikely reason for a natural death,'" Meduza, February 16, 2024. https://meduza.io/en/feature/2024/02/16/an-unlikely-reason-for-a-natural-death.

7 "Что известно о смерти Алексея Навального [What is known

about the death of Alexei Navalny]," Tass, February 16, 2024. https://tass.ru/obschestvo/20007143.

8 Roman Badanin and Ivan Osipov, "Я понимал, что сотрудничество с Навальным может быть угрозой для моей работы [I understood that cooperation with Navalny could be a threat to my work]," Forbes, April 25, 2012. https://www.forbes .ru/sobytiya/lyudi/81639-ya-ponimal-chto-sotrudnichestvo-s-navalnym-mozhet-predstavlyat-ugrozu-dlya-moei.

9 Viktor Feshchenko, "Верхом на хайпе: Что под капотом у медиамашины Алексея Навального [Riding the hype: what's under the hood of Alexei Navalny's media machine]," Sekret Firmy. https://secretmag.ru/navalnyi/.

10 "Прокуратура обжаловала арест Навального [The prosecutor's office appealed Navalny's arrest]," Forbes, July 18, 2013. https://www.forbes.ru/news/242368-prokuratura-obzhalovala -arest-navalnogo.

11 "Путин назвал приговор Навальному 'странным' [Putin called Navalny's sentence 'strange']," TV Rain, August 2013. https://tv rain.tv/teleshow/novosti_sajta/putin_nazval_prigovor_navalno mu_strannym-349275/.

12 Grigory Yavlinsky, "Без путинизма и популизма [Without Putinism and populism]," Grigory Yavlinsky, February 6, 2021. https://www.yavlinsky.ru/article/bez-putinizma-i-populizma/.

13 Recounted to the author, from a conversation with Mark Galeotti in Moscow in March 2012.

14 Kathrin Hill, "Navalny debates nationalist Girkin in attempt to broaden appeal," *The Financial Times*, July 21, 2017.

15 Kristina Sukhareva and Yekaterina Grobman, "Сторонники Алексея Навального собрались в 'Россию будущего' [Supporters of Alexei Navalny gathered in the 'Future Russia']," *Kommersant*, May 20, 2018.

16 "Все административные аресты Алексея Навального [All administrative arrests of Alexei Navalny]," *Vedomosti*, September 25, 2018.

17 Conversation with a Moscow oppositionist, Moscow, fall 2013.

18 "Навальный о Каце: 'Он непорядочный человек и просто проходимец' [Navalny on Katz: 'He is not a decent person and a grifter']," TV Rain, May 31, 2016. https://tvrain.tv/teleshow/choose_tvrain/navalnyj_o_katse-410433/.

19 Maxim Katz, X post, October 20, 2024. https://twitter.com/max_katz/status/1848017447011668315.

20 "Красная жара: заговор Рашкина ударил по репутации КПРФ [Red heat: Rashkin's conspiracy hit the reputation of the Communist Party of the Russian Federation]," *Moskovskii Komsomolets*, April 28, 2021.

21 "Рашкин признался в убийстве лося в Саратовской области [Rashkin admitted to killing a moose in the Saratov region]," *Izvestia*, November 18, 2021.

22 "'If it hadn't been for the prompt work of the medics': FSB officer inadvertently confesses murder plot to Navalny," Bellingcat, December 21, 2020. https://www.bellingcat.com/news/uk-and-europe/2020/12/21/if-it-hadnt-been-for-the-prompt-work-of-the-medics-fsb-officer-inadvertently-confesses-murder-plot-to-navalny/.

23 Vladimir Isachenkov and Daria Litvonova, "Putin denies involvement in poisoning of Kremlin foe Navalny," Associated Press, December 17, 2020. https://apnews.com/article/vladimir-putin-alexei-navalny-poisoning-325535308e61b232343514fb2cdfe3a5.

24 "Alexei Navalny: Putin critic arrives in Germany for medical treatment," BBC, August 22, 2020. https://www.bbc.co.uk/news/world-europe-53871617.

25 "'Он герой, и его больше нет.' Акции памяти Алексея Навального ['He's a hero and he's gone.' Events in memory of Alexei Navalny]," Svoboda.org, February 19, 2024. https://www.svoboda.org/a/akcii-pamyati-alekseya-navalnogo-on-geroy-i-ego-bolshe-net/32826008.html.

26 "'Мы находимся на войне.' Илья Пономарев о неизвестной до убийства Дугиной 'НРА' и своей роли в ней ['We are at war.'

Ilya Ponomaryov about the 'NRA,' unknown before Dugina's murder, and his role in it]," Spektr, August 23, 2022. https://spektr.press/my-nahodimsya-na-vojne-ilya-ponomarev/.

27 "Проект Акта о Переходном Парламенте [Draft Act on the Transitional Parliament]," Congress of Russian Deputies website. https://web.archive.org/web/20221106001550/https://rusdep.org/proekt-akta-o-perexodnom-parlamente/.

28 Transcript of Yekaterina Shulmann's podcast, November 9, 2022. "Программа 'Статус' сезон 06, выпуск 12 [Program 'Status' season 06, issue 12]," https://teletype.in/@eschulmann/status__s06_e12.

29 "Most of Russia's opposition is either dead, in exile abroad or in prison at home. What happens now?" Associated Press, February 19, 2024. https://apnews.com/article/navalny-russia-opposition-putin-8554f74e229c451f96956939b05d2a99.

30 "Navalny's widow vows to continue his fight against the Kremlin and punish Putin for his death," Associated Press, February 20, 2024. https://apnews.com/article/russia-navalny-death-56d3cf1d114e6be452465d5e312b4fad.

31 Tatyana Felgengauer, "'I vowed to turn the prison into a political anti-war platform. I believe I have succeeded.' In-depth interview with Moscow politician Ilya Yashin one year after his arrest," Mediazona, June 27, 2023. https://en.zona.media/article/2023/06/27/yashin_interview.

32 Dasha Litvinova, "For freed Russian opposition activist Ilya Yashin, resuming work against Putin is his priority," Associated Press, August 9, 2024. https://apnews.com/article/russia-yashin-prisoner-swap-putin-crackdown-ukraine-a74efa54bc6d033b57ee4dd10d1227b6.

33 Conversation, Washington, DC, 2022.

34 Conversation, London, 2024.

35 From Kovcheg's official website. https://kovcheg.live/en/ark/.

36 From the Russian Democratic Society's official website. https://www.rusdemsociety.co.uk/.

37 Natalia Zotova, "Кац обещает ничего не делать [Katz promises not to do anything]," *Novaya Gazeta*, March 16, 2012.

38 "Russia low but rising in charity rankings," BEARR Trust, December 3, 2013. https://bearr.org/regional-news/russia-low-but-rising-in-charity-rankings/.

39 Roland Oliphant, "Russian truckers 'March on Moscow' in biggest outbreak of industrial unrest in years," *Telegraph*, November 30, 2015.

40 "Russian truck drivers strike for 10 days against Platon tax system," *Moscow Times*, February 22, 2016.

41 "Дальнобойщики и КПРФ продолжают протестовать против Платона вместе [Truckers and the Communist Party of the Russian Federation continue to protest against Platon together]," news release, KPRF, November 12, 2016. https://kprf.ru/actions /kprf/160127.html.

42 "Путин снизил штрафы для дальнобойщиков в 90 раз [Putin reduces fines for truck drivers 90 fold]," Forbes.ru, December 15, 2015. http://www.forbes.ru/news/308359-putin-snizil-shtra fy-dlya-dalnoboishchikov-v-90-raz.

43 "Russian newspapers show rare solidarity with detained, beaten journalist," CBS News, June 10, 2019. https://www.cbsnews.com /news/ivan-golunov-arrested-russian-newspapers-show-solida rity-with-detained-beaten-journalist/.

44 See figures from OVD.info. https://donate.ovd.legal/.

45 "Russia blocks website of OVD-Info protest-monitoring group," Reuters, December 25, 2021. https://www.reuters.com/ world/russia-blocks-website-ovd-info-protest-monitoring-group-interfax-2021-12-25/.

46 "Дисциплина и апатия: кто претендует на мандаты на местных выборах 2024 [Discipline and apathy: who is vying for seats in the 2024 local elections]," Golos, August 21, 2024. https://golosinfo.org/articles/148268.

47 Anatoly Kurmanaev, "A prison at war: the convicts sustaining Putin's invasion," *The New York Times*, December 4, 2023.

48 See figures from OVD.info. https://ovd.info/content/aprel-2024
    -chto-my-sdelali-blagodarya-vashey-podderzhke.
49 "Destroy Putinism with Russian hands: the Russian opposition
    must transform into an armed resistance," *Ukrainska Pravda*,
    June 3, 2024.
50 Data on politically motivated criminal prosecutions in Russia,
    OVD.info, June 18, 2024. https://en.ovdinfo.org/old.
51 For a detailed comparison of how authorities handled the
    Novocherkassk strike and the Mezhdurechensk miners' strike
    in 2010, see Vladimir Shlapentokh and Anna Arutunyan,
    Freedom, Repression, and Private Property in Russia (Cambridge:
    Cambridge University Press, 2013), p. 148.

Index